Business, Religion, & Spirituality

THE JOHN W. HOUCK
Notre Dame Series in Business Ethics

BUSINESS, Religion, &Spirituality

A NEW SYNTHESIS

edited by
OLIVER F. WILLIAMS, C.S.C.

UNIVERSITY OF NOTRE DAME PRESS

Notre Dame, Indiana

Manufactured in the United States of America

Library of Congress Cataloging-in-Publication Data
Business, religion, and spirituality : a new synthesis / edited by
Oliver F. Williams.
p.   cm.— (The John W. Houck Notre Dame series in business ethics)
Includes bibliographical references and index.
ISBN 0-268-02173-2 (alk. paper)
ISBN 0-268-02174-0 (pbk. : alk. paper)
1. Business—Religious aspects.   2. Business ethics.   3. Spiritual life.
I. Willaims, Oliver F.   II. Series.

HF5388.B87   2003
291.1'785—dc21

                                            2002155285

∞ *This book is printed on acid-free paper.*

Contents

Introduction

OLIVER F. WILLIAMS, C.S.C.

The idea that people of religious faith ought to bring their religious values into the workplace and that these values ought to influence the quality of life and important decisions in business is not a new idea. The Center for Ethics and Religious Values in Business at the University of Notre Dame has been writing and researching about this issue for over twenty-five years.[1] In 2000 the Academy of Management, one of the primary professional organizations for those teaching in business schools, approved a new interest group, which focuses on the study of the relationship and relevance of spirituality and religion for management and organizations. Called the Spirituality and Religion (MSR) Interest Group, the unit, which has been fermenting for a number of years, has already attracted hundreds of members.

What is new, however, is reported well in a 1999 cover story in *Business Week*. "A spiritual revival is sweeping across Corporate America" and "perhaps the largest driver of this trend is the mounting evidence that spiritually minded programs in the workplace not only soothe workers' psyches but also deliver improved productivity."[2]

The new emphasis on spirituality in the workplace has been discussed by the *Wall Street Journal*, *Fortune*, and scores of books and journals in the last several years. Spirituality seems to be a basic human good essential for human flourishing.

Spirituality may be defined as "the desire to find ultimate purpose in life, and to live accordingly." Proponents argue that tapping into our inner depths can yield new power, energy, meaning, and knowing that can enhance life in the workplace. While spirituality has been historically

1

rooted in religion, the emphasis today is often on a spirituality disassociated from religion. Is this possible? Is it a good idea?

The Tradition: A Congruence between Inner and Outer Life

In order to understand the context for the current discussion, it may be helpful to outline some of the history of the interplay of religion, spirituality, and work. The Judeo-Christian tradition views work as essential and valuable, yet also as drudgery. Genesis 2:15 relates that God intended humankind "to cultivate and take care of" the world and that work is essential to human fulfillment. Genesis 3:17–19 goes on to portray work as a burden and a tribulation and blames this aspect of work on sin, humankind's turning away from God and his plan. Matthew 25:14–30, the parable of the talents, teaches that work and creativity are serious responsibilities, which ought not be avoided. The theme of the parable is that persons are gifted by God and that full use of their talents is the appropriate and loving response.

Lewis Mumford has suggested that the Benedictine monasteries of the sixth century were the founders of capitalism.[3] For monks work was an essential dimension; it was their conviction that through their life together, consisting of work, prayer, and recreation, they grew closer to God. In order to have ample time for prayer, meditation, and so on, labor-saving devices were developed. Tasks were standardized so that they might be interchanged among the brothers. As a result of their thrifty living, they were able to save money, and they used this accrued wealth to build better equipment—hence they were called the "first capitalists."

Arnold Toynbee draws a significant parallel between monasticism and capitalism when he points to the inner-directed motivation of a monk.

> The Benedictine Rule achieved what has never been achieved by the Gracchan agrarian laws or the Imperial alimenta, because it worked, not, as state action works, from above downwards, but from below upwards, by evoking the individual's initiative through enlisting his religious enthusiasm.[4]

The positive attitude of the monks toward work had an influence throughout the Middle Ages.[5] One could find dignity and self-respect in labor or craftsmanship: "To labor is to pray."

Thomas Aquinas

Thomas Aquinas (1225–1274), perhaps the best-known medieval religious scholar, brought together much of the biblical teaching and writings of the Fathers and other commentators in a grand synthesis with Aristotelian philosophy. Society during Aquinas's time was primarily based on an agricultural economy and was poor by any contemporary standards. The differences between the haves and have-nots (the feudal lords and the serfs) were large, and upward mobility was unknown. It was a static society, where lords, peasants, craftsmen, and merchants were each thought to have a "right" to whatever it took to perform their particular function in society. Members of society understood themselves in terms of the analogy of the human body, each class having a particular role to perform in the grand scheme of things, in accordance with the divine plan. While the manor might obtain goods from traders and guilds, the scale of commerce was minuscule compared to that of later centuries.

The church taught that all should have sufficient means for their particular state in life; accruing wealth beyond this level was sinful, the sin of avarice. In the medieval world commerce was suspect, and although it was tolerated, it could never be acknowledged as a good. The fear was that trade and commerce would accent and strengthen the acquisitive traits of one's character.[6] In the words of R. H. Tawney, the attitude of medieval thinkers toward the acquisitive appetites "was that of one who holds a wolf by the ears."[7] Extended reflections on just prices, usury, and trade occupied theologians as they sought to provide guidance to preserve the traditional standards of personal morality. It is worth noting that the point of their work was not so much to change social structures, for their perspective on society was the prevailing static view. Their work was an effort to formulate a code of ethics that would provide practical guidance for living a life of Christian virtue.

Because of advances in technology and in the social and human sciences, humankind has discovered how to increase productivity and accrue wealth. In our time there is a growing realization that, with appropriate advances, no one has to be poor in the future. What the Thomistic tradition has in common with the spirituality movement of our time is the movement's attempt to establish some congruence between the principles that organize life in the workplace and those that shape private lives. Tawney points out that the compartmentalizing of the various dimensions of life into an absolute dichotomy was totally foreign to medieval thought. He notes that in nineteenth-century England there was a common acceptance of this total separation; people came to believe that "[t]rade is one thing, religion is another," yet the strict division between private and public morality was something new.[8]

Because this sort of separation between private and public life would have been totally alien to Aquinas and the tradition of Aristotle, they might have something to say to our times. A retrieval of Aquinas offers us a social philosophy that points to one way of healing the breach between outer and inner life.

For Aquinas, the basis of moral goodness is God's *wisdom*, that is, the wisdom of God intends that creatures be in a proper relationship to each other and to him.[9] Thus moral goodness is constituted by being in harmony with God's plan of creation. Creation is taken to be that act of God that gives finite beings an existence apart from him. All things have a "nature," an essence, and various actions are required to bring that nature to perfection. For example, an acorn requires sun, water, soil, and so on if it is finally to become what it is destined to be—an oak tree. Knowing the End (the oak tree), one can determine the Means (sun, water, soil, and so on) to bring it to perfection. The centerpiece of Aquinas's reflection on the person is his understanding of the End of human life: "Man's ultimate happiness consists solely in the contemplation of God."[10] His thinking is marked by a teleological cast, that is, first one determines the End of human life (enjoying the presence of God), and then one ascertains the Means to attain it.

The means to attain the vision of God—which can only be fully attained in the next life—include a supernatural gift of grace, which enables one to become the sort of person who might enjoy this vision. Becoming this sort of person entails the slow process of appropriating the virtues; Aquinas's program combines the virtues enjoined by the Bible—faith, hope, and charity—with Aristotle's four cardinal virtues: wisdom, justice, temperance, and fortitude. Part of being oriented properly to God is the appropriate orientation toward the natural good. For Aquinas, then, ethics (moral theology) is the means by which one brings into actuality the sort of person one potentially is, a person capable of and suited for union with God.

Creation, as an act of God, mirrors his eternal law; this eternal law, insofar as it is implanted in creation, is called "natural law." This natural law is discerned by human intelligence as people in community seek to determine the right things to do and to be. For the Thomist-Aristotelian synthesis, a society ordered by law and custom discerned by right reason is a society in accordance with the divine plan. A law is taken to be just if it responds to the demands of reality, if it is arrived at by right reason reflecting on the many aspects of the situation. The context for this reflection is the end of humankind, and the role that society has in shaping persons for that end; the forming of virtuous persons is all-pervasive. In this account, the human will is not the source of the rightness of a law, but rather the human intelligence, for it is this faculty that reads the "imperatives of nature" implanted by God in creation. To be sure, God has not so specified things that there is only *one* concrete action, or *one* type of government, and so on to meet the demands of reality. Rather, natural law is a generalized pattern of action that may be concretized by persons in a variety of "just" ways. To be free means to be able to work out the concrete demands of reality for oneself; it does not mean to be purely spontaneous, as some utilitarians might suggest.[11]

All of creation has its own "natures," its own ends—and hence its own autonomy—and yet ultimately all is oriented toward the creator. The human intellect has the task of discovering what it takes to bring the various "natures" to perfection. For example, one might argue that humankind has recently discovered how to produce wealth, a relatively new skill in the history of the human race. But in the Thomistic vision this new skill cannot be allowed to dominate and must be subordinated to the end of life on this earth, *the formation of virtuous persons*. Economic activity is only a means, and it must be guided by reference to the moral ends. This is the heart of the teaching of Thomas Aquinas, and it continues to form the basis of church documents. Some seven hundred years later, the Second Vatican Council decree, "The Church in the Modern World," restates the point clearly: "economic activity is to be carried out according to its own methods and laws but within the limits of morality, so that God's plan for mankind can be realized."[12]

The Roots of Compartmentalization

The sociologist Daniel Bell, following a theme similar to that of Joseph Schumpeter, develops the point that there is a crisis of legitimacy in business institutions that ultimately stems from a loss of religious values.[13]

For Bell, the social system only made sense when work derived meaning and value from the Protestant ethic. In his judgment the Protestant ethic is no longer a significant influence in the culture, and hence the rational technocratic system so essential to capitalism is slowly being undermined. Some discussion of the Protestant ethic will illuminate what many take to be a crucial influence on the course of capitalism.

The rapid economic growth that marks what is known as capitalism was not to come for some eleven centuries after Benedict and five centuries after Aquinas. In the early–twentieth century Max Weber advanced the thesis that two key doctrines of the Protestant Reformers provided the force that enabled modern capitalism to come into being: Martin Luther's doctrine of vocation (*Beruf*) and John Calvin's teaching on predestination. What made capitalism unique, according to Weber, was the pursuit of profit by means of systematic and rational behavior.[14] He cited rational bookkeeping as a key characteristic of this entity called capitalism. Why was it that capitalism was able to marshal such enormous amounts of human energy for the cause of economic growth? Why was it that characteristic pre-Reformation Christian attitudes, which extolled the virtue of poverty, encouraged withdrawal from the world, and honored the intellectual life over commerce, were suddenly transformed into attitudes that fostered the development of business—attitudes of austerity, industry, thrift, frugality, and so on. The answer to these questions, according to Weber, lies in the theological teachings of Luther and Calvin and the way in which these teachings were passed along to the people by Reformed pastors. It is worth noting that R. H. Tawney and other scholars modified Weber's theory. For example, Tawney includes the influence of the bankers of Venice and Florence, and hence of *Catholic* ideas, in the ethos that spawned capitalism.[15] In any event, it is instructive to consider the original Weberian thesis.

Luther brought a fresh perspective to the notion of Christian vocation.[16] He taught that one's occupation in the world was not to be taken lightly, for doing the task well was the way to serve God and to give thanks for divine justification. This conviction provided motivation for high performance in one's station in life, whether it be as a scholar, craftsperson, or laborer. Yet Weber argues that the life pattern of systematic and rational activity that characterized capitalism was not sufficiently explained by Luther's doctrine of calling or vocation. He also examined Calvin's doctrine of predestination. In Calvin's theology, God elects some to be saved and others to be damned, and one is powerless to affect the outcome of God's sovereign will. In the face of the great uncertainty over salvation, there were many in these communities who suffered great anxiety. Weber suggests that one look to the advice given by Reformed pastors who were ministering to this salvation-anxiety problem in order to find the significant motive power for economic growth.[17]

In order to calm consciences, the pastors were saying that there were *signs* of election, and that these signs were material success in one's business. While one could not *attain* salvation by prudent management of a business enterprise, one could have some assurance that salvation was in line for a person if material prosperity prevailed. Thus everyone struggled to ensure that businesses were profitable, and this produced the driven quality in the "Protestant ethic." Although the pastors encouraged people to live frugally, to be austere, they were also counseling industriousness and persistence. This combination of advice enabled people to overcome their anxiety and also to accrue wealth. Since Calvinism taught that wealth would be an obstacle to holiness in that it led to pride and sensuality, this posed a problem. It was not long, therefore, before a new teaching emerged to account for the new condition. The doctrine of stewardship was developed; it taught that wealth was a trust and was to be used for the common good.

The crucial point in Weber's analysis is that making profits became a value in its own right. Since anxiety over possible damnation is calmed if one is materially successful, it "made sense" to be almost single-mindedly focused on material success. Thus the Protestant ethic changed history, for heretofore ethical values had always discouraged such a single-minded quest for profits. Weber goes on to show how the Protestant ethic eventually lost its religious roots and yet maintained its vitality with a secular vision. Benjamin Franklin epitomizes this secular vision. Reading Franklin's works, one is struck by the fact that all the values of the spirit of Christian asceticism are present, although the religious basis of these values has died. What remains is what Weber calls a "fundamental element of the spirit of modern capitalism: Rational conduct on the basis of the idea of calling."[18] Weber quotes Franklin:

Remember, that money is of the prolific, generating nature. Money can beget money, and its offspring can beget more, and so on. Five shillings turned is six, turned again it is seven and threepence, and so on, till it becomes a hundred pounds. The more there is of it, the more it produces every turning, so that the profits rise quicker and quicker. He that kills a breeding-sow, destroys all her offering to the thousandth generation. He that murders a crown, destroys all that it might have produced, even scores of pounds.[19]

The writings of Benjamin Franklin exhort the reader to practice austerity, honesty, frugality, thrift, industry, and so on—all the virtues of the Puritan ethic—not for the sake of the signs of salvation, but rather in order to accrue wealth and to live as a moral athlete—the best way to live.

Adam Smith: An Assumed Interplay

What is the relationship between business values and religious or spiritual values? Understanding the dynamic of a market economy sheds light on this important connection. Perhaps the most adequate understanding of the market economy is that presented by the moral philosopher Adam Smith (1723–1790) in his *Inquiry Into the Nature and Causes of the Wealth of Nations* (1776) and his earlier work, *The Theory of Moral Sentiments* (1753).[20]

In the *Inquiry,* Smith sought to understand why some nations were wealthier than others. Part of his answer was that nations that encouraged free competitive markets were wealthier. In a curious kind of way, when each person pursues his or her self-interest the common good is enhanced and all are wealthier. Given competition, the baker bakes the very best bread possible and sells it at the lowest price feasible so that he will have the resources to buy what he wants. Although motivated by self-interest, the result is that the community has good bread at a reasonable cost. Thus Smith showed how economic self-interest was beneficial for the community.

In my view, however, the crucial point in Smith's analysis is his assumption in *Inquiry* that is quite explicit in his *Theory of Moral Sentiments*: The "self-interest" of business people would be shaped by moral forces in the community so that self-interest would not always degenerate into greed and selfishness.

The point of religious social teaching is that the family and the church are some of the crucial moral forces that must be strong to enable people to keep their moral bearings in the business world, and to be the formative influence on self-interest so that it matures from selfishness to concern for all in the global community.

Compartmentalization in America

Tawney pointed out that what differentiates modern from medieval economic ideas is the modern assumption that economic criteria are the sole authoritative standard.[21] The single criterion of economic expediency, how to provide the greatest possible amount of material goods, replaces medieval natural law and its concern for providing guidance for a society of virtuous persons. One of the points of this volume is a challenge to the notion that economic criteria indeed offer the *sole* standard. We must recognize, however, that the churches have much less to say today than in the medieval world. In the face of this massive cultural shift, what guidance has been provided by the church leaders of the United States? In order to understand the present state of the discussion between religious values and business, a brief historical sketch may be helpful.

When it comes to considering the influence of religion on business life in the United States, we are, for the most part, speaking of Protestant denominations. Although today about 25 percent of Americans are Catholics, this sizable percentage represents a relatively recent phenomenon. In Colonial America, Catholics were a distinct minority. A 1708 Maryland census reported 2,974 Catholics in a population of 33,833 persons. Pennsylvania in 1757 recorded 1,365 Catholics out of some 200,000 persons. As the population of the United States was approaching 4 million in 1785, only 25,000 Catholics were recorded.[22] The nineteenth-century influx of Catholic immigrants from Europe achieved economic success only relatively recently. The same can be said for the Jewish people. The mass immigration of Jews did not take place until the twentieth century, and although their early positive influence was far greater than their numbers, they did not have a substantial role in shaping Colonial America.

The medieval ideal was surely not dead in the New World—at least not in the Massachusetts of the 1600s. The Puritan colony was governed with an overarching religious principle that claimed authority over the economy.[23] For example, prices and wages were fixed by leaders of the colony to reflect what they took to be a "fair" standard. The clergy, who were often the political leaders as well, wielded power over all dimensions of community life. The doctrine of the "calling" was elaborated by Cotton Mather, a famous Puritan cleric, in his work *Two Brief Discourses, One Directing a Christian in His General Calling, Another Directing Him in His Personal Calling*, published in 1701. Mather teaches that a Christian has two callings, one "to serve the Lord Jesus Christ," and the other, to pursue a particular vocation in which, in some fashion, one serves fellow community members. To portray the challenge of living a Christian life, Mather uses the image of a person rowing a boat toward heaven: each of the two oars (callings) must be given its proper attention in order to reach the shore. Thus one's worldly calling is essential to the attainment of eternal life, and business is actually taken to be God's work. Scholars have noted that this way of framing the doctrine of the calling contained within itself the seeds of its own destruction. Since their daily work was a religious task, merchants conducted their businesses with dead seriousness; they became so successful that they soon asserted their independence from clerical interference.[24]

Indeed just how independent economics was becoming in eighteenth-century America is illustrated by the writings of the Reverend Joseph Morgan; Morgan taught the famous "hidden hand" doctrine almost forty years before Adam Smith. In his *Nature of Riches*, published in 1732, Morgan says:

> A rich man is a slave to others, while he thinks others are Slaves to him. He is a great Friend to the Publick, while he aims at nothing but serving himself. God will have us live by helping one another and since Love will not do it, Covetousness will.[25]

Taken to its extreme, this position signals the abandonment of the medieval ideal and the acknowledgment that business and religion are indeed two discrete, impenetrable worlds.

Yet the struggle to keep one unified vision of life in which economics was subordinated to religion continued into the nineteenth century. There was a pervasive belief that economic success was intimately related to moral virtue. The comment of a Massachusetts Quaker merchant about settlements in Ohio was typical for the period: "With a population governed by such habits [industry, temperance, morality, and love of gain] the state must necessarily advance in improvement at a rapid rate."[26] There was also a continuous concern that acquisitive attitudes had overtaken the merchant class; sermons and clerical writings of the time stressed the need to bring Christian values to business practice. The Reverend Theodore Parker sums up the tenor of the times: "If religion is good for anything, it is as a rule of conduct for daily life, in the business of the individual and the business of the nation."[27]

The Protestant churches of the mid–nineteenth century became more and more identified with the wealthy and the powerful classes and had little attraction for the workingman. There was a prevailing opinion that hard work, moral character, and perseverance would bring the good life (material success) to all who would try it. The spirit of the times is perhaps best captured by the novels of Horatio Alger, a popular writer, who began his career as a Unitarian minister in Massachusetts. Alger's stories tell of poor boys rising to financial success through honesty, frugality, and persistence; these rags-to-riches stories were used as models by many of the clerics writing and speaking to their people.[28] Henry F. May, in *Protestant Churches and Industrial America*, notes that in 1876 Protestantism was almost totally identified with the status quo and was the source of little prophetic insight for business and political life. Prominent clerics, more often than not, opposed unions in favor of setting wages by the "natural law" of supply and demand.[29]

There was a dramatic shift in the posture of the churches as sensitive pastors saw their people locked in violent labor conflicts. The railroad strike of 1877, the strikes of 1886 culminating in the Haymarket bomb explosion in Chicago, and the series of conflicts over Carnegie Steel Corporation's threat to reduce wages all conspired to reorient the thinking of religious leaders to the plight of the worker. The turn of the century saw a new focus by leading theologians on the social teachings of Jesus. The Congregationalist pastor Washington Gladden in *Applied Christianity* (1886) and *Church and Modern Life* (1908) and the Baptist Walter Rauschenbusch in *Christianity and the Social Crisis* (1910) and *A Theology of the Social Gospel* (1917) set the new agenda for the Protestant world. Catholic scholars such as Bishop Francis Haas and Monsignor John A. Ryan made great contributions in defense of the American labor movement. Ryan's *Living Wage* (1906) and *Distributive Justice* (1916) were especially influential.[30]

Walter Rauschenbusch tells a story which illustrates the new consciousness of *social* sin that theologians were advocating. There was a farmer who belonged to a small religious community known for its strict observance and pietistic spirit. One day this farmer was caught shipping milk that was polluted. Upon being confronted with the violation, "he swore a worldly oath" in anger. The church censored the sinful farmer: "But, mark well, not for introducing cow-dung into the intestines of babies, but for expressing his belief in the damnation of the wicked in a non-theological way."[31] Rauschenbusch's point was that the churches often focus on minor sins and totally overlook major wrongs committed in the world of work. Changing history, making the world a better place, ought to be part of the Christian vocation.

Although the influence of the social-gospel movement was never pervasive, it did spark a general interest in reform of the marketplace and a concern for the problems of the poor. The Federal Council of Churches in America, formed in 1908, was an ecumenical group of thirty denominations that came to be the social conscience of Protestant America. Although the horrors of World War I destroyed the easy optimism of the Progressive movement and drew attention to the ever present evil dimension of humankind, the call for social reform was not to be forgotten. Adequate working conditions, child-labor laws, a living wage, and a host of other social issues were championed by the churches. In 1948 th World Council of Churches was formed to strengthen Christian influence throughout the globe. Although initially it was composed of some 152 member churches from Western Europe and North America, today the council is dominated by Third World members. At present there are some 295 Protestant and Eastern Orthodox member churches from one hundred countries. Periodical assemblies are held and position papers are issued; a 135-member Central Committee representing worldwide churches makes decisions when assemblies are not in session.

In 1950 the National Council of Churches was formed by twelve interdenominational agencies. Today its membership includes Methodists, Episcopalians, Baptists, Presbyterians, Lutherans, and Quakers, as well as the Greek, Syrian, Serbian, Ukrainian, Russian, and Armenian Orthodox communions. The 266-member governing board of the council takes positions on social issues and offers guidance to church members (some 40 million in all) in the United States.

As mentioned earlier, until recently Catholics were not especially influential in shaping America. Their major contribution has been their role in the labor movement and their activities on behalf of social justice for the worker. In 1920 the bishops of the United States organized the

Social Action Department of the National Catholic Welfare Conference under the leadership of Monsignor John A. Ryan. The conference was to be a vehicle for making pronouncements in the name of all the U.S. bishops on matters of concern. Usually it met once a year and considered a number of issues. In 1920 the Administrative Committee of the conference approved a major statement on social issues, drafted by the talented moralist John A. Ryan. *Social Reconstruction: A General Review of the Problems and Survey of Remedies* provided a general framework for considering social concerns in a moral perspective and made suggestions on issues such as unemployment and health insurance, minimum-wage laws, child-labor laws, the rights of labor to organize, public housing, and so on. From our perspective today, the document is rather moderate in tone, and many of its recommendations have been implemented in law. The significant point, however, is that the program was highly controversial when first released, and it was even taken to be subversive in some quarters. The president of the National Association of Manufacturers wrote a strong letter of protest to Cardinal Gibbons in response to the statement:

> It is pretty generally assumed that the Roman Catholic Church of the United States is, and always has been, unalterable in its antagonism to all forms of Socialism. It is our belief that a careful reading of this pamphlet will lead you to the conclusion we have reached, namely, that it involves what may prove to be a covert effort to disseminate partisan, pro-labor union, socialistic propaganda under the official insignia of the Roman Catholic Church in America.[32]

The conference document prevailed, however, and today its major proposals are taken for granted as the minimum requirements of justice in a democratic society. In 1966 the National Catholic Welfare Conference was reorganized and named the United States Catholic Conference—an administrative arm of the National Conference of Catholic Bishops. The key function of the conference remains, namely, to develop and promulgate guidance on social and economic questions of the day. That this guidance is heard and practiced by those in business today is highly doubtful. For a host of reasons, business people find a great dichotomy between the values they cherish in their personal lives and the reigning values in the workplace. In large measure, the quest for a "new spirituality" by business people reflects this void.

A New Development: Spirituality and Changing Unjust Social Structures

There is no question that moral and spiritual nourishment are essential to the mission of the church. How is it that the churches are increasingly involved in social and political issues? How are these concerns part of the church's mission? These are crucial questions for many today, and some background may be helpful.

As discussed above, the overarching Catholic vision was stated in systematic form by Thomas Aquinas (1225–1274), and this perspective continues to guide the church today.[33] Aquinas, drawing on the biblical teaching and the writings of the church fathers, wove an enduring tapestry with an Aristotelian and Neoplatonic philosophic framework. All of creation flows from God and finally will return to him. The goal of life on this earth is to become the sort of person who will finally enjoy the vision of God in the next world. "Man's ultimate happiness consists solely in the contemplation of God."[34]

Becoming the sort of person who might enjoy this vision, becoming virtuous, is only thought to be possible because of a gift of God (a supernatural gift of grace). Appropriating the virtues over a lifetime is the *Means* to the *End* of human life. Then one is oriented properly to God and may see him in the next life. For Aquinas, however, all creation is fundamentally good, and being properly oriented to God entails as well the appropriate orientation toward the natural good.[35] Aquinas highlights the key biblical virtues—faith, hope, and charity—but he also stresses the need to form character in Aristotle's four cardinal virtues—wisdom, justice, temperance, and fortitude.

For Aquinas, then, moral and spiritual nourishment was crucial, for this was the way one prepared for life in the next world. The focus was on personal morality, and in this context the medieval theologians wrote much about just prices, trade, and usury. The efforts of the moralist were largely directed to individual Christians and were designed to ensure that each kept faithful to a path of personal virtue.

While the churches have never forsaken their role of shaping the character of individual Christians through preaching, teaching, and liturgy, there has been a new realization that the Christian mission also entails criticizing unjust social structures and transforming the world. Aquinas lived in an era when it was generally assumed that society was static. People most often remained in the socioeconomic group where they were born, as lord, peasant, craftsman, or merchant. "Justice" was understood to mean that each person was entitled to whatever their particular role in society required. Thus, in justice, a lord had considerably more material goods than a peasant. Viewing the world in terms of the analogy of the human body, each class of society was seen to have a different role to perform in society, but all were united in an organic whole.

How is it that transforming the world and hence involvement in social and political issues have come to be understood in the church as an integral part of its mission, as a "constitutive dimension of the preaching of the Gospel?"[36] On one level, it could be argued that in the United States only in recent years have Catholics assumed positions of power in business, government, and the wider society. It would have made little sense to speak of changing the social structures to the immigrant parents or grandparents of the current generation of American Catholics. As a result of education and the upward mobility of their parents, present-day Catholics are often influential in the United States. In 1891 Pope Leo XIII issued the encyclical (a pastoral letter written by the pope as the chief shepherd of the church) *Rerum Novarum*. This encyclical was published in face of the impact of the industrial revolution and the church's growing concern over severe working conditions and the exploitation of the workers. American Catholics were largely blue collar people, and the pastoral championed their cause—political and economic rights. Today the descendants of these poor workers probably do not need to hear a comforting word but rather a challenging one—a call to continue to fashion a world that is more humane for the poor and the powerless.

Unlike the United States, Europe has long had a tradition of Catholics being directly active in social and political issues. Theologians reflecting on the relationship between temporal progress and salvation have deepened our understanding of the Kingdom of God. The Jews of Jesus' time believed that in some ways the Kingdom of God was already present. It was experienced in the historical acts of God (2 Samuel 7:12–16), yet it was also future (Judges 8:23). Jesus preached that where people are conforming their lives to the will of God, there the Kingdom is coming (Matthew 6:9–13). In his many stories, Jesus portrays the characteristics of the Kingdom—peace, justice, forgiveness, and harmony. Following the resurrection, the disciples of Jesus came to realize that the Kingdom of God had come into the world in the very person of Jesus, the Christ. The church today has come to realize that human work furthers the Kingdom of God. Pope John Paul II in the 1981 encyclical *Laborem Exercens* (On human work) reiterates this point.

> Let the Christian who listens to the word of the living God, uniting work with prayer, know the place that his work has not only in earthly progress but also in the development of the Kingdom of God.[37]

Tying "earthly progress" with the Christian vocation is now a well-established fact in Roman Catholic teaching. "Moral and spiritual nourishment" that simply focuses on personal virtue to the exclusion of a social dimension would indeed be a deficient diet in the Catholic context.[38] John Paul II quotes the Vatican II document "The Church in the Modern World" to make this point: "People are not deterred by the Christian message from building up the world, or impelled to neglect the welfare of their fellows. They are, rather, more stringently bound to do these very things."[39]

In *Laborem Exercens* John Paul II brings together the traditional emphasis in Christian teaching on the need to become virtuous persons with the relatively recent focus on transforming the world. Work has a subjective and an objective dimension, and the development of the Kingdom of God entails both. John Paul understands the Book of Genesis to mean that the most important purpose of work is to develop the human qualities of the person (the subjective dimension of work). When Genesis speaks of human "dominance" over nature, this is indeed an invitation for humankind to share in the work of creation, to be co-creators and transform the world (the objective dimension of work).

> Man ought to imitate God, his creator, in working, because man alone has the unique characteristics of likeness to God.[40]

And again,

> Man shares by his work in the activity of the creator.[41]

To be sure, salvation is more comprehensive than present liberation from dehumanizing environments. Insofar as the Kingdom of God reaches the human heart, it overcomes sin and floods a life with the love that strikes at the root of social and political injustices. Yet, because God has acted and continues to act to realize his Kingdom on earth, his creatures are called to respond and mirror his love by actively changing the world in accord with his intentions. The Kingdom of God will come finally and completely only in God's good time.[42]

At root, this discussion of the development of the Kingdom of God draws on the theological issue of how the divine and human contribute to the economy of salvation. Although no exhaustive explanation is possible for such a mystery, the work of theologians such as Walter Kasper and H. Richard Niebuhr is most helpful.[43] Knowing who God is, his mighty deeds in the past and his present work, Christians are called to conform their action to God's action. Sometimes called the "indicative/imperative" approach of biblical ethics, this interpretation helps to understand how the human response is a sign and a mediation of God's activity, while in no way exhausting all of the divine initiatives. The human response is indeed essential, yet no one plan of action can be construed to be God's plan or *the* plan.

Recent church documents stress the primacy of the spiritual, yet these documents are misunderstood if this emphasis is taken to mean a flight from social and political concerns.[44] The church vision here is one of integral humanism which considers the concrete person enmeshed in social and political structures. Redemption affects all creation, and efforts to overcome unjust aspects of the world are part of the spiritual task. The gospel proclamation is one of love but also one of justice and peace. Thus the emphasis on the spiritual is not meant to imply that the Christian can escape from involvement in the world; rather, it calls for a more profound engagement with it. That which is truly human is spiritual. Pope John Paul has repeatedly taught that Christ and the church shed light and offer hope to the person in his or her world. The mission of the church is to speak and act in the concrete situation.

> Man in the full truth of his existence, of his personal being and also of his community and social being—in the sphere of his own family, in the sphere of society and very diverse contexts, in the sphere of his own nation or people . . . , and in the sphere of the whole of mankind—this man is the primary route that the Church must travel in fulfilling her mission: *he is the primary and fundamental way for the Church*, the way traced out by Christ himself.[45]

Thus it is clear that while the Roman Catholic Church can never forsake its role of shaping the character of Christians by its preaching, teaching, and liturgy, this task does not exhaust its mission of providing "moral and spiritual nourishment."

Recent Attempts to Retrieve the Medieval Synthesis of Spiritual and Economic Values

In 1986 the U.S. bishops issued a landmark pastoral letter on the U.S. economy, *Economic Justice for All*, and in 1991, the hundredth anniversary of *Rerum Novarum*, Pope John Paul II published the encyclical *Centesimus Annus*.[46] These documents try to analyze our times and, in particular, our economy in the light of the Gospel and point us toward a more humane community.

In my view, the key challenge to our times identified by Catholic social teaching is to discern and implement those institutional arrangements that will promote and protect a society of virtuous persons, and the major impediment to realizing this vision is "idolatry of the market." Paragraph 39 of *Centesimus Annus* states the problem well:

> If economic life is absolutized, if the production and consumption of goods become the center of social life and society's only value, not subject to any other value, the reason is to be found not so much in the economic system itself as in the fact that the entire sociocultural system, by ignoring the ethical and religious dimension, has been weakened and ends by limiting itself to the production of goods and services alone.

The remedy proposed for this idolatry of the market is to strengthen the moral and religious institutions so they might have a more influential role in shaping people and communities. *Centesimus Annus* says we must "create lifestyles in which the quest for truth, beauty, goodness and communion with others for the sake of common growth are the factors which determine consumer choices savings and investments" (para. 36).

While acknowledging a crucial role for the market, an endorsement that is stronger and more explicit than any previous statement of Catholic social teaching (para. 40), and while acknowledging a significant role for the state in regulating the market and creating the conditions for job creation (para. 48), Catholic social teaching is primarily concerned to reinvigorate "mediating institutions," those "various groups and associations which make up society" (para. 48).

The insight here is the age-old one that becoming a virtuous person in community, preparing for a final destiny with God, is what life is all about.

> People lose sight of the fact that life in society has neither the market nor the state as its final purpose, since life itself has a unique value which the state and the market must serve.

The Church's "specific and decisive contribution" is the understanding we have of ourselves and of our own destiny (para. 41). One premise of Catholic social teaching is that the person is social by nature, not by choice, that the need for others, for community, is a constitutive dimension of the person. This is the basis for commutative as well as distributive and social justice in Catholic thought.

What happens when the market dominates life in society, without significant influence from other institutions, is that often the person is shaped to be greedy and insensitive, and social and distributive justice pale in importance.

Only when the social nature of the person finds an important part of its fulfillment in institutions other than the market, especially in the family and the church, can we expect a humane community. *Centesimus Annus* stresses that authentic fulfillment of the person is "realized in various intermediary groups, beginning with the family and including economic, social, political and cultural groups" (para. 13). The family is given special recognition because it is there that the person "first receives formative ideas about truth and goodness and learns what it means to love and to be loved, and thus what it means to actually be a person" (para. 39). One of the tasks of the state is to support and strengthen the family with its social policy. The personal character necessary for a humane community will, in large measure, be formed in the family.

In order to overcome today's widespread individualistic mentality, what is required is a concrete commitment to solidarity and charity, beginning in the family with the mutual support of husband and wife and the care that the different generations give to one another (para. 49).

The Need for New Institutional Arrangements

Catholic social teaching offers an integrative vision that calls business persons to higher values and obligations. It calls for morally constrained behavior and the strengthening of those institutions that foster such behavior. Morally mature Christians will come to see that "self-interest" is best realized when all have the possibility of a humane life and that selfish behavior has little cash value in a Christian perspective.

Yet, the teaching is not naive about the power of economic rationality. The huge loss of jobs in recent times because of plant closings resulting from off-shore moves and the spate of hostile takeovers has been a sober reminder that economic rationality can demoralize even the most loyal and virtuous workers.

With this in mind, the teaching has suggested new institutional arrangements that might help overcome the growing distrust in the workplace. For example, *Centesimus Annus* "recognizes the legitimacy of workers' efforts to obtain full respect for their dignity and to gain broader areas of participation in the life of industrial enterprises" (para. 43).

Economic Justice for All is more specific in making suggestions designed to cultivate the loyalty of workers in the face of an economic system that requires tough decisions. It offers the following rationale.

> The virtues of good citizenship require a lively sense of participation in the commonwealth and of having obligations as well as rights within it. The nation's economic health depends on strengthening these virtues among all its people, and on the development of institutional arrangements supportive of these virtues. (para. 296)

The document proposes that American business experiment with some new forms of worker participation that may enhance the possibility of community in the face of economic rationality.

One proposal discussed often in the management literature is known as "stakeholder theory": The idea that management is accountable not only to stockholders—although they obviously are a key constituency—but to all the stakeholders ("workers, managers, owners or shareholders, suppliers, customers, creditors, the local community, are the wider society").[47]

The idea here is to devise some way to hear all constituencies when important decisions are made. The objective is not to paralyze decision making but rather to listen to all those who may be affected by a decision, before making it. Management has an opportunity to hear many points of view and also to communicate its response.

Another suggestion offered is the cooperative ownership of a firm by all workers. Some companies have ESOPs (Employee Stock Ownership Plans) and many firms offer stock to workers, but other experiments in employee ownership are relatively rare.

A third suggestion designed to foster community in the workplace is to involve the workers in plant closing and movements of capital decisions. This would allow the workers to face the economic rationality question and the value trade-offs heretofore restricted to management.

Major challenges

Whether these suggestions are the final answer or not, what is clear is that business leaders and all citizens have to face some major challenges if we are to promote and protect the possibility of a virtuous community in the workplace. In summary, we must attend to:

1. Strengthening those institutions in society such as the family and the church that shape self-interest and serve as the moral forces that keep the market in perspective. Then service to the poor and the needs of the global community will seem more urgent.
2. Seeking new institutional arrangements that will involve more employee participation and serve to overcome the distrust and cynicism that comes from *uncritically* accepting economic rationality.

Some Concluding Remarks

What becomes clear from this brief summary is that churches have had a fairly constant record of trying to cultivate the spiritual life of its members while at the same time challenging capitalism to be more humane and just. From the religious perspective, profit is not an evil in itself, but simply an index of success—a report card, if you will. But profit was to be sought in the context of the higher religious and cultural values—love of God (Benedictine monks), a sign of salvation (Calvinists, Puritans, and others), the virtuous life (Thomas Aquinas, Benjamin Franklin), and so on. Religious persons, through their spiritual values, are motivated to work well, to strive to provide some coherence and direction to the business enterprise, and to set some limits to the acquisitive appetites.

It is well to remember, however, Max Weber's ominous warning. Weber feared that once people abandoned the interplay between spiritual or religious and business values, civilization would be on the decline. In the closing pages of *The Protestant Ethic and the Spirit of Capitalism*, Weber expresses his fears:

> Where the fulfillment of the calling cannot be directly related to the highest spiritual and cultural values, or when, on the other hand, it need not be felt simply as economic compulsion, the individual generally abandons the attempt to justify it at all. In the field of its highest development, in the United States, the pursuit of wealth, stripped of its religious and ethical meaning, tends to become associated with purely mundane passions, which often actually give it the character of sport.
>
> . . . For of the last stage of this cultural development, it might well be truly said: "Specialists without spirit, sensualists without heart; this nullity imagines that it has attained a level of civilization never before achieved."[48]

One of the most obvious signs that Weber's warning is being heeded is the contemporary revival of the interest in spirituality and business. As the essays that follow indicate, however, the revival is of a spirituality most often divorced from religion. Is this viable? Why has religion become so unfashionable, almost in proportion as spirituality grows in fashion? How can a new synthesis be effectively communicated? These and other important questions are addressed by the essays that follow.

Toward a New Synthesis

All the scholars and managers writing in this volume are proponents of spirituality in the workplace, yet all have some questions. As this movement to integrate spirituality into business and health care continues to grow, what are the moral questions that should guide leaders? Is spirituality being treated as simply an instrumental good, valued for its usefulness in enhancing productivity and well-being? What are the responsibilities of business leaders? Of faculty? Of business schools? Of churches? With these questions in mind, the Center for Ethics and Religious Values in Business asked a number of prominent persons and distinguished scholars to contribute to a volume.

The common thread that links all the authors of these essays is that all have distinguished themselves in their respective fields or professions and all are concerned to advance spirituality in business. The women and men writing here present a sober, but positive, prognosis for this new spirituality growth and offer some direction for the future.

Martin Marty, the revered professor at the University of Chicago Divinity School, presents the opening chapter. His basic thesis is that "religion" and "spirituality" cannot easily be separated, and he presents a six-part matrix to develop his analysis. For Marty, spirituality is crucial for it can "help enlarge imagination and vivify both religion and business," but so is religion, for it includes essential critique and community possibilities. Marty sees the contemporary spirituality movement as a work in progress.

Laura Nash, in chapter 2, asks why there has been so little effective church leadership on the spirituality-in-business issue. She has researched this question and offers her findings. The essay concludes by distinguishing three levels of religious engagement and demonstrating that, with the proper level of engagement, objections from both the business community and the churches are likely to diminish.

In chapter 3, Robert Kennedy offers an insightful analysis providing the reader the philosophical conceptual tools to understand spirituality in abstraction from any religious tradition. Drawing on the work of Germain Grisez and John Finnis, Kennedy focuses on the role of spirituality in human fulfillment and how the Christian manager might play a role.

André Delbecq and James McGee have led seminars with senior executives on bringing spirituality into the workplace, and they offer their reflections in chapter 4. This essay shows how business can be a vocation, a spiritual calling, that influences the day-to-day work of organizational leadership.

The next four chapters discuss how some of the major religious traditions might induce spirituality in the business person and in organizational life. Edward Epstein, in chapter 5, focuses on the contribution of Judaism; Krishna Dhir provides the reader with insights from the Hindu tradition in chapter 6. In chapter 7, Jamal Badawi focuses on the teachings of Islam. Lawrence Cunningham offers some reflections on the relationship between spirituality and religion and shows how these influences shape a life in the Christian world in chapter 8.

Chapters 9–12 all focus on what business people have to say about spirituality in the workplace. In chapter 9, the scholar Ian Mitroff presents reflections based on extensive interviews with business leaders and summarizes their hopes and fears of spirituality in a business setting. Most fear religion in the workplace but cherish spirituality there. Mitroff also highlights the organizational aspect of spirituality in business, the implication being that this new movement will ultimately lead to "new roles, job descriptions, and governing structures that will allow people to express, maintain, and develop their spirituality." Mitroff's essay is followed by a response by a business leader, John Ryan, who has often reflected on these issues.

Chapter 10 is authored by a retired CEO, John Caron. Caron is one of those unusual business leaders who was an advocate and practitioner of spirituality at work long before it became fashionable. He offers some reflections on how to move ahead with the program today.

Claudia McGeary has found the spirituality of Henri Nouwen helpful in her professional life. In chapter 11, she offers a brief summary of Nouwen's spirituality and several case studies of people who live by Nouwen's approach.

Chapter 12 argues that one cannot practice business ethics well without having a vision of the sort of person one ought to become and the sort of communities one ought to form. The author further argues that this vision ultimately is provided only by a religion and its spirituality. Making these significant points would be a challenge for a seasoned academic, but the chapter is all the more remarkable because it is written by a retired officer of Morgan Stanley, Buzz McCoy.

The final three chapters discuss specific ways to develop authentic spirituality both on the individual and the organizational level. Chapter 13 by Stephen Porth, David Steingard, and John McCall uses the tools of Catholic social teaching to provide "a foundation to illuminate the distinction between an authentic spirituality of business and a trendy, superficial new management approach."

Gerald Cavanagh, S.J., in chapter 14, asks whether it is possible to tap the rich resources of religion in order to develop a personal spirituality without activating the divisive elements of religion. He answers in the affirmative and outlines the Ignatius spirituality of St. Ignatius Loyola as one that offers valuable lessons for business people.

The final chapter is written by a woman who served as CEO of a major health care system. Patricia Vandenberg, C.S.C., in chapter 15, tells the reader how to bring spirituality into organizational life by recounting the experience of her own organization. This insightful essay is followed by three responses from professionals in the health system: Mary Kathryn Grant, Peter Giammalvo, and John Gallagher.

I am most grateful for our many benefactors who helped support the work of the Center and, in particular, this volume, especially William Lehr Jr. and the Hershey Foods Company Foundation. Also, a thank-you is in order to Deb Coch, administrative assistant at the Center, whose work enabled this project to move from an idea to a finished product. Finally, I want to thank all those who contributed to this volume and added to our understanding of spirituality in the workplace.

NOTES

1. The Center for Ethics and Religious Values in Business has published several volumes with a focus on religion, spirituality, and business. See O. F. Williams and J. W. Houck, *Full Value: Cases in Christian Business Ethics* (San Francisco: Harper and Row, 1978); J. W. Houck and O. F. Williams, eds., *Catholic Social Teaching and the U.S. Economy: Working Papers for a Bishops' Pastoral* (Washington, D.C.: University Press of America, 1984); and J. W. Houck and O. F. Williams, eds., *Co-Creation and Capitalism: John Paul II's* Laborem Exercens (Washington, D.C.: University Press of America, 1983). For a brief survey of the history of the interplay among religion, spirituality, and business, see O. F. Williams, introduction to *The Judeo-Christian Vision and the Modern Corporation,* ed. O. F. Williams and J. W. Houck (Notre Dame, Ind.: University of Notre Dame Press, 1982), 1–21. Much of the material presented in this introduction has been previously published by me in these earlier volumes: pages 6–8 in *Catholic Social Teaching;* and pages 5–18 in *The Judeo-Christian Vision.* See also O. F. Williams, "The Economy and the Christian Business Leader: The Vision and the Challenge of *Centesimus Annus,*" *The Priest* (October 1992): 33–36.

2. M. Conlin, "Religion in the Workplace: The Growing Presence of Spirituality in Corporate America," *Business Week,* 1 November 1999, 150–58.

3. Lewis Mumford, *Techniques and Civilizations* (New York: Harcourt, Brace, 1934), 14.

4. Arnold J. Toynbee, *A Study of History* (London: Oxford University Press, 1947), 226.

5. Cf. Thomas Aquinas, *Summa Theologica*, II-II, 187, 3.

6. Ibid., 77, 4.

7. R. H. Tawney, *Religion and the Rise of Capitalism* (New York: New American Library, 1958), 37.

8. Ibid., 4.

9. Aquinas, *De Veritate,* 23, 6.

10. Aquinas, *Summa Contra Gentiles*, III, 37.

11. See Aquinas's "Treatise on Law" in *Summa Theologica*, I-II, 90–97.

12. "Pastoral Constitution on the Church in the Modern World," in *The Documents of Vatican II*, ed. Walter M. Abbott, S.J. (New York: Guild Press, 1966), para. 64, p. 273.

13. Daniel Bell, *The Cultural Contradictions of Capitalism* (New York: Basic Books, 1976); Joseph A. Schumpeter, *Capitalism, Socialism, and Democracy*, 3d ed. (New York: Harper and Brothers, 1950).

14. Max Weber, *The Protestant Ethic and the Spirit of Capitalism*, trans. Talcott Parsons (New York: Charles Scribner's, 1958), 15–31.

15. Tawney, *Religion and the Rise of Capitalism*, 76.

16. Weber, *Protestant Ethic*, 84–86.

17. Ibid., 98–112, 229 nn. 47, 48.

18. Ibid., 180.

19. Ibid., 49.

20. Adam Smith, *The Wealth of Nations*, ed. Edwin Cannan (Chicago: University of Chicago Press, 1976); *The Theory of Moral Sentiments* (Indianapolis, Ind.: Liberty Classics, 1969).

21. Tawney, *Religion and the Rise of Capitalism*, 227.

22. The statistics on the Catholic population in America are from John Tracy Ellis, *American Catholicism*, 2d ed. (Chicago: University of Chicago Press, 1969), 21, 82.

23. The discussion of the influence of Protestant denominations in the United States follows closely the work of Thomas C. Cochran, *Business in American Life*. See also Marquis W. Childs and Douglas Cater, *Ethics in a Business Society* (New York: New American Library, 1954).

24. Cochran, *Business in American Life*, 37.

25. Quoted in ibid., 38.

26. Quoted in ibid., 106.

27. Quoted in ibid., 109.

28. Horatio Alger, *Struggling Upward and Other Works* (New York: Crown Publishers, 1945).

29. Cf. Henry F. May, *Protestant Churches and Industrial America* (New York: Harper and Brothers, 1949).

30. Cf. George A. Kelly, *The Catholic Church and the American Poor* (New York: Alba House, 1976).

31. Walter Rauschenbusch, *A Theology for the Social Gospel* (New York: Abingdon Press, 1945), 35.

32. Quoted and discussed in Ellis, *American Catholicism*, 145.

33. See Oliver F. Williams, introduction to *The Judeo-Christian Tradition*, 1–21.

34. Aquinas, *Summa Contra Gentiles*, III, 37.

35. The Second Vatican Council decree, "The Church in the Modern World," reiterates this important point for the sphere of economics: "economic activity is to be carried out according to its own methods and laws but within the limits of morality, so that God's plan for mankind can be realized." See Abbott, *The Documents of Vatican II*, para. 64, p. 273. All citations of Vatican II documents are to this edition.

36. The following sentence from the documents of the 1971 World Synod of Bishops has been called "the most notable development to date in the history of modern social teaching": "Action on behalf of justice and participation in the transformation of the world fully appears to us as a constitutive dimension of the preaching of the gospel or, in other words, of the Church's mission for the redemption of the human race and its liberation from every oppressive situation." See "Justice in the World," in *The Gospel of Peace and Justice: Catholic Social Teaching Since Pope John*, ed. Joseph Gremillion (Maryknoll, N.Y.: Orbis Books, 1976), 514. For an analysis of this statement, see Charles M. Murphy, "Action for Justice as Constitutive of the Preaching of the Gospel: What Did the 1971 Synod Mean?" *Theological Studies* 44 (1983): 298–311; and Francis Schüssler Fiorenza, "The Church's Religious Identity and Its Social and Political Mission," *Theological Studies* 43 (1982): 197–225.

37. John Paul II, *Laborem Exercens*, para. 27. All citations are to the text published by the United States Catholic Conference, publication no. 825, Office of Publishing Services.

38. For a comprehensive study of the social dimension of the faith by twelve authors, see Houck and Williams, *Co-Creation and Capitalism*.

39. *John Paul II*, Laborem Exercens, para. 25.

40. Ibid.

41. Ibid.

42. The Vatican II document "The Church in the Modern World" alludes to the dialectical aspect of the Kingdom. "On this earth that Kingdom is already present in mystery. When the Lord returns it will be brought into full flower," para. 39.

43. Cf. H. Richard Niebuhr, *Christ and Culture* (New York: Harper, 1951); and Walter Kasper, *Jesus the Christ* (New York: Paulist Press, 1977).

44. Pope John Paul II, in his first encyclical letter, *Redemptor Hominis*, portrays his vision of integral humanism. See para. 14.

45. John Paul II, *Redemptor Hominis*, para. 14. All citations are to the text published by the United States Catholic Conference, Office of Publication Services.

46. *Centesimus Annus* and *Economic Justice for All* are published by the United States Catholic Conference.

47. For an excellent discussion of stakeholders, see James E. Post, Lee E. Preston, and Sybille Sachs, *Redefining the Corporation: Stakeholder Management and Organizational Wealth* (Stanford, Calif.: Stanford University Press, 2002).

48. Weber, *Protestant Ethic*, 182.

PART I

Developing a Framework for Discussion

ONE

Non-Religion, Religion, and Spirituality

Competing for Business

MARTIN E. MARTY

Setting the Stage

▋ *Thesis: The triumph of the market casts issues relating religion and spirituality to business into new forms.*

The forces, movements, and energies that today we call religious, spiritual, or faith-based have related through the ages in diverse ways to the spheres of life that today we call economic and that we see embodied in business and commerce.

These relations have been particularly vivid in the scriptures, traditions, and communities that derive from prophetic faiths, the Abrahamaic or Jerusalemaic, namely Judaism, Christianity, and Islam. At the same time, ties between religious and economic spheres are also easily traceable in other traditions, for example, the Confucian, Buddhist, and Hindu.

Some of these relations have been and are positive. The texts and traditions encourage or command believers to be stewards, to carry on their missions, and to live out their vocations in commerce, whether as individuals or in communities. Other elements of these traditions have been and are critical. They impel their adherents to be responsible in respect to material possessions, to be concerned over the temptations of riches and the sufferings of the poor, to develop ethics of buying, selling, and sharing, and to organize individual and collective business ventures in ways congruent with the norms of their faith.

31

That such positive and critical intentions grew more complex with the rise of modern corporate life has been documented at great length. The prophetic leaders and communities made many efforts to show their awareness of these changes in economic life.

At the turn of the millennium, that centuries-long trend of complication had increased immeasurably. The new factors on a global scale are "the triumph of the market," along with debates over the enlargement of the concept of individual freedom in market involvement and technological developments, including, most recently and most emphatically, the "e-revolution."

Concurrent with the realization of those three factors have been changes within religious communities and in their cultural environments. The most vivid illustration in the West, and particularly in North America, has been the invention and refinement of "spirituality," a phenomenon particularly suited to a pluralistic, free, free-market society.

Spirituality has become an advertised instrument for helping individuals cope with and interpret their place in the stressed world of business and commerce. For example, an advertisement in *Newsday*, 3 March 2000, asks: "Ever lose your *glasses* just to find them on top of your . . . *head?* Everyone today is looking and looking for *Spirituality*. Maybe they're looking in the wrong place. If you're Jewish, maybe you should *look here*. To your Judaism. To your special heritage. For Judaism has always taught that spirituality can be found in one's own home and community."

Similarly, many leaders in the corporate world have examined the role spirituality can play in helping provide meaning in the economic realm and debated whether its presence may enrich and deepen performance and participation by their employees in companies.

That this new development has considerable potential and promises some positive effects will be obvious to anyone who hears the testimony of people who would replace religion and faith communities with this individualized spirituality. It is likely, however, that spirituality will also continue to be seen as both complementary to and in rivalry with religion. The disadvantages of religion in the eyes of many in business and commerce relate to the fact that it connotes tradition that is not always adaptive, institutions that can be perceived as "sectarian" and self-seeking, and the like.

In this emerging cultural situation, it is time to take up issues concerning both religion and spirituality, against the background of non-religion. Contending that both have their place, I would like the following effort to be seen as an endeavor to render perceptions and employments of religion somewhat more "easy" and those of spirituality more difficult in the eyes of those who would have in mind the interests of individuals, companies, cultures, and global economies alike.

The motive for doing this has nothing to do with "selling" one at the expense of the other or simply trying to perceive and help effect a "level playing field" for both. I will contend that what religion has represented, while challenging to business and commerce, includes some critiques and community possibilities that evaporate when individualized and eclectic spirituality dominates. Meanwhile, spirituality can help enlarge imagination and vivify both religion and business and commerce.

A Six-Part Matrix for Observing and Discerning Our Subject

■   *Thesis: The positive effects of religion and spirituality on business and commerce cannot easily be separated.*

Before pointing to what I mean by business, let me present what I will call a "matrix" for examining non-religion, religion, and spirituality. I want to point out elements that are not unique to religion but are also visible in spirituality, many forms of non-religion, and many expressions in business and commerce. These elements are often associated only with religion.

The base for this matrix is not a definition but a pointing-to of religion, one that I have found serviceable through the decades. Historians tend not to overdefine subjects, but they do need to find and set some provisional boundaries for their analyses and narratives. They are less interested in preparing a priori molds into which everything should fit. My method calls for me to note in each case what observers of numerous cultures through different periods have tended to call religion. Thus, having been one of eight editors of *The Encyclopedia of Religion* (Macmillan, 1987) and someone who had to help decide what topics to include as religious, I often describe the venture by saying that "religion is the kind of stuff you write about in a book with such a title."

If all but one or two of the following characteristic elements are observable in a phenomenon, both in common speech and scholarly usage, we find reason to locate it in this matrix.

Ultimate Concern

First, there is *ultimate concern*. Paul Tillich's word serves well to point to this dimension. In whatever culture and circumstance they find themselves, most people have some center, some focus, and usually some object outside themselves to which they direct their passions, their most profound thoughts, their intentions and commitments—often to the point that they are willing to die for these. People can direct such ultimate concern to God, to the nation, to success or sex (in Tillich's own illustration), and, for that matter, to their vocation and profession and, yes, business. By itself, however, we would not necessarily call such a commitment or ultimate concern "religious" unless it focused on God or the Sacred or the Numinous, *or is accompanied by a number of the characteristics I shall discuss below.* (Remember, there are many nontheistic and humanistic religions, e.g., many expressions of Buddhism.)

Myth and Symbol

A second feature in this matrix reveals a predilection by individuals or groups to express themselves through myth and symbol. Most of the time religious, spiritual, faith-full people may operate with conventional modes of rationality, as their culture conceives these. Most of their discourse will be of the ordinary linguistic and rational sort. But some events of their lives, for example those that deal with being born and wedding and dying, or aspects of living that call for commitment by larger groups to causes, as in the case of devotion to the nation, evoke mythosymbolic language. These can be the myths of ancient Greece, the symbols of Egyptian religion, or the myths and symbols our nation has recognized when elicited by sacrifice, as at Gettysburg, or realized in Abraham Lincoln's rhetoric: "Fourscore and seven years ago . . ."

The Star of David, the Rising Sun, the Cross of Jesus, the accounts of creation in Genesis or in the Navajo story would all exemplify this dimension. Might we also observe a kind of sacral power in the text of a written national constitution, or, in some economic instances, a dollar sign? At this point we would not insist on a simple "yes" answer; this is merely a signaling, an alert.

Rite and Ceremony

Third, in this matrix of the spiritual, the religious, the ultimate, we characteristically look for a favoring of rite and ceremony. That to which one attaches mythic and symbolic value, such as being born and dying, or greeting the times of day and the seasons of the year, the falling of rain or an approach to battle, causes most people to ritualize the reality. There is so much terror, so much ecstasy in the world that most sentient beings could not bear existence were there no ritual compression and condensation of complex phenomena available to them. The public response to assassinations of beloved leaders illustrates this as much as do Yom Kippur or observances of New Year in many religions issuing from Asia.

For a third time, again offered a bit playfully but not without some serious intent, we can ask: might we do well to look at the graduation ceremonies for master of business administration achievers, or the mounting of the certified public accountant diploma on the wall; or, similarly, initiation into the modes of corporate life in particular companies, as belonging to this matrix? In each of these cases we must be careful not to overextend the game and overplay the provocations. Appropriately, it has been said that "if everything is religious, nothing is religious." There is some danger that we might diffuse concepts of the religious and quasi-religious so much that nothing distinctive remains in respect to this matrix. But we might equally underdevelop them. So, here is another alert.

Metaphysical Backdrop
Fourth, expressions of the spiritual, the religious, the faith-full, the ritually practical tend to assume that there is some sort of—I use this word with caution—metaphysical backdrop. That is, behind the visible routines of everyday life within a given sphere, groups and individuals often suggest that there is something more important, not always and not easily accessible on empirical terms, that gives meaning to it all—some *real,* and not metaphoric, "invisible hand."

Such an assumption is certainly evident among all theistic faiths, all outlooks based on some concept of divine epiphany or revelation, and all philosophies that cherish metaphysical concepts. In most sanctioning of wars by modern nation-states such appeals also have been regular; a nation acts "under God" or in the name of some bigger story that exacts sacrifice of life.

I venture to propose that such implied metaphysical claims attach themselves to most inclusive economic philosophies. This becomes obvious in any retrospect of Marxist socialism. That ideology included a prophecy, on no empirical grounds, concerning the inevitability of the emergence of a classless society and the decline in the value of the nation-state. And the cruel eye of the historian shows Marxism to have been based on a quasi-metaphysical assumption.

Many of the claims associated with capitalism, from roots in the Protestant ethos as discerned by R. H. Tawney, Max Weber, and others, from Adam Smith down to modern metaphysicians of the market, qualify. To isolate these in their contemporary forms, one does well to observe Pope John Paul II. During the years when he had to be preoccupied no longer with opposing Communism he has turned his energies to addressing many capitalist outcomes and side effects in the form of "consumerism" and "commodification." He sees these to be making quasi-religious claims on many in the free and free-market world. Some theologians in the prophetic tradition speak of these as idolatrous. Protestant theologian Harvey Cox combined the playfulness of discernment that we are here including with some prophetic insight in a widely circulated article, "The Market as God." We may think of market language as being grounded in secular rationality, but philosophers of science and historians of philosophy are increasingly discerning a quasi-metaphysical commitment among rationally "cool" analysts in economics as well as in many other areas of human activity.

Behavioral Correlates

Fifth in this matrix is an observation that some behavioral correlates accompany the other features. Thus: If you believe this, then you don't eat that; or you raise your children thus. You observe these days on the calendar, and you call this or that action "good," while a person of another faith community or commitment is equally serious about other courses. In all these cases, faith, religion, and spirituality are not conventionally confined to the ideal, mental, and abstract worlds. They call for agency, practical action, usually of sorts that follow certain specific patterns of injunction.

Can we observe this feature also in respect to themes we associate with vocations, professions, and careers, including those in business? The Hippocratic oath in medicine is an illustration of an at least quasi-sacral call for certain behavioral consequences, as are many codes in the business world. A person or a firm is allowed to compete mercilessly and even go as far as the destruction of the other within the confines of these codes. But the same person is penalized if such actions are carried on in "lay" circles or away from the active business scene. Oaths, vows, and affirmations behind various ethical prescriptions and codes tend to "fit" the business sphere.

Social and Communal Life

Finally—and for the first time there may be less consistency of application to "spirituality" and "non-religion"—religions, faiths, cultures of belief and practice tend to advocate and issue in *social and communal* life. The individual characteristically cannot bear the weight of divine revelations, hierophanies, experiences of conversion, the witnessing of the uncanny, or the miraculous. She seeks company. And if one is to act upon ultimate concerns, myth and symbol, rite and ceremony, metaphysical commitments, and behavioral correlates, these are ordinarily best nurtured and sustained by groups, by communities, and through social organizations.

In this sixth case, a late-modern, postmodern tendency in the religious zone makes it necessary to qualify some aspects of this matrix when introducing, not the word "religion," but "spirituality." Thanks to the explorations of social analysts and prophets like Thomas Luckmann, Robert N. Bellah, Robert Wuthnow, and hosts of others, we observe many people, at least temporarily or in a certain personal or cultural phase, pursuing their course apart from and even rejecting community, institution, and organization. A mantra heard frequently on television or in bookstores and at health clubs is: "I am not a member of the institutional church; I am against organized religion; I am not even sure I am religious. But I am *very* "spiritual.""

While some casual countertrends toward community are apparent in this market—witness that advertisement about spirituality and Judaism quoted above—this trend presents sufficient cultural valence and offers sufficient promise to have to be taken seriously. And in many ways this spiritual endeavor leaves the seeker, the searcher, isolated, even determinedly lonely. As such his or her agency matches well many aspects of business life in a competitive society.

At the beginning of this section I mentioned that I would note what I mean by "business," and now we can add "commerce." Since it is not my intention to offer anything original on that subject, let dictionary terms suffice: "The occupation, work, or trade in which a person is engaged"; "a specific occupation or pursuit"; "commercial, industrial, or professional dealings"; "a commercial enterprise or establishment"; "commercial dealings." And commerce: "The buying and selling of goods, especially on a large scale." I will leave refinements or criticisms of those definitions to others who are experts and who see reasons for adducing special definitions in relation to the present topic.

Non-Religion Competing for Business

■ *Thesis: Issues concerning religion and spirituality have to be seen in relation to the non-religious dimensions of business and commerce.*

All the talk about cultures in which business and commerce dominate can depend upon elements of sleight of hand or altering-by-definition of phenomena. In ordinary discourse, depending upon practical and common sense observation, there is no question that the cultures about which we are speaking are not religious, "faith-full," or spiritual. Individuals who participate in the economic order may bring to it all kinds of private commitments. There may be some small businesses and maybe even some corporations that self-consciously set out to embody and exemplify specific religious commitments. There are, after all, Christian Yellow Pages, and one can point to exceptional executives who speak with great clarity about faith commitments and then set out to put them to work in their firms and spheres.

Still, in post-Enlightenment times, in most Western cultures, an implied and sometimes formal commitment to the use of "secular rationality" is privileged when people are in "the original position" (John Rawls 1971) determining values, justice, and the like. We do not look for Mormon brain surgery or Baptist renology or Confucian blood transfusions; so also we do not look for Adventist bidding and selling on the market; only casually and even flippantly do people talk about "economic miracles" or an almost supernatural rewarding roll of the dice in the stock market. Usually the whole enterprise is calculated on empirical, testable, rational grounds.

Such observations lead me to say that among the main spheres of life, business is one of the more difficult in which to put to work religious, faith-full, and spiritual, especially communal and social, norms. In the Public Religion Project (1996–99), a three-year endeavor sponsored by the Pew Charitable Trusts through the University of Chicago, we found no difficulty tracing and dealing with explicit individual and communal religious expression in the media, politics and government, education on all levels, and more.

It was much more difficult applying the same norms and bringing similar inquiries to the area we code-named "Business and Commerce." This despite the fact—or the hunch—that more leaders in that area were personally religious than are many mass communicators and academics. (Let's leave politicians out of this for the moment; they cannot *not* appear to be religiously motivated and committed in the current climate.)

Just how are religious norms put to work on the stock market; in pricing; in competitive realms? To put that question is no license for religious critics to attack the business and commercial worlds for being what they are and perhaps largely have to be. Instead, we advance them to bring a dose of realism to our proceedings and implicitly to offer a challenge to those who would make discernments and prescriptions in this world, especially those who suggest that there is an easy fit between religion and business.

In other words, it is easier to find company for *homo religiosus* among *homo politicus, homo educationis,* and the like than in the leadership or among the agents of *homo economicus.* The world of business and commerce may make its appeal to the mind (as through advertising) and the spirit (through extraordinary appeals), but it sets out to be, and ordinarily has to be, steadfastly material. It deals with buying and trading "things," usually while being oblivious to religious concerns.

Of course, an advertiser knows he takes risks if his advertisements insult the rabbis, the pope, and certainly Allah and the Prophet. And, including a larger "of course," some religions do make explicit economic stipulations, as in the case of Islam and the prohibition of charging interest. But in most semisecularized Western cultures, the zone of business and commerce comes across as one of the most secularized, by most definitions of that term.

We have thus far treated business too monolithically. Its spectrum includes an enormous range of basic commitments depending upon whether and how it relates to the personal or the impersonal, the individual or the corporate, the unmonitored (e.g., by government) or the monitored, the independent or governmentally stimulated (e.g., in Keynesian economics), the theoretical or the practical, the disfavored or the favored. The old story about Margaret Fuller uttering, "I accept the universe," and the follow-up comment of Thomas Carlyle, "Gad, she'd better!" can apply to the universe of business and commerce.

Such a universe is inescapable among all but the Robinson Crusoes of the world. The moment Trobriand Islanders or Afghan villagers barter, purchase, or offer natural products or handmade goods for sale, they are engaging in some of the basics that have corollaries in the worlds of high finance and speculation. We live, willy-nilly, in political worlds and so, also, in economic worlds. Insofar as they are non-religious, they are puzzling to those who would make prophetic discernments.

Business, Non-Religious or Not: A Subject of Prophetic Scrutiny

▌ *Thesis: In any dynamic culture, the world of business is to be subjected to critical scrutiny from religious vantages.*

We would not be preparing a book on business, religion, and spirituality if everything were perceived as being in order in the business world. The contributors and authors tend to be ethicists, theologians, philosophically self-conscious businesspersons, and the like. Most of us may well find much to affirm in the expansive worlds of business. Indeed, a simply negative and disparaging approach to them would not likely get much of a hearing. Nor can many critics stand sufficiently apart from the assumptions of the business world to have the credentials for expressing such utter condemnations. But I suspect that many do share the assumption that there should be *krisis*, judgment, scrutiny of anything that encompasses so much of life and determines so many human destinies as do business and commerce.

There is a long tradition of prophetic criticism of business in the Hebrew Scriptures and later rabbinic glosses, the New Testament and the Christian tradition, the Qur'anic literature, and elsewhere. Sometimes it is directed against the monarch, sometimes against the religious leader, but most frequently against misusers of material possessions. A cynic has described the Old Testament prophets as spokespersons of the party out of power. Had they sidled up to the king and the rich and whispered only affirmation in their ears, they would have shown that they had not been called to be prophets or been categorized as such. They were acting in accord with the job description of the prophet-by-vocation.

Some of them discerned and pointed to a religious dimension to the business and commerce of their times. They adduced a religious justification for dealings that exacerbated the tension and enlarged the gap between seller and buyer, rich and poor, accumulator and sharer. The norm the classic prophets employed was to be witness to a jealous God, who sees material possessions to be among the main challenges to theocentric living and a healthy community. Henri desRoche says that religious forces face essentially three options when dealing with the powers that be. They may *attest* them, which means "affirm them to be correct, true, or genuine" overall. And most religionists have tended to do so. It is this tendency that often produces what is perceived as the self-preserving character of "organized religion" and that turns many away from it.

Second, they may *protest* egregiously unjust practices and arrangements within an approved, but ambiguous, system. Or they may *contest* the system and all practices within it, as if from without. This is what radical materialist Marxist criticism set out to do, however blind it was to the ideological flaws that were part of its own system. This is what Hutterites and the Amish and other peaceful "dropouts" of the surrounding economic order, set out to do by example.

In our culture, most of the criticism, including, I suspect, most of what appears in this book, is in the *protest* category. That is, it "accepts the universe" of the market, is aware of its triumph, at least in the phases manifest in our contemporary world, and recognizes many of the mixed blessings of that triumph. But it measures that market triumph also by norms outside it, finds some aspects seriously lacking, and makes counter-proposals to change its ways.

Such a task of critiquing and proposing is extremely difficult today. Change in the business world, especially in our new cybernetic, e-commerce, and e-business contexts, is so sudden, so vast, so drastic, that it is hard to gather data and find perspectives for offering judgment. One evidence of this is the meagerness and tardiness of analysis and critique. The shelves of books by and for religious ethicists on some themes are extensive and coherent: the civil rights struggle; issues of war and peace; even those that have to do with the environment or with health-and-medicine themes are abundant and, again, coherent.

The shelves of the new world of business and commerce, however, are scantier, the databases more scattered, the generalizations more questionable, and the ethical norms not as firm as in some of the other areas.

W. W. Rostow liked to speak of the Industrial Revolution as a "take-off" in economic growth and invention. The current business revolution is such a new take-off. A half century ago or less, there was no talk of the e-revolution, little in respect to globalization in the economy, or of corporate mergers and takeovers. It was not yet the time to offer a retrospect on the failure of alternatives to business and commerce worlds, as in communism or radical socialisms. It was not yet the time to discuss a cultural tilt in vocational and professional interests. (Witness the enrollments in business and career planning among collegians whose parents or grandparents made a "leftist" or "Greening of America" assault on business.) Criticism of the adjustment of other institutions such as government, education on all levels, and religious institutions to this revolution was only beginning to develop.

One small, but not unimportant, observation that demands attention comes not from Catholicism, Judaism, or mainstream Protestantism, but from the one-fourth of Americans who make up the Evangelical cohort. As late as H. Richard Niebuhr's *Social Sources of Denominationalism* (1927) these belonged to or were prospects for "the churches of the dispossessed," who brought critiques of the "possessors" to match. Long after that time they still housed what was left of what Max Weber called "ascetic Protestantism."

Some of these attracted and nurtured millennial apocalypticists, who showed little interest in the larger questions of the economy in a world soon to pass away. Most of them saw spiritual validity in "Sunday closing laws," in economic injunctions to "love not the world, neither the things that are in the world," in restraint and, on spiritual terms, shunning of the material. They were by then only distant heirs of the world the Tawneys and Webers described as the progenitor of capitalism. But they had chosen to stress contentment with one's position in life and to scorn affluence.

I do not think it an inaccurate observation or an unfair judgment to say of this Evangelical world and its corollaries that the periodicals, the radio and television programs, the curricular accents, the celebration of celebrities in this sector show it to be at least as "worldly," materialistic, and—outstripping its competitors—"market oriented" in its religious activities as the non-religious. Critics and liberals in the personalist traditions, the Martin Bubers and Paul Tillichs, the liberation theologians and others who worried about commodification and consumerism railed against the depersonalizing, dehumanizing aspects of corporate life. Meanwhile, many of these religious conservatives "out-moderned" them and often replaced them as entrepreneurs in their religious and cultural locations.

There are significant exceptions to that observation, but I propose it for research, confirmation, or what I believe can only be partial disconfirmation. Consult the writings of people like Jacques Ellul, John Howard Yoder, Jim Wallis, Tony Campolo, Ron Sider, and other intra-Evangelical critics for particulars. They continue critiques from the narrow line between *protest* and *context* approaches.

While such voices can be heard in the preaching, the prophetic, the critical aspects of ethical and spiritual appraisal, no doubt most specialists in these fields today work within the context of the market world that has emerged. On its terms, they are asking how to humanize it, speaking of *dignitatis humanae*, as does the Pope. They ask questions about government-business and rich-poor relations in the context of the given within our culture without wishing it and its mixed blessings away. In sum, I believe that the next direction for most in this field will have to do more with *krisis*, making critical judgments, than with prophecy of a "contesting," culturally transcendent sort, at least in respect to its intentions.

Religion and Spirituality Competing for Business

■ *Thesis: Religious and spiritual interpretations of life and prescriptions for action compete with non-religious aspects of business and commercial enterprises.*

I've tucked a kind of wordplay into the phrase, "competing for business." Advocates of both compete for the ear of business agents; the different voices are competing for the ear of those who make decisions in business. Left and right, regulated- and free-market advocates compete to be heard, so they might make some difference in the world of business. They have an "ethics business" to promote and sell.

At the same time, the phrase recognizes that what today is called "religion" on one hand and "spirituality" on the other uses different strategies to address and alter business world assumptions and practices.

In what way do their attempts show up?

First, they compete in respect to the *interpretation of life*. Their task is made more difficult in the domestic world described by Alasdair MacIntyre's book title *After Virtue*. Contending interests go "after virtue" but do so "after" the time when they share premises sufficiently to engage in meaningful argument. They find new difficulties when the various schools of thought and religious and non-religious communities do not share enough presuppositions to have the kind of disagreements out of which arguments can emerge. It is vastly more difficult to engage in ethical discourse or religious interpretation in the global business and commerce, where cultural assumptions that proceed out of Islamic, Confucian, Shintoist, and other such matrices confront them.

However, they aspire to do so. We can find testimony to the fact that there is uneasiness even where there is affirmation if we consult the record of papal encyclicals and actions on the economy; the ruling of various Islamic agencies; the controversies over the economy among Jewish religious thinkers; the mainstream Protestant conciliar (as in World Council of Churches, National Council of Churches) efforts; the turns of National Association of Evangelicals leaders and forces; the critical voluntary associations.

I sometimes tell of a round of University of Chicago alumni talks in partnership with a global economist. He regularly proclaimed Good News and Bad News. The good news was that the market had won. It had swept the competitors away. The market represented the present and dominated the future. That was good. (Remember, he was from the University of Chicago, where economists get Nobel Prizes for contributing to "market" talk!) Now, his bad news: "we" have not the faintest idea with what personal and social philosophies to greet this change at the millennial turn. The colleague was in effect uttering the kind of challenge this volume set out to address.

A second range of critiques and proposals directed to business and commerce and based on the acts of listening and research by ethicists and public philosophers or theologians has to do with *personal life and action*. If we divide that personal life, as opposed to the *Weltanschauungen* just mentioned, into four levels—vocation, profession, career, and work and job—it does not take long to see some challenges that need to be addressed.

How does one live out a *vocation*, a calling, especially in theistically oriented ethical systems and responses, where God somehow does the calling, but especially now in a sphere where classic aspects of "calling" are not easily applied? It might have been easier for the farmer, the monk, the homemaker, the small-business person to live out such a vocation within a culture that privileged religious discourse. It is not impossible, say advocates and exemplars, to live out a vocation in corporate, global, complex, ever changing business life, but it needs a fresh approach.

What do the *professions* mean in a time when change undercuts their assumptions? Joseph Schumpeter has spoken of the "creative destruction" that is integral to self-replacing capitalist achievements. But that creative destruction can take a toll on personal lives of professionals who find their professions rendered obsolete, their qualifications questioned or irrelevant, their justifications unheeded. People therefore "change professions," which can be a creative act. But it is different from the situation when a business calling meant pursuit of a consistent profession.

Career: this has become the key sphere in today's business. It represents a narrowing of profession and certainly of vocation, even as it is an application of both. It is in career, where status matters so much in definition, where takeovers and mergers and new technologies lead to aborting of trajectories that we see many of the psychological manifestations that the religious and the spiritual would address. Among these are *Mangelkrankheit*, a classic German diagnostic term for deficiency, voiding, "work-sickness"; assaults on marriage and family life; uprootings and replacements that make it difficult to sustain religious traditions; and more. Again, career mobility has its assets as an expression of freedom and as being evocative of creative responses. But it calls for a new appraisal and agenda.

Finally, *work and job.* This is the area that absorbs much of the energy of religious appraisal and spiritual counsel. What happens to vocation in the era of piecework? asked the critics of the early-Industrial-Age factory and the assembly line. How can one find meaning in isolated activity that has little relation to the end product? Such centuries-old questions acquire a new edge in the e-business and e-commerce world, which comes, as most change does, with a package that includes assets and liabilities.

One could move from the personal to the corporate and must then ask, what about the *vocation* of a business? How does it work out its "mission" and of what, and how is it a "steward?" How can one honor the sense of mission and stewardship of the employees and leaders?

Another dimension to which fresh inquiry is given has to do with *governmental involvement* on global and local levels alike. A business ethic that is based on the assumption that governments have either nothing or everything to do with regulating and attending to the interaction of markets is not likely to touch ground in the ever changing world of regulation. Some free-enterprise advocates tend to negate the instruments by which government involvement enhances their work and enables them to compete. Others do little but complain about what is occurring. Some critics of the free-enterprise system believe that regulation will help in their task of humanizing business, but the record of the twentieth century gives them less credibility than they might need as they seek a "third way."

This set of obversations again is not made in order that one can dismiss either school but to call for reflection upon the fact that the agenda has changed. How to bring, say, a Catholic viewpoint based on encyclicals as old as *Rerum Novarum* (1891) to this world of multicultural transactions, among nations and polities that have no concern for or curiosity about what popes say? How to relate what popes say about what Catholic (and other) business people do? What kind of a hearing do pronouncements about the economy based on *shari'a* get in non-Islamic cultures? Illustrations in the form of questions abound.

Particular Problem Areas

▌ *Thesis: The turn-of-the-millennium cultural context evokes fresh approaches to business themes by the religious.*

I hope that this essay will help provide a framework for discussion, which is what I have been trying to do. If readers accept any part of the picture of challenge and possibility outlined up to this point, they may check with me some problem areas for advocates and ethicists (and ethicist advocates) to address, if not now, then in the future. I will necessarily be brief and do little more than point to those areas.

First, the complexity of business and commerce. There are now so many massive corporate and monolithic levels that the language appropriate to the entrepreneurs, so honored in society today, does little justice to the *complexity of the large companies and transactors* (which the successful among the enterprisers become). In a pluralist world, these firms cannot be organized around particular views of ultimate concern or particular faith commitments. And even if they were, their agents deal constantly with others that do not share those commitments.

Second, *pluralism* within firms, locally, nationally, and globally. It would be unrealistic to say that locally based firms in homogeneous cultures—Mormon-led in Mormon country, Baptist-managed in Baptist cultures, Islamic in Islamic national isolation—found no problems in communicating even with constituencies that share many of their assumptions. But there were some advantages. For example, they could, without much controversy, easily use company profits for charitable activities, often religiously based, in ways that are more difficult to pursue where management, labor, and milieu are made up of people with vastly differing commitments.

Third, *secularity*. I introduced this subject in discussing the "non-religious" assumptions in commercial and business ideal and practice. We have to give attention to the way in which the characteristic modes of operating in such cultures, modes based on "secular rationality," do not do justice to other ways of addressing reality. When people make basic decisions in personal and, they might hope, in business and corporate life, they are often guided also by tradition, intuition, community, memory, affection, and hope. All these are jostled in the pluralist, secular world, where they are not shared by the diverse constituencies of firms and markets. Yet they are to be somehow put to work; they *are* being put to work. How bring this element forward and deal with it equitably?

Fourth, the "*interests*" of religious institutions. These organizations, as communions and also at home and in the world, are shaped by business and commerce. Clerical leaders have long had to be adept at dealing with the politics and economics of pulpit and pew. Not to put too fine or too inelegant a point on it: as their critics observe, they also are operating businesses, usually small ones, but connected in many cases to large ones.

Do their political and economic advocacies reflect this set of interests? We think of occasions when a Catholic or other religiously based hospital is struck by labor forces, who claim that the church is not just to its own workers while it calls and works for justice in the society at large.

As the late Father John Courtney Murray used to say of the Catholic church, and as one might say of others, the Catholic church is a "thing" into which one bumps. It is not a vapor, escapable, evadable, invisible, inoffensive.

For the reasons associated with that reality, many have addressed spiritual dimensions of the business world in our time by the invention and celebration of "spirituality," the term we have least discussed to this point.

The Invention of Spirituality and Its Relation to Business

▌ *Thesis: There are three competing strategies in the advocacy of spirituality; the most popular emergent form has more in common with religion than might appear at first sight.*

This is not the place to undertake a full-dress historical or phenomenological study of the rise of "spirituality" in our culture. But to achieve what I hope to do in the final pages, I have to ask especially younger people with shorter memories to undertake an act of imagination with me: imagine yourself a sentient, informed, culturally alert adult as recently as a third of a century ago, say, in 1967. That is when I was called to produce an article on the subject for *Daedalus* of the American Academy of Arts and Sciences. The terms "spiritual" and "spirituality" were virtually unavailable, they were very rarely used in public discourse. The Catholic publishers that had once produced books on the subject—Kennedy, Bruce, Newman, and others—were going out of business. Mainstream Protestant leadership tended to be favoring models of ministering to and among and by what was then called "secular man," who would have been embarrassed by spirituality. Judaism, in its Reform and Conservative wings, had not yet recovered cabalistic or Hasidic "spiritual" expressions. Theologian Paul Tillich, who urged us never to bury or repudiate a concept in religion, did think that "spiritual" and "spirituality" could not be retrieved. He said this in his book *Life in the Spirit*, the third volume of his *Systematic Theology*, as recently as 1963.

Consult the *Reader's Guide to Periodical Literature* and you will find from 1900 to the 1960s some references to what I call "spirituality with adjectives": Catholic, Jewish, medieval, mystical, and other spiritualities. Then in the 1970s authors of some articles began to argue that "spirituality" was too rich a term to let the religious have a monopoly on it. Let humanists be spiritual too. Very soon a variety of popular journals, including the best-selling women's magazines, were advertising spirituality as something everyone could have, should have.

It is important to listen carefully to the different claims about spirituality made in respect to the world of business. Not all advocates and critics mean the same thing by it, and not all are careful when using such words. I am going to propose three areas in which they are heard and to which they are directed.

Sometimes spirituality is equated simply with what I would call *human soulfulness,* as when one responds to the wondrous with a sense of wonder. In a lineage traceable from Aristotle to Leon Kass, one finds the soul spoken of not as something uncanny or as a ghost in a machine. Instead, the soul is the vital and integrating power of any organic body, something that represents its openness to possibility, to futures. Dealing with it does not pull one into the sphere religion occupied. There are no claims for dealing with the supernatural, suprahuman, or transcendental. An agnostic or atheist can be, and often is, more "soulful" than many of the pious. Devotion to spirituality as human soulfulness, whether or not it is relevant to discourse about business—although it usually is—does not crowd the spheres we have seen in the sixfold matrix above.

Second, there can be, and there is, a revival of "*spirituality with adjectives.*" Sociologist Robert Wuthnow in his recent book *After Heaven* speaks of it as "dwelling in" as opposed to "seeking" spirituality. I like to call it "moored" instead of "unmoored." It is anchored in specific texts, traditions, communities. People may deal with these sources and contexts syncretistically, on "interfaith" grounds, or borrowing from or depending on more "sectarian" sources. Thus a Catholic may learn Buddhist meditation techniques, and Christians may learn from Jewish or Buddhist pursuits of health. This spirituality with adjectives, the "moored" sort, is a challenge to and a revivifier of many standard religious bodies and communities that had neglected it. Such spirituality has its own kind of place—close to that of religion—in all talk of business ethics, philosophy, expression, and action.

If development of human soulfulness represents the least difficulty for those who would apply it to business, spirituality with adjectives, because of the traditional and communal bases, represents the most problematic, though in some ways more promising, approach.

The third form is one that is most frequently advertised and which I think should be seen as a kind of stealth plane flying low under the range where people can target "religion" in flight in our culture. Advocates of such spirituality often use the word "God," though not necessarily referring to a transcendent one, a "thou," but instead to the god "within us." More often they make claims about "energy" and "connection" in the universe as the backdrop. Think of that as *disembodied,* or *spiritual, spirituality*, or as the spirituality that relates to a metaphysic of universal energy and connection.

Dean Winnifred Sullivan in conversation has given me her definition of spirituality: it is what is left after people take religion and then take out of it all the things they don't like. Thus, organization, institution, community in continuity, dwelling, mooring, focus get replaced by eclectic elements that help individuals produce a collage, a montage, an assemblage pleasing to themselves. One sees this approach evidenced on the shelves of megabookstores, where the sign Spirituality above shelves may include noninstitutional religion, inspiration, self-help, New Age, holistic and alternative medicine, African and Asian religions, ancient and occult and metaphysical texts, and the like. Ephemeral communities may form in the coffee shops of such bookstores, among the readers of spiritual bestsellers, or followers of spiritual and charismatic leaders.

This form of spirituality is advocated most frequently as a new source for interpreting and energizing the business world and the people in it.

Listen, however, and it will become clear that the sixth element of our matrix, *social and communal*, alone is not integral to the spirituality of an emergent sort. I need not illustrate this, but ask you to observe by opening the books, reading the advertisements, listening to the gurus, attending retreats: certainly "ultimate concern" is at issue; there is an ambitious resort to myth and symbol and usually to rite and ceremony. The reference to "energy" and "connection" and cognate terms suggests a metaphysical commitment, and there are elaborate behavioral correlates: meditating, breathing, and the like are constants.

I point this out not in derision, denunciation, or simple celebration of this kind of spirituality. My interest is in locating it so that we deal with it frankly when it is offered as a solution or the solution to spiritual problems that come with business today. Advocates of such spirituality may indeed make major contributions, but I think we have to say "Handle with Care" when it is presented as something that is religiously independent or neutral.

On the old assumption that, as with thieves, so with religious people "it takes one to know one," we might observe the ways in which religious traditionalists and fundamentalists have resisted corporate retreats and managerial policies or practices devoted to Buddhist or Tao-te-ching or Confucian exercises. Most of us may look at them as cultural glosses and practices. But the fundamentalists do not have to be too pecksniffian to see these also as out-and-out religious rivals. There is some substance to their contention that such spirituality should have the same status as would Baptist, Muslim, or Catholic religious spirituality—which, of course, need not mean "not any."

Assets have come with the invention of the new expressions of spirituality. They surely point to a human who is more interesting than the old computer-with-legs called "secular man." This spirituality does more justice to the discontents and passions of many humans than does secular counsel. Spirituality of this sort has shaken up and confronted religious institutions, spurring them on to recover their own lost treasures, to reform. If it enhances wonder, curiosity, alertness, and the esthetic dimensions of life, there are few reasons to complain in a world so often full of boring, indifferent, apathetic, tone-deaf citizens. This eclectic spirituality is an expression of human freedom and individuality, part of which makes it a good match for many aspects of business life.

If the role of religious communities in respect to business has tended to be of the "throw-our-weight-around" sort, that of spirituality has often been more instrumental than intrinsic. Most of the profoundly spiritual geniuses in the various faiths have stressed that spirituality has its own rationale and outcome. In the managerial and entrepreneurial world the instrumental dimension matters: be more spiritual and you will be more productive. You will advance. Your firm will prosper. You will find interpretations available when failure comes and will have a basis for celebration of ambitions fulfilled, of success.

All that advocacy should disturb the proponents of the spiritualities more than it might the business agents, who will find out on empirical grounds how, and even whether, this particular instrumentality, this "utility" worked.

This spirituality helps the individual cope with many aspects of corporate life but is less poised than classical ethical, philosophical, religious, and communal heritages to engage in *krisis*, protest, and reform. Manifestly it helps many in their personal and private lives and may inspire a sense of vocation and aspects of stewardship and mission. To the degree that it does so, there seems little reason to demean or scorn it.

As for the firms themselves, there is a temptation to use this form of spirituality without regard for the sensitivity of employees who bring other approaches to the spiritual life. This spirituality is virtually powerless in respect to governments, globalization, and multinational corporations. "Spirituality does not make house calls," one might say in the world of organized associations, though, of course, many of the advocates of seeking spirituality may themselves be generous, good people.

Without going into extensive praise or critique, I would put a bottom line under this by saying: if we regard spirituality as highly individualized, but eclectic, religion, *but still religion*—religion not yet having taken communal and social and institutional form but poised to do so—then it may have a chance to win its case on an equal playing field with religions and religious philosophies. It might well demonstrate the results of its promise, without relying on illusion or delusion, but on the free market of beliefs, ideas, and contentions.

REFERENCES

Cox, Harvey. "The Market as God." *Atlantic Monthly* 283, no. 3 (March 1999): 18.

DesRoche, Henri. *Jacob and the Angel: An Essay in Sociologies of Religion.* Amherst: University of Massachusetts Press, 1973.

MacIntyre, Alasdair. *After Virtue: A Study in Moral Theory.* Notre Dame, Ind.: University of Notre Dame Press, 1981.

Murray, John Courtney. *We Hold These Truths: Catholic Reflections on the American Proposition.* New York: Sheed and Ward, 1960.

Niebuhr, H. Richard. *The Social Sources of Denominationalism.* New York: Henry Holt, 1929.

Rawls, John. *A Theory of Justice.* Cambridge, Mass.: Harvard University Press, 1971.

Rostow, W. W. *The Stages of Economic Growth: A Non-Communist Manifesto.* 3d ed. Cambridge: Cambridge University Press, 1991.

Schumpeter, Joseph. *Capitalism, Socialism, and Democracy.* New York: Harper and Brothers, 1950.

Tillich, Paul. *Systematic Theology.* Vol. 3, *Life and the Spirit and History and the Kingdom of God.* Chicago: University of Chicago Press, 1963.

Wuthnow, Robert. *After Heaven: Spirituality in America since the 1950s.* Berkeley: University of California Press, 1998.

TWO

A Spiritual Audit of Business

From Tipping Point to Tripping Point

LAURA L. NASH

What a sea change! Ten years ago a book on spirituality in business would generally be regarded as a lunatic undertaking by a fringe group of superstitious crystal tappers. Today there is widespread interest in the notion that spirituality can be a desired and effective force in daily life, including today's business environment. More than a fad, the current spirituality "market" flies in the face of earlier predictions that modern society would become fully secularized, with science and technology—the very stuff of the new economy—being the primary carriers of secularism. Instead, intuitive, nonrational "ways of knowing" have taken business science by storm to form a new cognitive framework for decision making. Adam Smith's invisible hand of the marketplace has been shaken by the firm clasp of a *sacred* "invisible made visible" (one definition of religion). For some, this development smacks of a general blasphemous idolatry of the market in today's society. For others, it represents a retrogressive superstition. But to many people, the current spirituality in business movement is a serious attempt to bring their deepest convictions to and through the way things work in business.

An Idea Whose Time Has Come?

How many? Hard to tell. Depending on one's definitions of spirituality and religion, a web search will identify 7,500 Christian web sites on Yahoo or 135,000 sites for spirituality in general. Steve Covey and Deepak Choprah's book sales each reach well into the eight figures (i.e., tens of millions), supplemented by substantial corporate investment in their training and coaching services. They are joined by a host of best-selling authors from a multitude of traditions, ranging from the secular psychologist James Hillman (*The Soul's Code: In Search of Character and Calling*) to the Evangelical management consultant Laurie Beth Jones (*Jesus CEO*) to the ultimate syncretist, Ken Wilber (*A Brief History of Everything*). At last count I found over seventy-five academic programs with some reference to religion or spirituality and leadership. Practices range from Woodstock Business Conference's monthly meetings (now up to sixteen chapters and growing) to nonaffiliated individual "questers" lighting candles before a business meeting to focus everyone's spirit.

In his latest book on U.S. religious attitudes, George Gallup has called this rising tide of lay religious interest America's "epic soul quest."[1] If one adds in so-called secular spirituality programs for corporations, the epic is a true blockbuster. The forms of spiritual practice are so varied, the definitions of spirituality so fuzzy, and the focus of these efforts often so vague that the description "Spirituality in Business" is almost useless for providing a head count of comparable activities.

What we can safely conclude is that America is still a nation of commerce and a nation of religious people, even as Tocqueville described it in the early-nineteenth century. According to the *New York Times Almanac 2000*, there were 6.7 million businesses in 1996 (the last year for available statistics and not including the vast informal business sector), employing over 102 million people (1998) out of a national population of 270 million; 169 million adult Americans claimed affiliation with a religious group, 159 of which were affiliated with a Christian church. George Gallup's surveys consistently show about 9 in 10 Americans expressing a belief in God.[2]

As Martin Marty noted long ago in *Pilgrims in Their Own Land*, the history of American religion is one of constant change, diversity, and competition for souls.[3] Today these forces are, if anything, intensified by the emergence of significant non-Christian populations and syncretic, noninstitutionalized religious quests, to use Wade Clark Roof's term.[4] Competition for the soul of business people is particularly intense.[5]

Notre Dame's volume on business, religion, and spirituality invites us to identify the parameters of this interest, to understand the sources and content of the new spirituality and business programs, and, most importantly, to assess the trend in religious and business terms. Is spirituality in business of any significant religious or practical worth? What can and should academia and the religious community add to the general lay-person's spiritual search?

In my experience, many religious and business professionals will not find this last question appealing. There is a great chasm between the two communities, especially regarding their religious interpretation of economic life and personal economic activity as an agent of a corporation. Many have given up hope that the "other side" is at all capable of developing a suitable understanding of "spirituality in business." Business people say, as Ian Mitroff's surveys indicated, "I'm spiritual but not religious," deliberately distancing themselves from organized religion. Church professionals and secular academics alike dismiss the current business interest as "spirituality lite" (Wendy Kaminer's term).[6]

As Scotty McLennan and I argue in our forthcoming book, this attitude is deeply entrenched and very destructive in terms of the church's ability to speak to the business community with positive impact. In the tradition of business ethics, popular spirituality is particularly vulnerable to academic and religious superciliousness, and the intellectuals have not missed the opportunity to heap a little scorn. I was recently approached to comment on a television program on spirituality in business that was being planned by a group of theologians. They had decided to call the show "Mickey Mouse, Margaret Thatcher and the Marketplace." I declined to participate.

There is considerable anxiety among religious professionals that today's spiritual seeking in business is too human-centered, too referenced on the self, without being anchored in more eternal truths. Without a broader grounding, the critical capacity of individuals (their *krisis*) may be too limited to reflect a mature religious point of view. These concerns deserve serious consideration, whether the goal is to spiritually strengthen one's own business behavior or to increase the church's ability to be an effective influence on business thinking.

The problem is to find the right mirrors against which to hold up the many expectations and claims about religion and business being made today. Craig Dykstra rightly points out that the primary "mirror" in spirituality in business programs is the notion that life—and people—are basically OK.[7] Having recently reviewed over a hundred of the new spirituality books (both secular and overtly Christian in orientation), I share his concern. Much of this material is highly limited in its scope even as it takes a refreshingly empowering view of the individual in business. Hard questions are avoided in favor of cultivating mental techniques for reducing stress and achieving higher performance. In business terms, even if you can't put your finger on spirituality, you know it when it's blocked—you feel powerless, stressed. If your team lacks spirit, it finds itself engaged in self-defeating behaviors.

Not surprisingly, more traditional religious orientations find difficulty with a worldview that reduces the state of the soul and important social issues such as poverty and family dysfunctionality to stress factors in the workplace. It is inaccurate, however, to portray the entire spiritual and religious interest of business people in these terms.

Ian Mitroff, for example, suggests a very different conclusion, writing with great understanding about the various social contributions to the corporation alleged to be derived from spirituality.[8] This paper makes no attempt to assess these contributions from an empirical standpoint. I do agree, however, with the John Templeton Foundation that substantive empirical work needs to be done on the effects of spiritual activity, whether these effects are on personal health or economics. Such knowledge is essential if we are to understand more fully the nature of spirituality itself.

Some people feel no such need to assess the authenticity of the claims that spirituality is making an impact on business. Like natives who bang on a drum during an eclipse to make the moon come back, many enthusiastic disciples of Steve Covey's leadership principles are content to say, "This works for me, so it must be true." This strong element of "positive-thinker" philosophy in the current movement (which is as eclectic and dependent on "little tradition"[9] exoticisms as were the nineteenth-century movements described by William James)[10] suggests on the surface that today's business spirituality is, as the conference brochure indicated, a "mere" exercise in corporate performance enhancement or narcissism.

It would be a mistake, however, to jump to such a conclusion. James himself was careful to point out that certain "optimistic types" (he included business people in this category) tended to be drawn to forms of religious expression that seemed unpalatable and intellectually thin to the more "pessimistic" types such as mystics, clerics, and academics. Unvarnished claims of bottom-line payback for today's spiritual programs may be more a reflection of the need to secure corporate funding than of an intrinsically materialistic content in the spiritual message. The actual content of these programs is often paradoxically directed at both increasing business acumen and escaping its more narrowly defined purposes, as much at romanticism and longing for transcendent truths as a hope for business success.

The Spiritual as a "Tipping Point"

It is true that most of the new business spirituality methodology is bent on empowerment. This spirituality involves an intensification of internal resources that is assumed to lead to effectiveness, whether an intensification of aesthetic awareness, one's problem-solving abilities, or one's knowledge of God. On this view, spirituality is the invisible ingredient that puts a person over the top. The new spirituality is essentially like Malcolm Gladwell's "tipping point."[11] A tipping point is the seemingly unpredictable moment when a slight incremental difference creates a disproportionate momentum for change. Gladwell cites the example of water in a beaker. Slowly, drop by drop, a beaker fills with water. Eventually the surface tension puts the water above the glass line, and yet it does not spill over. Then that one extra drop breaks the tension and causes quite a bit of water to spill. A simple tipping point event can contain the seeds of enormous social change, as when the crime rate in New York City's subway system abruptly dropped following the eradication of graffiti.

Spirituality in business is regularly celebrated as the tipping point for success. Many of spirituality's little successes—such as improved stamina, creativity, or ability to cooperate—can be seen without much effort to be factors of performance. Terms for this wondrous state abound: the Zone, the Buddha Within, the Spirit of the Enterprise.

As the terms indicate, this road to personal intensification is embedded in larger metaphors of meaning such as holism, sacredness, or connection to universal fellowship that transcends mundane, everyday impulses. The cosmology or theology varies dramatically from program to program, but the business seeker's pursuit of effectiveness is not without these larger frameworks of individual transcendency. In our forthcoming book, Scotty McLennan and I identify four directions in the current spiritual quest, all of which may be subject to goals of empowerment and spiritual intensification. They are:

- Search for sacred self
- Search for balance according to a sacred cosmology
- Search for community
- Search for religiously or humanistically consistent ethics

The emphasis here is on self-empowerment but not selfishness. A good example is Steve Covey's popular executive workshop, "Principle-Centered Leadership." Covey suggests a framework for "igniting the fire within" that responds to what he calls "four basic categories of need." They are the physical/economic, mental/intellectual, social/emotional, and spiritual/holistic. Several of the categories demand bearing responsibility toward others, as does the last, which is about "contribution and integrity." Says Covey: "[Principle-centered] leaders realize that people want to contribute to doing something that makes a difference. They ensure that people be part of meaningful tasks with worthwhile outcomes."[12]

As the mainstream churches and evangelical lay groups embrace the spirituality movement, some are firmly pursuing an updated version of the positive-thinker tradition of Norman Vincent Peale, while others deplore any suggestion that the soul could ever be about one's own profit.

Today's dramatically different expectations and assessments of spirituality in business are understandable. They reflect a general state of confusion about religion itself, about the place of specific traditions within a holistic and pluralistic ethic of tolerance, about long-standing conflicts between church and business elites, and about a rapidly changing understanding of spirituality and science that departs from the social and historical roots in which the wisdom texts of Christianity developed. The absence of a common language for examining what we mean and want from spirituality or religion in business places serious limitations on the sense of possibility for religious or business transformations of the type being sought. Individuals cannot create a shared set of understandings upon which to base collective action. Religious institutions cannot provide constructive assistance.

Important as it is to create this common ground, *it is first necessary to understand the key reasons why it has not been created so far.* Every day I hear of a new congregation or university program eagerly setting out to "do something" about spirituality and business in a way that is consistent with the Big Traditions of their religious orientation. In the absence of a few signposts for accomplishing this task, Christian spirituality in business quickly turns from tipping point into tripping point. One or both of the professional communities becomes "turned off" by the juxtaposition of business and a Christianity-affiliated spirituality, which necessarily means religion once the institutional church is involved.

Understanding the Tripping Point

A number of the most strongly supported programs in this area have reported repeated failure to engage the business community in the way they would like. The turn-off comes in many forms, from polite dismissal of proffered programs to outright hostility and negative stereotyping among business and church professionals toward each other.

Without naming names, I think we have to respect the integrity and quality of these organizations and consider their experience as indicative of a serious obstacle to relevancy, for whatever reasons. While secular spirituality "takes off" as a multimillion-dollar market and secular business ethics programs become a billion dollar industry,[13] there has not been a single Christianity-based effort of equal impact outside the lay Evangelical community.[14]

I am particularly concerned in this chapter with the question of how and why the somewhat tardy attempts of Christian religious communities to tap into the new spirituality interest seem destined prematurely to hit a wall. My main concern here is to address certain predictable aspects of the tripping point before making normative conclusions about how this spirituality in business should be audited. In exploring this question I will suggest a broad framework for rethinking the terms in which we approach the question of religion, spirituality, and business.

In the past few years, with the support of the Lilly endowment, my coauthor, Scotty McLennan, and I interviewed over a hundred clergy and business people and reviewed or participated in extensive samples of the spirituality books and programs. Despite a common interest in spiritual or religious matters, there is a great distance between pew and pulpit on questions of business. Both groups construct negative stereotypes and rationales for discounting each others' views.

Our interviews indicated that this distancing effect is both underestimated by the professional Christian religious community and, to the degree it is recognized, assumed to be justifiable. Our work seeks to help church communities to self-identify and critique the causes of tripping points in their approach to business and spirituality, causes such as worldview, language, assumptions about legitimate moral authority, and the necessity for pluralism in the corporation. The way these issues are played out frequently cuts off mutual discussion or support for the businessperson's pursuit of the spiritual in professional life. By comparison, the so-called secular spirituality programs are clearly making an impact on the spiritual experience and daily thinking of many business people, even though in many cases the content falls far short of what a Christian theology would see as a significant transformation in business. Not surprisingly, the church itself cannot claim to have achieved—or even attempted—such a transformation in its own management behavior.

Building on these findings, I would like to present for consideration and discussion three common problems in the professional religious Christian culture that seem to lie at the source of the tripping points:[15]

The Source of the Tripping Point

Religious Problem #1: A History of Nonengagement in Business Problems from a Personal Standpoint

For many theologians and members of the clergy, business simply does not compute as a legitimate focus of religious expression. To use Patricia Werhane's term, they lack "moral imagination." For many pastors, the management aspects of their jobs are their least favorite and least valued tasks. Many academicians are only interested in the theological tradition and the theoretical framework. Their institutional status is dependent on reinforcing this stand. Take, for example, the professor of a divinity school who taught liberation theology. When asked whether he had ever engaged in a discussion with managers of a multinational corporation with responsibilities in a developing country, he answered with surprise, "Why should I do *that?*" He was quite certain, however, that he understood the psychology of the businessperson, which he saw as selfishness, greed, and lack of theological grounding.

One might expect such a response from a liberal academic professional, but the same pattern of indifference can be seen at the congregational level, even in the nondenominational conservative Evangelical churches with strong social service programs aimed at being "market sensitive" to their members. An example would be the church in Boston that sponsored an adult Bible class for members in business. The class was run by a businessperson and attempted to sustain a dialogue and Bible study around the problems people faced at work. Between twenty-five and a hundred members regularly attended this class. After four years the seminar leader was asked, for the first time, to report on the program to the board of ministers. Not one of the ten had had any interest in evaluating the program. They were totally surprised at what had been occurring right under their roof.

As with this parish, the church's nonengagement in the world and worldview of business people is often taken for granted, on the assumption that the personal activities of business people are hardly authentic occasions for significant religious or spiritual attention. A parent reported with sadness and some anger an incident at his church's youth fellowship. A group of high school students had raised money to go on a mission overseas during the summer to build housing for the poor. The pastor initiated a churchwide prayer and blessing of the group's effort. This parent's son was not going on the trip. The boy was staying home to work a summer job.

The parent approached the pastor and said, "Hey, wouldn't it be great to deliver a blessing to all the students who are going off to their first job this summer?" His pastor was baffled. Politely, but firmly, the cleric ignored the request. Reported the businessperson:

> My pastor wasn't hostile. He just didn't get it. He couldn't understand why going off to work in business would be grounds for a blessing. *Mission* work was what was important from a religious standpoint.

Fear plays an important role here: fear of corruption, fear of the style of business, fear of abandoning a language that does not have the poor as its focus. An examination of the curriculum content of most seminaries quickly explains how this kind of devaluation of business is institutionalized early in the churchperson's professional training. We surveyed twenty top seminaries to discover almost no courses on business, very little exposure to business leaders during seminary work, and what was there tended to be framed as prophetic stances against big business, articulated at a macroeconomic level.[16] Jesuit business schools may be the key exception to this type of institutionalized indifference. Most of the programs on religion and business today are in Jesuit business schools, and even here the divide between academic and businessperson can be very strong. The University of Notre Dame, founded by the Holy Cross Fathers, has a priest as director of the Center for Ethics and Religious Values in Business, but this is a rare occurrence. All too often the explicitly "business" part is farmed out to a layperson who works with little support or collaboration from the religious professionals.

Religious Problem #2: Vague But Deep Ideological Hostility to Capitalism and the Modern Corporation

Tap into the foundational assumptions of many religious professionals and there is still a strong thread of suspicion that capitalism primarily represents selfishness and destructive individualism at the expense of the less fortunate. The expectation of a *spiritual* focus, on this view, remains with the poor in a literal economic sense and excludes the rich, however poor in spirit. Capitalism's increasingly disproportionate rewards to the victor do not suggest a reason for seeing the successful capitalist (read businessperson) as a potential contributor to solutions to poverty unless that involves reward to the corporation.

Theologians from Max Stackhouse to the U.S. Council of Bishops have questioned the liberal church's extreme opposition to capitalism. Nonetheless, many members of the clergy are still constructing a theology marked by, at most, two levels of separation from socialism either in statist form or in some vague assumption of informal ecclesiastical control over economic choices. Every failure of capitalism confirms the suspicion that the more prophetic the stance, the more *unlike* capitalism it will be. Given the lip service being paid to former errors in the liberal church's uncritical support of communist regimes, I call this the crypto-communism of today's religious community.

Not every religious professional critical of business condemns capitalism outright, but ideals of communal life and church- or state-governed social welfare are so favored as to be considered a condition of religious thinking in many Christian communities. The unexplored dimensions of this stand are very much like the attitude toward what is called medical necessities. Medical necessities are the tests, drugs, or therapies that define minimal good health care. When legislators actually try to define these terms or medical professionals try to apply them, it turns out that unanswered and complicated questions remain to such a degree that the term cannot be applied. The same holds true for many of the automatic foundational assumptions of religious necessity, such as the bias toward the communal. Moral and practical difficulties of application are not rigorously attended to, such as the lack of models demonstrating sustained wealth generation and the preservation of nuclear families in long-term communal forms of life.

Like discussions of medical necessity, the key economic principles and virtues of religious necessity with regard to business life fail to provide applicable guidance. Much of the religious literature and even more of the attitudinal foundations in the religious community are most notable for their defiance of pragmatism in favor of utopianism. As one person commented on the Jubilee movement to cancel Third World debt, "It doesn't really matter *what* the developing countries do with the forgiven debt." What about buying arms to further ethnic violence? Ignore or struggle? Yet another tripping point.

For those whose religion requires a single-focused negative prophetic stance on capitalism's worst exploitations, empowering programs on spirituality for business are not only not of great interest, they seem shockingly indifferent to the poor. The most common characterization of business people in our interviews was that they did not "care." Failure to scold or to take an oppositional activist stand seems to indicate a lack of religious seriousness. Even worse, the notion of emotional and spiritual *support* to the businessperson suggested a cop-out.

Some members of the clergy hid these feelings for the sake of congregational peace, but lived with an inner guilt and hostility that came out in their comments. These fears are only fed by the many uncritical apologetics that are easily found among the romanticized portrayals of the business-religion connection, especially from some quarters of the conservative Right. A religiously based argument entitled "God Wants You to Be Rich" is far from reassuring.

Meanwhile, the so-called laity reports the ever increasing opinion that the workplace is a setting in which spirituality can be relevant and even cultivated. This is a serious division in the church community writ large, and the flight to secular spirituality programs is a good wake-up call.

Religious Problem #3: A Historical Tradition That Associates Spirituality with Settings outside Business and the Modern Activities of a Corporation
Consider this remark from a Congregational pastor in New England:

> I love the people in my church who are in business, and I want to bring them closer to God. I think spirituality may be a great way for us to talk about religion at work, but frankly, I don't really have much to say about business. The way I can best bring them to God is to offer my support and give them perspective. Take their minds out of their own business concerns and remind them of others, particularly the poor.

What *is* spirituality from a Christian standpoint? The most vivid examples come from people and events closely associated with the church. Theresa of Avila's spirituality is contextualized by her life in the convent and her struggle with the powers of the church. Religious spirituality such as this often implies a strong element of suffering, self-denial, or an ecstasy of paradoxical proportions. Extreme acts of hermitage, charitable service, or courageous stands against authority, sometimes ending in martyrdom—this kind of spirituality we can easily understand as being religious. Even NPR can speak of Dorothy Day's "spirituality" and expect to achieve general understanding among its jaded secular-humanist audience, however controversial her spirituality may have been from a psychological standpoint. Day's religious views caused her to seek God in a certain unique and painful way, and the new knowledge of God that she so obtained motivated her to heroic action on behalf of the poor. This spiritual profile, however, does not suggest a managerial temperament or setting. Far from it. How, then, to reconcile these visions of spirituality with Karl Rahner's joyous "mysticism of everyday life, the discovery of God in all things; there is the sober intoxication of the spirit."[17]

Christian religious tradition posits a spirituality that is at heart an *imitatio Christi*. But neither Christ—nor even the aristocratic Buddha on whom the Dalai Lama claims to build a secular spirituality open to all— ever climbed a corporate ladder. Historical embodiments of spiritual depth in *business* tend to be extremely controversial and subject to endless reconstruction as to their ethical and spiritual value. Jean Strouse's new biography of J. P. Morgan gives a good example.[18] The mogul who clearly profiteered in the Civil War was an anti-Semite and hard-driving deal maker. He also had a close relationship to Bishop Henry Codman Potter, a friend of Samuel Gompers and activist in the labor movement. Morgan's syndicate launched a singlehanded attempt to stave off the run on the New York banks, buying up the plummeting shares while other leaders turned tail. Morgan's religious respect for Codman and his own Episcopal priest was deep.[19] Was Morgan a spiritual man? Was his sense of community religiously consistent in any way? Clearly the problems attached to making such assessments suggest inherent stumbling blocks in the understanding of Christian spirituality as it applies to business. Do our preconditions of religious authenticity eternally condemn the successful businessperson to a position of spiritual inferiority?

In *Anatomy of Disgust,* William Miller coins the term *moral menial* to describe people in society who perform tasks that are generally regarded as unappealing but necessary. [20] An executioner would fall into such a category. In medieval times the Jew, whose unchristian ability to charge interest kept the lending system going, was also a moral menial. Miller points out that society has often coped with its moral ambivalence toward these people through the twin reactions of tolerance limited by disgust. Personal traits such as smelling bad are assigned to the hangman or the Jew, offering physical reasons for the aversion we feel, without necessarily going so far as to suggest pogrom.

Today's church frequently puts the businessperson in the role of moral menial. The emblems of disgust are more generalized than toward a hangman, but the gut sense of aversion that accompanies moral menials can easily be detected. Much of this ostracism and moral superiority is inadvertent and hardly acknowledged. I have interviewed literally scores of business people and members of the clergy who report having a close, personal relationship with each other. But when I pressed them for concrete examples of some church engagement with business activities of those parishioners, some interest in the roles they play, some acknowledgement of religious influence on their religious life that would emplify this closeness, I found there was little there besides an enthusiastic opinion that the business parishioner was a good person. As long as the clergy keeps its distance, this relationship seems good. What is not tested, however, is the religious professional's ability to *penetrate* the problems and perspective of the businessperson on tough business issues.

From a personal standpoint I am frankly enraged that business people continue to be assigned the role of moral menials. More dispassionately, I fully appreciate the enormous obstacles in Christian tradition and professional religious culture that hinder active engagement in business people's search to bring spirituality to their professionals lives.

My concern here is that these three tripping points be addressed more deliberately before being allowed to uncritically shape the essential terms in which we assess business spirituality from a religious standpoint today. My concern is both from a theological standpoint—I am not convinced that New Testament teachings demand a radical stand against individual property rights—but also from a pragmatic one. These biases create enormous obstacles to mutuality in the search for religious spirituality in business. The language, worldview, and tradition of church activity all provide a sharp contrast to modern business, despite capitalism's undeniable roots in Protestantism. As such, they divide, rather than engage, the corporate actor. Take language. As Scotty McLennan and I discuss, the church conventionally adopts a language of weakness and suffering to promote religious awareness. It seeks compassion for people exhibiting these qualities and assures us of God's compassion for the same weaknesses in ourselves.

Business people are drawn to a language of empowerment as they think about their responsibilities, even in their spiritual quest. The church's language of weakness and self-sacrifice is threatening to the business person; it seems unpragmatic and goes against the responsibilities the individual believer assumes at work. While the church considers the nuances of weakness a path to spiritual empowerment, the religiously consistent connection to empowerment in daily business life is generally not indicated by the church. Profit continues to be a sign of the damned. These patterns leave the businessperson suspicious and unable to fulfill his or her spiritual hunger with Christianity-based notions.

Meanwhile, the stresses are high. The new business interest in spirituality is surely driven by a deep existential and moral confusion over the state of economic life in today's cyber-economy. Business people want to understand how things work in the new economy and social order. They see their most fundamental assumptions turned on end, from the new melding of science and religious "ways of knowing" to the apparent demise of market rationality such as the correlation of stock price and profitability.

In the absence of robust church responses to these changes, it is no wonder that the businessperson looks elsewhere for new sources of spiritual guidance. A Steve Covey speaks their language. A syncretistic Meg

Wheatley or Joe Jaworski understands new paradigms of science and religion, but they do not explain the relation of these models to practicing
Christianity. Evangelical offerings frequently fail to address the deep-
seated popular belief that proselytizing and the J-word are not appropriate in a business institution. The J-word is often used in such a way as to
make a claim on the listener to acknowledge the testimonial as true or at
least plausible. Trivialize this meaning and the J-word becomes blasphemous. Clearly a problem here.

Before conducting our spiritual audit of the corporation, we need a
more robust articulation of the parameters of Christian spirituality and religion in the social context of the modern corporation. While there is not
room to develop these parameters here, I would like to suggest a way out
of some of the most frequent tripping points that I have mentioned. These
will help sustain our effort to bring some form of Christianity-based spirituality to the questions of business leadership in the modern corporation.

The first step is to clarify our understanding of the term "religion," so
as to remove all implication that Christian spirituality in business necessarily means proselytizing or lockstep modeling of business in a way that
replicates the church's historic economic stands. As Martin Marty points
out, "religion" is one of the least clear terms in the English language, and
we see this confusion in the contradictory response of business people
who affirm a Christian affiliation and believe it has nothing to do with
business. Take this banker who has been deeply involved in Episcopal
and Presbyterian churches:

> I love the church, but sometimes I look at what we do in the
> company, the nonprofits we work with, the daily policies, and I be-
> lieve in many cases we [business] have found a more effective vehicle
> for these concerns outside the church.
>
> I begin to wonder, you know, "What is the religion part of social
> action or business ethics, when so much of what we do resembles
> what the church does but without the involvement of any formal
> religion?"

Says another businessperson:

> You can't argue religion has a role in business. *They're totally different.*
> Sure, my inner values overlap, because that's who I am, but that's not
> religion.

As these remarks indicate, the boundaries of religion, psychology, and social conscience are blurring in their calls to action. Why care about one's fellow human being? Religious persons might claim, "because the Bible tells us so." Psychologists might claim, "because you'll live longer and happier." Social geneticists might claim, "because we are hard-wired to care and cooperate." But they all recommend caring. The modern individual with some belief in Christianity probably draws on *all* these frames of reference for the same act, but will find it difficult to single out the specifically "religious" element of caring for others *in a nonreligious setting.* Corporate caring, then, is "spiritual but not religious."

Aside from its obvious drama and exoticism, so-called secular spirituality may be having such a strong reception because conceptually it sits at the liminal point where the boundaries of religion, science, and psychology blur. Futhermore, it operates in the contexts where people live most of their lives. Their success suggests that the churches need to establish greater clarity at the lay level about the meaning and contexts of religion. For this to occur, it would be helpful to distinguish between contexts and understand that there are multiple forms of religious expression, some more fitting to a business setting and context than others.

Three Levels of Religious Engagement

As a start, I would suggest that "religion" be characterized not as a monolithic activity associated with the church, but as having three basic forms: (1) espoused, (2) catalytic, and (3) foundational.

Espoused Level

The first category represents publicly proclaimed expressions of religion (personal or institutional). These would include specific denominational statements and sectarian forms of allegiance; vocalized proclamations of religious awareness that imply some invitation to the listener to agree or disagree; proselytizing; and social action claims for justice associated with specific formal religious bodies. This first form is closest to the root of the word "religion," namely, the forms that *bind* similar believers together in some formal or informal religious affiliation.

I believe that general opinion favors very few of these forms as being appropriate in the corporation or as regulators of corporate decision making. Wearing your church affiliation on your sleeve, favoring a specific religious authority at business gatherings, or proselytizing, however allegedly voluntary the invitation, are all unfit for a corporate context. The same is true for affiliations of business people within one corporation based on religious preference. Fears of promoting intolerance are simply too high to approve of such activities to the nonbelongers.

Exceptions can be found in forms of espoused religion that are highly privatized and personalized, such as wearing an item of personal clothing carrying religious symbolism—a head scarf or yarmulka, a cross on a chain. Another privatized form of espoused religion in the workplace is the business chaplain, who makes himself or herself available for confidential counseling help to individuals. Another is the ecumenical setting directed at a common cause that goes beyond a single business or industry. The White House annual prayer breakfast would be one such example, where leaders from many faiths gather for a morning of prayer and speeches directed at the country's common good.

As a rule of thumb, any form of generalized public religious expression at work that treads on democratic values of tolerance and pluralism is inappropriate.[21] A firm line should be drawn between activities conducted in an espoused way (such as a private fellowship retreat of Evangelical businessmen) and workplace efforts to address spiritual and ethical issues. To the degree that current Christian efforts to address spirituality and business make triumphalist claims of the espoused church's authority, they cross this line.

Catalytic Level

Level 2, the catalytic form of religion, describes a more personalized, interior form of religious worship and consciousness that is more easily detached from institutional religion without losing all religious content. Largely based in *experiential* religious activity, the catalytic is both a way of deepening one's knowledge of the spirit (or the nontheistic equivalent) and being personally empowered by this knowledge to act in the world. The current spirituality movement is located at this level. Its focus on empowerment is essentially catalytic, effecting access to a deeper, authentic self even as it rests on that which is beyond the individual. Personalized, syncretic, and directed to the mind, body, and "secular" sociability of the individual, this level of religious experience is easily distanced from the espoused form.

My own definition of spirituality is "access to the sacred force that impels life." This understanding of spirituality allows for many forms of access to occur—from meditation to cosmological study—and for many names for the sacred force that impels life, from the gift of knowing God to the structure of the genetic code. "Sacred," however, raises this force to a transcendent position, capable of eliciting the awe and reverence that Rudolph Otto posited; "life," because spirituality is inherently connected to acts of creation rather than destruction.

Today's spirituality in business seizes on all three aspects of this definition, but with the least emphasis on the phenomenon of sacredness. Many of the techniques for catalytic religion are drawn from Eastern or native sources, but without being posited as hostile to the symbols of transcendency that are totally Christian. This seems to me the best entry point for Christianity and its particular understanding of the sacred in the context of business. Here the weight of the tradition that impedes the bridge to relevancy is lightened as a more personalized, experiential form of religion takes hold. The acceptance of God that Tillich proposes would clearly be located on the catalytic level.

It could rightly be asked whether the catalytic form of spirituality is so personalized in this definition that it inherently must discount obvious social concerns of Christianity. On the contrary, most of the spirituality emphasizes the self in relation; cosmic systems and holism underscore the interdependency of life forms.

Foundational Level

The third level, the foundational form of religious activity, helps overcome the problems of narcissism and selfishness that occur when even the "genetic logic" of cooperation and attention to the common good fail to provoke compassion. "Foundational" refers to the time-tested, anchoring worldview, convictions, and narratives of religious traditions and theology. These provide a deeper, less personalized perspective to the businesspersons' consciousness and experiential search. They do not depend on self-generated religious articulations alone.

The current spirituality movement is very "thin" on religious tradition, as was pointed out earlier. This thinness will begin to show as individuals capture the personal and catalytic only to encounter gaps in their own interpretations of the ethical or the cosmological. Uncontrollable difficulties such as social disruption, illness, or other forms of misfortune—even the achievement of sudden great wealth—are likely to spur the kind of identity crisis that is associated with spiritual quest. These quests will be frustrated unless nourished by the collective wisdom found in foundational texts. Popular religious interest already appears to be expanding from its spirituality and self-help focus to the foundational level. George C. Gallup Jr.'s recent surveys seem to have picked up an emergent interest in the core convictions and roots of Western religion, including Christianity.[22] One sees a rising interest in adult education courses in biblical study; business people are taking "time out" to study religious tradition at lunchtime or even attend divinity school. Book publishers, an important indicator of new intellectual trends, are suddenly churning out numerous popular guides to religious texts; the churches celebrating Mass in Latin have jumped from 6 to 131 since 1990. Exposure to the foundational is essential to the spiritual development of business people. The chief task today for religious professionals is to forge new links between level 2 and 3 in dialogue with business people. As it is now, the catalytic tends to stand separate from the other two levels. Here the universities and lay groups can play a strong role in providing a more pluralistic context for the examination of foundational religion and its possible meaning for modern life.

The point of distinguishing these forms of religious activity is that the breakdown helps place the diverse aspects of an individual's religious life in some coherent framework that acknowledges a separation and difference between "religion at church" and "religion at work." It allows business people to entertain deeper examinations of Christianity without having to defer to an espoused platform that offers little crossover to the business setting. The religious communities have no such need and may be somewhat insensitive to its urgency for the business population. This is not to say that the explanations of duty, meaning of human existence, or perspective on corporate life should be entirely free of religious tradition, but rather that this tradition must be responsive to the pluralistic, pragmatic demands of the corporation and *find a catalytic form of expressions as well as foundational link*. This cannot occur if the first presumption is that utilitarian aspects of spirituality are religiously illegitimate. Part of the business quest for spirituality is to be empowered to get out of the box wherein the symbols and acts associated with ultimate meaning are associated only with a nonbusiness context.

This is not to suggest that espoused and collective religious expression is irrelevant to the businessperson, but rather that it should be maintained as a private activity. Ideally, heightened activity at levels 2 and 3 would be supplemented (not supplanted) by private commitment to espoused religion. The point here is that the professional religious must not assume that the espoused should be a precondition of the church's attempts to address the religious dimension of business.

Conditions for a Spirituality Based on Christianity

With a firmer distinction established between espoused, catalytic, and foundational religious forms, some of the traditional espoused tests of spirituality become inappropriate. We will have to rethink the very terms on which spirituality is held up as a religiously consistent standard against which business activity is assessed, or audited. I would like to end this essay with four conditions that I think would be appropriate for this reworked understanding of a Christianity-based spirituality in business.

A Catalytic Focus
Exploration of Christian spirituality should occur primarily at the catalytic level with regard to business activity.[23] Christian spirituality must speak to the businessperson on a personal, experiential level that does not require negation of his or her role as businessperson. This means accepting the notion that personal empowerment directed at some business activity is a valid goal and not necessarily "against" religious conscience. The test to determine which business activities are potentially an expression of spirituality is whether they are consistent with promoting "access to the sacred force(s) that impel life." This starting point should discipline the development of any spiritual audit. One test might be whether the application of a proposed religious view "kills" the spirit of the business actor to pursue life-enhancing solutions to economic problems. All too frequently well-intended economic programs with an espoused religious agenda have ignored life-destroying aspects of the business being created, such as the dependence on monopoly or poor accounting practices.

Not all catalytic activities must be personal. Social goals are extremely important to most people's sense of spiritual wholeness. But the catalytic does suggest that more attention should be paid to personal relationships even in the most systemic social activism. I know of one venture capitalist who is finding his spiritual life deepened the most through his personal relationship with a minority entrepreneur his company is backing. These two leaders discuss their foundational religious convictions openly, but do not have the same espoused affiliations. Jim Wallis's Call to Renewal program is one example of how social action can include the personal spirituality of the poor as a significant catalyst in shaping economic participation of the underemployed .

Reconciliation to Capitalism

The new spirituality should be framed in language, metaphors, and embodiments that do not set business and religion in dualistic opposition, or force a choice for religion and against fundamental principles of capitalism. As the business historian Thomas McCraw has argued, there are many developing forms of capitalism that do not exclude social responsibility from their foundational principles.[24] These ideas need to be studied and critiqued by the religious community. In this area, I suspect the language of poetry and use of biographical narrative will be more powerful than the language of theology.[25] I have not seen evidence of significant catalytic force in the many academic theories of ethics and the economy except within the academic community itself.

Again, the secular spirituality programs give a clue: most adopt a language that is highly evocative, personally accessible, and strongly weighted toward the empowering and the therapeutic. The challenge for Christian spirituality is not to counteract these forces out of fear of promoting self-regard, but to help the businessperson extend these forces for compassion and emotional maturity to a wider arena and more difficult cases.

Contextualization

Spirituality should provide specific penetration of the business setting and the businessperson's roles. As H. Richard Niebuhr said, "Active practical self-definition issues from response to challenges rather than from the pursuit of an ideal."[26]

New Institutional Linkages to Foundational Level of Religion

Despite the need for new frameworks, as suggested here, Christian spirituality in business must establish better linkage to the core foundational concepts of Christianity. No doubt, many of the new spirituality's ends seem trivial or even religiously misguided as they are applied to business (that's code for "sinful"). To speak of the soul of a corporation or team "spirit" with the same reverence as one speaks of the deeds of sacred figures like Jesus or David seems blasphemous or idolatrous. To suggest that the discovery of the inner person, the soul of one's uniqueness, is for the creation of a new brand of toothpaste is hardly grounds for canonization.

Craig Dykstra has posited that the new spirituality fails to do what religion has been best at from a moral sense, making *claims* on its members. For the religious community—lay and professional—it is important to test whether or not the ends to which spirituality is put conform to fulfillment of religiously defined ends, such as the advancement of the Kingdom of God as traditions define it, or the fulfillment of true personhood from the standpoint of religious meaning. Reintroducing the foundational level will allow these claims to be voiced without raising the specter of church dominance over business. This is not to disavow the espoused forms of religion, but to emphasize that people should engage in these espoused forms outside the business setting and that their application to work will necessarily be perceived as privatized and limited.[27]

Conclusion

No doubt, some of the scorn and alarm over the shallowness or crass commercialization of spirituality is deserved. Despite the deliciously tacky packaging of some of the programs—my favorite being the seminar on the three Ds: Diet, Discipline, and Deity—I am less dismissive. I find it helpful to remember William James's comment that the positive thinker literature was "nearly unreadable to the average educated person," yet he cautioned that such an experience should not be dismissed as inauthentic on these grounds.

The same could be said for the spirituality movement today. Hard as it is for some to read of "secular Buddhism," the "Tao of negotiation," or dollops of "chicken soup for the soul at work," there are deeper currents driving this business quest for the spiritual. These currents flow very close to the ultimate concerns of Christianity but within the unfamiliar and perplexing context of technologically precocious, postmodern capitalism. Dismissing the claims for a "corporate soul" seriously underestimates the connection between the production of seemingly trivial products for sometimes extraordinary profit and the complex set of human experiences that go into the organization and accomplishment of these ends.

The current spirituality movement is about much more than the material and financial accomplishments of a corporation—it is about a search to connect the reality of the sacred to one's daily life. It is about securing generalized prosperity and meaning in the large sense of these words. Recalling the fourfold needs of spirituality that were described earlier, I would suggest that religiously driven spirituality and business programs must seek at a normative level to accomplish transformations in all four areas.

Fulfilling the preconditions described here would require a new level of acquaintance with business, new forms of religious and spiritual expression within the Christian tradition, and a willingness to refrain from triumphal proselytizing on occasions of successful dialogue. Most importantly, the development of the spiritual must be conducted *in concert.* As the academic and religious communities attempt to bring a clearer understanding to this tipping point we call spirituality in business, and as both business and religious professionals attempt to bring the lessons of the Big Tradition, they are unlikely to succeed in isolation from each other . Traditional religious understandings of spirituality are not adequately prepared to address the new configuration of pragmatism, social conscience, and self-conducted religious experience that is being evidenced among the business community and popular guru programs.

On the analogy that poverty programs should include the direct voice of the poor in shaping the very terms of policy, spirituality in the business arena should include the religious voice *and* the business voice in the shaping of its goals. There are many reasons to assume that a true dialogue of this sort will not be particularly welcomed by either group, and those who do welcome it may nonetheless find difficulty in being heard.[28]

The ability of the two communities to retain a necessary mutuality in this quest will depend on a much higher sensitivity to, and avoidance of, the patterns of argument that separate them the most. By being aware of the many tripping points in the current approach of the church toward business, it is possible to begin to set the conditions for moving forward. Some of these have been set forth in this essay, and I look forward to their discussion by my colleagues.

NOTES

1. George C. Gallup Jr. and Timothy Jones, *The Next American Spirituality: Finding God in the Twenty-First Century* (Colorado Springs, Colo.: Cook Communications, 2000).

2. John W. Wright, ed., *New York Times Almanac 2000* (New York: Penguin Reference, 1999); George C. Gallup Jr. and Jim Castelli, *The People's Religion: American Faith in the '90s* (New York: Macmillan, 1989); and Gallup and Jones, *Next American Spirituality.*

3. Martin E. Marty, *Pilgrims in Their Own Land: Five Hundred Years of Religion in America* (New York: Penguin Books, 1984).

4. Wade Clark Roof, *Spiritual Marketplace* (Princeton, N.J.: Princeton University Press, 1999).

5. I concentrate here on people with some affiliation to Christianity but who are not seeking to organize economic institutions around deeply sectarian or fundamentalist principles. An example of the latter would be the long-standing Christian Business Men's Committee. Founded in 1930, this organization has been dedicated to a three-part strategy of "spiritual multiplication" in the marketplace. Offering support and access to biblical Scripture and prayer through meetings and follow-up activities, the goal of this organization is to fulfill the Great Commission by seeking out people in the marketplace. (Description taken from the organization's materials, especially "The Why and How of a Christian Business Men's Committee," CBMC of USA, Chattanooga, Tenn.)

6. Wendy Kaminer, "The Latest Fashion in Irrationality," *Atlantic Monthly* 278, no. 1 (July 1996): 103–6.

7. Craig Dykstra, "Religion and Spirituality," *Responsive Community* (Winter 1996): 6.

8. Ian Mitroff and Elizabeth A. Denton, *A Spiritual Audit of Corporate America: A Hard Look at Spirituality, Religion, and Values in the Workplace* (San Francisco: Jossey-Bass Publishers, 1999).

9. The term is Robert Redfield's.

10. William James, *The Varieties of Religious Experience* (New York: Macmillan, 1961), 90. As James noted, the positive-thinker programs were grass roots in origin and a syncretistic blend of Berkleyan idealism, mind-cure psychology, Hinduism, spiritism with its emphasis on progress, and scientific evolutionism.

11. Malcolm Gladwell, *The Tipping Point: How Little Things Can Make a Big Difference* (Boston: Little, Brown, 2000).

12. Steve Covey, *Principle-Centered Leadership,* Publication of Covey Leadership Center, Module 2 (1996), 18–19.

13. Estimate according to *Ethikos.*

14. Three examples having widespread impact and equally negative reactions from some mainstream business people are Laurie Beth Jones's *Jesus CEO*, and Bob Briner, Norman Vincent Peale, and Ken Blanchard's *Management by Values*.

15. Many of these findings confirm Robert Wuthnow's work. See especially *After Heaven: Spirituality in America since the 1950s* (1998), *The Crisis in the Churches: Spiritual Malaise, Fiscal Woe* (1997), and *God and Mammon in America* (1994). Our conclusions, however, are specifically drawn from more recent activity and comments on business spirituality.

16. Laura Nash and Scotty McLennan, *Church on Sunday, Work on Monday: The Challenge of Fusing Christian Values with Business Life* (San Francisco: Jossey-Bass, 2001), 145–46, 151, 190.

17. Quoted by Karl -Heinz Weger, *Karl Rahner: An Introduction to His Theology* (New York: Seabury Press, 1980), 95.

18. Jean Strouse, *J. P. Morgan: American Financier* (New York: Random House, 1999).

19. See E. Digby Balztell, *The Protestant Establishment: Aristocracy and Caste in America* (New Haven, Conn.: Yale University Press, 1987).

20. William Ian Miller, *The Anatomy of Disgust* (Cambridge, Mass.: Harvard University Press, 1998), 184 ff.

21. Such efforts, though increasing in number, are clearly not compatible or desirable for the mainstream public corporation; how inappropriate is unclear. See Alan J. Wolfe, *One Nation After All* (New York: Viking, 1998), 55; and Gallup and Jones, *Next American Spirituality,* 72 ff. Alan Wolfe's surveys reveal a deeply embedded pluralism in America and strong opinions that religion should not play an official and didactic role in guiding public morality. The workplace is clearly "public" in this sense. Gallup and Jones have concluded that there is new evidence that Americans do not see the workplace as cordoned off from spiritual concerns and suggests they are becoming less reticent about their own spirituality inside the workplace. When asked, "Did you have occasion to talk about your religious faith in the workplace?, 48 percent answered affirmatively. The only example Gallup and Jones offer is hearing a worker say to a coworker with a medical problem, "I will pray for you." Alan Wolfe is careful to stress that his survey was not extensive enough to represent the entirety of public opinion, and Gallup and Jones's twenty-four-hour survey was based on telephone interviews with a national random sampling of one hundred adults aged eighteen and older.

22. Gallup and Jones, *Next American Spirituality,* 79 ff.

23. Note that these preconditions are for development of programs on business and Christian spirituality and should *not* be understood to apply to all spiritual exercises and contexts.

24. Thomas K. McCraw, ed., *Creating Modern Capitalism: How Entrepreneurs, Companies, and Countries Triumphed in Three Industrial Revolutions* (Cambridge, Mass.: Harvard University Press, 1998).

25. See, for example, David Whyte, *The Heart Aroused,* or Thomas Moore, *Care of the Soul* and *Reenchantment of Everyday Life.* The Trinity Forum program for executives regularly reprints classic biographical and fiction narratives of religious questing from Tolstoy to Lord Shaftesbury.

26. H. Richard Niebuhr, *The Responsible Self* (San Francisco: Harper and Row Publishers, 1963), 59.

27. A discussion of the types of limiting mental models for inclusion of religion in business thinking is discussed in our forthcoming book on business spirituality.

28. An earlier example of productive mutuality is to be found in the discussion between the theologian James Gustafson and the business leader Elmer Johnson in an earlier conference at Notre Dame. See James M. Gustafson and Elmer Johnson, "The Corporate Leader and the Ethical Resources of Religion: A Dialogue," in *The Judeo-Christian Vision and the Modern Corporation,* ed. O. F. Williams and J. W. Houck (Notre Dame, Ind.: University of Notre Dame Press, 1982), 306–29. One would hope for another such dialogue between these two greats, directed at a specific problem in business.

PART II

Conceptual Foundations
for Understanding Spirituality

THREE

Spirituality and the Christian Manager

ROBERT G. KENNEDY

When I was a child, I spoke as a child, I judged as a child, and I thought as a child; when I became a man I abandoned the things of a child. At present we see [spiritual realities] as puzzling images in a mirror, but later we will see them directly; now we know imperfectly, but later we will know directly.

1 Corinthians 13:11–12

Just as human activity proceeds from man, so it is ordered toward man. For when a man works he not only alters things and society, he develops himself as well. He learns much, he cultivates his resources, he goes outside of himself and beyond himself. Rightly understood, this kind of growth is of greater value than any external riches which can be garnered. . . . Hence, the norm of human activity is this: that in accord with the divine plan and will, it should harmonize with the genuine good of the human race, and allow people as individuals and as members of society to pursue their total vocation and fulfill it.

Second Vatican Council
Gaudium et spes, para. 35

Americans have always been a people deeply sensitive to the spiritual dimensions of life. This is hardly surprising when considering the nation's roots in the quest of its early colonists for religious freedom, or considering the faith that sustained the generations of immigrants who crossed oceans and tamed America's wilderness. Americans can be roused to accomplish great things, and never more so than when there are goods of the spirit to be protected.

Still, two of the themes that tell the story of the twentieth century are the retreat of religion from public life and the emergence of religious pluralism from a once self-consciously Christian nation. Yet another theme is the success of American business, which has created unprecedented material prosperity. It is no accident that these themes from the last century now combine to create a challenge for management in the new century. This is the challenge of integrating faith and spirituality into the workplace.

Spirituality in the Workplace

Diversity is not a new experience for Americans, though an argument can certainly be made that the factors contributing to modern diversity in the workplace are more numerous than they once were. More so than most peoples, Americans have coped with diversity and grown strong because of it. Our means of coping with it, however, have generally either involved rendering it superficial in comparison with a deeper commonality or excluding its manifestations from common life and making it a private matter. The former method has often been applied successfully to cope with diversity in nationality, while the latter approach has helped us to manage religious differences that have stirred other nations to open hostility.

At the beginning of the new century, however, it is becoming clear that it is not possible to privatize faith any longer. Whatever it might once have been, America is no longer a Christian nation, in the strong sense of that term. Too many of us are Jewish or Muslim or Buddhist or representative of another of the world's faiths. Christian faith is no longer one of the deep commonalities that unites Americans in spite of other differences, and faith is no longer content to be merely a private matter.

These new realities are causing turbulence in education, in cultural affairs, in politics (especially local politics), and in the workplace. The tacit agreement we once had, for example, not to bring personal matters to work is no longer viable. We now realize that we employ whole people, not just pairs of hands, or legs, or strong backs. We employ people with children, with elderly parents, with mortgages and grocery bills, but also people with passion and a desire to make a difference, with clever minds and new ideas, and even people with a faith commitment that shapes their lives. Management is learning how to deal with some of these dimensions of employees' lives, but it must learn to deal with the faith dimension as well.

The practical challenge presented to management by this faith dimension takes several forms. On one level, management is challenged to deal with expressions of faith that reflect the pluralism of the society but also have the potential to undermine the harmony of the workplace. In attempting to address it we seem to be caught on the horns of a dilemma. On the one hand, spirituality seems to be closely tied up with faith commitments and religious practices. In pluralistic societies one hardly knows how to create space for spirituality in organizations without opening the door for conflict between employees. It seems better to sanitize the workplace and avoid the problem altogether (though this would seem to be a retreat to a view of work as simply the performance of tasks and not the active collaboration of persons).

On the other hand, many organizations recognize the hunger for a spiritual dimension in the lives of their employees and experience the pressure to create some outlet for that yearning. Can this be done in a way that avoids imposing a certain set of beliefs and is respectful of everyone's views, including those who do not wish to participate? Or would any such effort be so bland and sterile as to trivialize spirituality and offend all employees while benefiting none? The problem becomes even more acute for managers who themselves have deep faith commitments that shape their lives. Must they compartmentalize their lives or can they find appropriate ways to integrate faith and career?

A second challenge concerns the relationship of spirituality to productivity and efficiency. The nineteenth century saw the first successful efforts at the rationalization of manual labor. These efforts flourished in the twentieth century and created stunning improvements in the productivity of labor, resulting in higher wages and lower prices. The twenty-first century must find ways to introduce similar improvements to knowledge work, but this is inherently a more complicated problem. As Peter Drucker points out, the rationalization of manual labor is always directed by the work to be done, and the work to be done is a given.[1] Knowledge work, on the other hand, is not defined by the task at hand, but instead begins by defining the task. Most knowledge work demands innovation and requires autonomy. It depends on the mind of the employee in ways that manual work does not. Many companies have tried to attend to this by introducing training and enrichment programs that, in one way or another, attempt to enlist spirituality in the service of efficiency and productivity.

A third challenge has to do with another aspect of the changing nature of the workforce. Given the retirement of the boomer generation and the smaller size of the succeeding generation, we can expect to see a shortage of highly qualified employees well into the future. The problem of retention will be a fact of managerial life, and it will not be solved merely by cash. For a significant number of knowledge workers noncash benefits will strongly influence where they work and what they do. Among these noncash benefits will be the "spiritual" satisfactions they derive from their work and their working environment. Managers who attend to this can expect to retain more of their employees, while others can expect to spend more time interviewing replacements.

The purpose of this chapter is not to offer a set of concrete guidelines and exercises for managing spirituality at work, but rather to suggest a framework within which spirituality and its relevance to business organizations might be understood and to offer some reflections on the role of the Christian manager. Our starting point will be the question of whether spirituality is necessarily bound up with a particular faith, or whether there might be a foundational spirituality prior to any faith tradition. To pursue this we need to inquire into the role of spirituality in human fulfillment and so to ask what spirituality might mean in a philosophical context rather than a theological one.

A Theory of Human Fulfillment

One of the conceptual novelties of the modern era is the consideration of spirituality abstracted from a particular faith tradition. Only within the last two centuries have we begun to speak about spirituality as distinguishable from the practices of this or that faith or religion.[2] Prior to this time, one's spirituality was evident in one's religious practice, not in the generic pursuit of spiritual well-being. Today, however, we are able at least to ask what is common about the doctrines and practices of established religious traditions in terms of spirituality considered in general. To do this effectively, though, we need to be clear about what spirituality really is.

Over the past two decades or more two philosophers, Germain Grisez and John Finnis, have articulated a restatement of classical moral philosophy that will give us the conceptual tools we need to understand what spirituality is in abstraction from any religious tradition.[3] To be sure, both Grisez and Finnis are deeply committed Catholics, but their moral philosophy, while compatible with Christian moral theology, is not derived from or dependent upon it. In fact, it will allow us to understand how a variety of traditions and practices may be authentically called spiritualities.

At the heart of their theory is the notion of *integral human fulfillment*. Humans, they argue, naturally seek and find fulfillment in the possession of a set of *basic goods*. These basic goods correspond to the richness of human nature and cannot be reduced to one another, nor is any one category of basic goods merely an instrument for the possession of another. As a consequence, genuine human fulfillment consists in the integrated possession of the basic goods, and the moral life is the practical pursuit of these goods in ways that permit persons to remain open to each.

Grisez and Finnis divide the basic goods into two sets. One set consists of goods that we may share or participate in, to some degree, without making a deliberate choice to pursue them. These include the good of life and health, the good of knowledge and beauty, and the good of excellence in work and play. At least initially, every human being experiences these goods as received from others and not deliberately chosen and pursued. That is, at first we simply experience life and health (or illness), we learn about our world, we enjoy beauty and action largely as things that happen to us, not as the results of our deliberate choices.

The second set consists of goods that are possessed only as a result of deliberate choice and pursuit, that is, self-determining action. These goods all entail harmony of some sort and the avoidance or overcoming of conflict and alienation. They include what Grisez and Finnis call the good of personal integrity or self-integration, which is harmony within the person and resolution of the inner urges and tensions that cause conflict within the self. A second good in this category is practical reasonableness or authenticity, which is harmony between knowledge, will, and action. We all have the experience, for example, of conflict between what we know to be right and what we actually choose to do. Practical reasonableness is really nothing less than the order that reason imposes, or should impose, on action.

A third basic good is harmony between persons, or friendship, which entails genuinely willing the good for other persons and participating with them in peaceful collaboration and community life. The fourth and final good in this set is religion, or harmony between the person and the Creator, the source of our being. However it might be understood by different persons, this good involves at minimum an alignment between the life of the individual and the order built into Creation, and perhaps even friendship with a personal God.

I submit that we may understand spirituality, in the broadest sense, *to be the pursuit of harmony in oneself and in one's relationships with others*. To put it another way, while the goal of a truly good human life is integral human fulfillment (the integrated presence in a person's life of each category of the basic goods), spirituality particularly concerns the second set of basic goods (and perhaps especially the fourth of these goods). Moreover, where spirituality constitutes a plan or a set of practices for realizing and integrating these goods in one's life, it is good or bad to the degree that it is (1) fully oriented to the truth about humans and extrahuman realities and (2) realistic in its prescriptions for successfully bringing people to genuine fulfillment.

Spirituality, then, may indeed be conceived in a meaningful way in abstraction from any specific religious tradition. Ignatian spirituality, Hindu spirituality, Scientology, animism, witchcraft, and voodoo all offer some plan for achieving human fulfillment. Nevertheless, they are not equally good spiritualities, and because the ways to go wrong in this area are so many, something else is required to ensure that the two criteria just mentioned are adequately fulfilled.

Spirituality and the Role of Religion

The pursuit of basic goods in the second set must, by definition, be deliberate, and, as we know from experience, is never easy. There are too many ways to go offtrack. Three of those distractions merit some further attention.

The pursuit of spiritual goods involves a sort of paradox. The first category of basic goods we discussed is defined by our ability to possess them without deliberate pursuit. We receive life (and usually health) from our parents and take it as a given. When we are young, we believe that we are immortal and invulnerable. At first, we soak up knowledge and appreciate pretty things without effort and only later, when we are in school, do we need to discipline ourselves to study and to cultivate our tastes. At the same time we take pleasure in the things we do well naturally, as a result of the talents we have inherited, but it requires maturity to develop the skills that we need but for which we lack talent.

The paradox is that while these goods are first experienced as received from others in some sense, we do not initially require others to possess them. We possess them without serious effort, and so no help or training is required. On the other hand, the basic goods of the second set (which we might call spiritual goods) cannot be received from others. We must cultivate them as a matter of choice. Nevertheless, we probably cannot do them well unless others show us how. Despite their furious protests to the contrary, adolescents need the guidance, direction, and discipline of their parents in order to resolve their inner conflicts and to learn how to form friendships and to live in harmony with others. Unless we learn from others that there is more to life than the first set of basic goods, we are too often willing to settle for pleasures and material possessions to the virtual exclusion of the other goods. Paradoxically, while we can possess the spiritual goods only through our own deliberate actions, we can probably not pursue them successfully without others.

A second distraction concerns what we might call the emotional companions of genuine fulfillment. We are quite capable of accepting an emotional satisfaction in place of what is really fulfilling. For example, it is usually a pleasure to be honored or complimented as a result of someone's recognition of our accomplishments. Some people, though, are quite content to pursue honor without the accomplishment. A sense of peace rightly accompanies the achievement of real self-integration, but this sense of peace (or its surrogate) can be induced in the absence of self-integration by other means, such as drugs and self-deception. Or we might be content to accept a sort of superficial sociability as a substitute for the effort of maintaining real friendships. In its worst manifestations, this distraction causes people to reject real goods in favor of mere emotional companions when the real goods do not generate the same emotional experience. It was with this in mind that Cicero admonished his son always to prefer being worthy of honor without recognition to being honored without merit.

A third distraction is related and involves self-deception. We may achieve a kind of harmony either by conforming ourselves to the truth or by reconceiving reality to conform it to ourselves. In either case we resolve an inner conflict. To give a simple example, a friend may need our assistance at a very inconvenient time, and this request creates a conflict. We may resolve the conflict either by honoring the reality of our friendship and giving the required help, whether convenient or not, or by deciding that he is not a real friend after all and so does not deserve our help. While both options resolve the conflict (at some level), only one respects the truth about the relationship. We could think of many other examples along the same lines. In the context of spirituality, though, the most prominent example has to do with a person's relationship with God. The conflict created by sin can either be resolved by repentance and reform or by the denial of sinfulness, or even of God's very existence.

These distractions are worth considering because they, and others like them, are very real problems for a spirituality abstracted from a faith tradition. At the very least, a spirituality rooted in a faith tradition provides a tested plan for pursuing the spiritual goods and a counterbalance to the temptations to accept substitutes and engage in self-deception. It provides a benchmark, a measure of authenticity that is supported by the successful experience of numerous predecessors. Since the human desire for friendship with God and harmony with Creation is too strong and deep to be frustrated, we should not be surprised to see such traditions emerge in virtually all cultures. Indeed, in very important ways these traditions actually shape human cultures. They represent the best human efforts to reach out to the divine and often contain profound insights about the human condition.

Some religious traditions—most notably Judaism and Christianity—go one step further and claim an authority superior to collective experience: revelation. While we can construct a spirituality of sorts quite in abstraction from any religious tradition (and the last two centuries have certainly seen many created *ex nihilo*), Judaism and Christianity—if their claim to possess revelation is true—constitute a far superior basis for spirituality than any other. In such a case, as fallen creatures subject to misdirection, self-deception, emotional intoxication, and the like, it would be thoroughly irrational for us to prefer a humanly constructed spirituality to one based on authentic revelation. To reject authentic revelation is to prefer the "puzzling images" of which Paul spoke to the Corinthians.[4]

Spirituality and Management

This might suggest that a Christian manager or, for that matter, any manager whose life is formed by a faith commitment should attempt to shape the workplace according to the insights of his or her faith. After all, if revelation is a superior guide to human fulfillment, do managers not have a duty to use it to benefit their employees? To some degree, if faith is well integrated in their lives, this will be inevitable, but it need not give rise to conflicts.

The relevance of spirituality for management and the workplace depends upon the recognition that persons are fulfilled by both sets of basic goods. In other words, while both are genuinely good and worth pursuing, there is more to a truly satisfying human life than health, knowledge, aesthetic experience, and skillful performance. At the very least, the recognition that humans need bodily *and* spiritual goods requires management to organize work in such a way that these goods are not impeded by employment. This is a moral minimum that we have come to recognize at the level of bodily goods (safe working conditions, physical comfort, reasonable wages, and so on) but often recognize only dimly at the level of spiritual goods.

Managers with a faith commitment will probably see the importance of the spiritual goods more clearly than others, but this does not mean that they ought to use the practices of their faith to organize and structure the workplace, or even to articulate the goals of the organization. The insights of their faith, however, should give rise to a commitment to create an environment at work that is truly open to the realization of spiritual goods in the lives of employees and actively supports the pursuit of those goods where possible. Even so, the nature of the workplace (whether a business, a not-for-profit organization, or a unit of government) imposes some limits on what a manager should and may do.

Classical moral philosophy recognizes generally three types of human associations: the family, the political community, and a rather vaguely defined intermediate category that we might call "specialized associations."[5] A crucial distinction between specialized associations and both families and political communities is that specialized associations are organized for specific, limited purposes. Families and political communities, on the other hand, are by their very nature designed for the comprehensive fulfillment of their members. No element of the well-being of its members truly falls outside the concern of families and political communities. With specialized associations, however, this is not the case. These voluntary associations are not formed to support the comprehensive fulfillment of their (sometimes temporary) members, but to pursue limited goals of common interest and benefit. The members of a garden club, for example, might feel sympathy for another member who is searching for a new job, but it is not the purpose of the club as such to provide employment counseling and placement services.

Similarly, a business is organized to pursue a limited set of goals that may be achieved by the collaborative efforts of the employees and managers, but the comprehensive human development of each of the collaborators is not one of these goals. Despite the rhetoric we sometimes employ, businesses are not families and managers are not parents. It may sometimes be expedient for businesses to provide certain kinds of extraordinary benefits or support in order to make it possible for employees to continue to collaborate, but when they do so, it is to make up for the failure of the family or the political community.

As a consequence, managers—even those with deeply held faith commitments—do not have a duty, as managers, to pursue or ensure the spiritual development of their subordinates. They do, however, have a duty to make sure that the structures and activities of the workplace are not hostile to this spiritual development and, where it does not conflict with the legitimate goals of the association, might even positively support such development. In discharging their duty, Christian managers are neither hobbled by their faith nor bound to give explicit witness. Instead, they may be assisted by their faith to see more clearly what will truly contribute to spiritual development, regardless of the faith of the employee, and be more strongly motivated to create those conditions.

Some Specific Duties for Christian Managers

Christian managers should be powerfully aware that all the persons associated with their enterprises—customers, employees, investors, creditors, and so on—are individuals beloved of God and destined for eternal life. As a result, they need to pay attention to the impact of their operations on several categories of basic goods, especially what we have called the spiritual goods.

First, managers must ensure that the work product of the members of the association serves genuine goods. The work of persons is too valuable to be wasted on phantom goods, or no goods at all. For example, many businesses in the developed world generate products and services that serve no real good at all (empty snacks or mindless entertainment) or may even promote evil (pornography, prostitution, many kinds of weapons, or drugs, tobacco, and alcohol). At best these products and services simply waste resources, and at worst they corrupt consumers. Inevitably, they also demoralize the employees who produce them and who are not yet desensitized to what they are doing. Management has a duty to see to it that what an organization does genuinely promotes human well-being, no matter how mundane the good served, and that employees share in the satisfaction of this by understanding clearly just what goods are served by their work.

Second, managers must be attentive to the self-integration of employees. This may emerge in the workplace in several ways. Since self-integration is the resolution of conflicting desires and inclinations within the person, a sound organization will not aggravate or exploit these inner conflicts. For example, many people experience a conflict between a desire for success in a career and family responsibilities. Managers should not aggravate this problem by forcing employees to choose between their families and their careers, or by penalizing employees who require some time or some flexibility to tend to their family responsibilities. Neither should they take advantage of a particular employee's inclination to over-work—an inclination that is a result of poor self-integration—however beneficial this might be for the company. In the United States, some industries, notably computer firms and financial services, are notorious for their willingness to exploit employees in this way.

Third, managers must be attentive to the development of practical reasonableness, or authenticity, in employees. Among other things, this means exercising care to avoid creating a working environment in which employees are faced with conflicts between what they are expected to do and what they think they are morally obliged not to do. This could include such acts as lying to customers or other employees, cheating customers, abusing subordinates, or even deliberately producing products of poor quality. Managers must also take care that incentive systems do not create such conflicts unintentionally.

Fourth, the workplace has the potential to be a community of sorts. Human beings, as social creatures, naturally tend to form friendships with others with whom they work. Friendship, in fact, is part of the cement that ensures effective collaboration. As a consequence, managers must be attentive to ways in which they can foster the development of the organization as a true human community, moving beyond a mere aggregation of individuals. They fail to do so when they stimulate unnecessary competition, when they exhibit favoritism toward some employees, or when they politicize the workplace.

Finally, managers need to be attentive to the consequences of work and participation in the organization's activities for the employee's relationship with God. For the Christian manager, at least, this may be understood on two levels. First, each person has a vocation, a role to play in the working out of the divine plan, and a set of gifts suitable for that vocation. Managers should be attentive to the gifts displayed by employees as signs of that vocation and willing to provide resources and opportunities, as appropriate, for employees to recognize and fulfill their vocations. There are countless stories of good managers who have recognized the potential in an employee and helped her to flourish by developing that potential. There are also countless examples of managers who saw employees merely as tools to accomplish specific tasks and who thereby wasted their human resources. The history of American business is replete with examples of gifted individuals who were smothered in one organization and went on to great success in a competing organization.[6]

A second level concerning the good of religion has to do with the practice of religion itself. As Pope John Paul II has commented many times, businesses must be attentive to the religious freedom and the religious obligations of employees. This may mean permitting individuals some tasteful and appropriate display of religious commitment in the workplace and perhaps even providing opportunities for individuals to pray together during the working day. It also means permitting employees to celebrate holidays and to refrain from working on days discouraged by their faith. And it certainly means avoiding any unjust discrimination based on the faith commitment of employees.

Spirituality in the workplace does create a set of problems and questions, not least because we tend to see things of the spirit as "puzzling images" and often disagree sharply about how to interpret what we see. Christians may indeed see these things more clearly because of revelation, but the spiritual goods cannot be imposed on others; they must be willingly and deliberately pursued. As a result, Christian managers cannot take responsibility for providing spiritual goods, but can only offer opportunities, ever respectful of the liberty of individuals to choose.

NOTES

1. Peter Drucker, *Management Challenges for the Twenty-First Century* (New York: Harper Business, 1999). See especially pp. 135–48.

2. The 1933 edition of the Oxford English Dictionary does not give clear evidence at all of the usage of the term "spirituality" outside of a definite religious context.

3. For the most comprehensive statements of their theory see Germain Grisez and Russell Shaw, *Beyond the New Morality*, 3d ed. (Notre Dame, Ind.: University of Notre Dame Press, 1988), and Grisez, *Christian Moral Principles*, vol. 1 of *The Way of the Lord Jesus* (Chicago: Franciscan Herald Press, 1983). See also John Finnis, *Natural Law and Natural Rights,* Clarendon Law Series (Oxford: Oxford University Press, 1980). For a joint presentation of their theory, with annotated bibliography, see Germain Grisez, Joseph Boyle, and John Finnis, "Practical Principles, Moral Truth, and Ultimate Ends," *American Journal of Jurisprudence* 32 (1987): 99–151. A more recent discussion of some key points, including critical essays, may be found in Robert P. George, ed., *Natural Law and Moral Inquiry* (Washington, D.C.: Georgetown University Press, 1998).

4. See 1 Corinthians 13:11–12.

5. In the *Politics,* Aristotle speaks of the family, the city, and the village, which he understands to be larger and more loosely related than a family, but not truly self-contained like a city. For the most part, philosophers have ignored this third category, but the dramatic proliferation of organizations in modern life has brought about a renewed interest in specialized associations.

6. Two computer companies in California, Xerox and Fairchild Semiconductor, are well known for their inability to develop talent in the 1960s and 1970s, and as seedbeds for individuals who left to form major, competing businesses, such as Intel and Apple Computer.

FOUR

Vocation as a Critical Factor in a Spirituality for Executive Leadership in Business

JAMES J. MCGEE &
ANDRÉ L. DELBECQ

What Motivates Organization Leaders in their Search for Spirituality?

For a number of years executives who participate in courses in our MBA program and in our executive center at Santa Clara University had requested a course in spirituality for senior leadership. Due to their interest a number of seminars have been offered in "Spirituality for Business Leadership" for both CEOs and working professional MBAs. Programs have also been presented to other organizational leaders, such as physician administrators. Each of the seminars begins with this question to the seminar participants: "What motivates you as an organizational leader to explore spirituality?"

Organizational leaders offer a variety of reasons. Sometimes executives have been in destructive work settings, and they are determined that their leadership must shape a healthier organization culture. Sometimes executives are going through problematic leadership challenges and are seeking strength to cope with their difficulties. Others cite the fast pace and chaotic context of contemporary competitive settings. But in the end, one reason is stated most frequently: the desire to integrate two important parts of life—the inner journey and the professional role. Contemporary organizational leaders yearn to integrate their deepest inner desires with the day-to-day experience of their professional role. One CEO who attended the seminar commented:

My feelings at the start of our seminar were one of great relief. I was being given a perspective to explore the integration of the two most important halves of my life.

This concurs with the findings of Ian Mitroff and Elizabeth Denton in their recent empirical study (Mitroff and Denton 1999).

For this reason, our seminars begin with the topic of "calling," or "vocation." Unless a leader feels that his or her organizational role is a "calling," the heavy burdens of leadership become separated from the spiritual journey, a separation that often contributes to burnout and cynicism. Furthermore, this particular lens for understanding the role of business leadership underscores the value of self-transcendence, so essential to the distinctive character of spirituality and so much a key to the mature leader's identity, perception, and motivation in decision making and action.

Organizational Leadership as a Noble Calling

Presently, a unique window of opportunity exists in which interest in contemporary leadership, new organizational forms, and spirituality are coming together with the potential for reshaping the institutional setting in which most individuals in modern societies spend the greatest part of their day. The organization is often the contemporary "village" for many people, and each day the organization is one of the most formative and influential "cultures" affecting their lives. Within these organizations individuals employ their skills and talents, find self-expression, often seek community, and serve others. As modern business and service organizations evolve to greater and greater "knowledge work" within more and more decentralized organizational structures, it is often in the workplace that the highest intellectual capabilities are engaged—resulting in enormous discovery, innovation, and creativity. As business is the principal source of employment in the United States—84 percent of the adult population is employed in the private sector—spirituality within the business context is of critical importance to the spiritual lives of a majority of citizens.

In addition, business not only provides the majority of goods and services we depend upon for the quality of our daily life but also the advanced artifacts of intellectual and artistic expression. Business is also the principal means of wealth distribution in modern economies, because most individuals participate in the economic order through salaries and wages rather than inherited wealth. And it is the private sector that creates the "surplus" wealth through which government, education, churches and temples, parks, the arts, environmental causes, and other essential good works are supported. Further, if many share in the potential of wealth accumulation, the market system keeps a stagnant oligarchy from controlling philanthropy.

Such an emphasis on the nobility of business leadership is not an attempt to ignore the dark side of organizational life and the business enterprise. A vibrant spirituality is one that is in tune with, and therefore able to speak to, the culture in which it finds itself. This harmony does not deny the radical gospel criticism of destructive elements in our society, but "if one's understanding of the spiritual quest is divorced from the daily round of one's activities, neither a vital spirituality nor a prophetic stance for justice can prosper" (Dreyer 1994, 27). Thus, a mature spirituality also looks at the dark side of life (the individual, the organization, and the systemic paradigm) and at the realities of imperfection, failure, and sin: greed, exploitation, environmental degradation, abuses of power, and failures of stewardship. Yet, without the realization of the nobility possible in the work of business, and in the particular work or organizational leadership, awareness of the enormous consequences of such imperfection is actually diminished.

In order to bring to the surface and develop spirituality for business leadership, then, the starting point is the acknowledgement that business is an enterprise of potentially great good. Perhaps an analogy might be made with the "daily examen" of Ignatian prayer, in which the faithful disciples take account of their relationship with God. Ignatius insists that, after giving thanks and praise to the Creator, one begins the self-examination by recalling one's expressions of goodness throughout the day. After such a reflection, the disciples look at their shortcomings during the day's events with confidence in God's mercy and with the promise of reform. Following this format, Ignatius of Loyola hoped to preserve the foundational Christian belief that all of Creation, no matter how tarnished by imperfection, is innately good. In doing so, Ignatius hoped that the "examiner" would never lose confidence in her or his nobility and the ultimate graciousness and mercy of God. So, too, with the "examen" of the business enterprise and the experience of organizational leadership. The starting point is the expressed goodness of the experience. And from such conscious awareness one becomes all the more awestruck by the enormous potential of the business enterprise, as well as the seriousness of its existing shortcomings.

In the present day the need is urgent to come to a deeper understanding regarding both the centrality of the organization as a pivotal institution in modern society and the centrality of executive leadership as a critical factor in the culture and operative values within an organization. Then the enterprise of business and the experience of corporate leadership can truly be *avodah*—a word from the Hebrew Scriptures that can be translated as both "work" and "worship."

Challenges to Contemporary Executive Leadership

The central challenge of leadership, as opposed to routine management, is vision. The organizational leader must bring a vision that transforms the organization into a true service entity, because its innate purpose is more than its self-perpetuation and maximization of profit. In this sense, a transforming vision can "cocreate" a new organizational reality. It is a spiritual challenge to discern such a vision for which the leader must be the primary spokesperson. How does the leader find the courage to purify and articulate this vision and then engage others in actions to make the vision a reality? How can the executive leader be sure the vision is not a product of greed and ego? How does the leader arrive at inner integrity so that the vision is communicated with transforming vitality? These are not trivial spiritual issues.

Recent scholarly research asserts that personal integration is crucial to successful visionary leadership. According to extensive studies in this arena, within the most effective companies there is a correlation between the values of the corporate CEO and the values of the corporate entity. For example, researchers have demonstrated that "value-based leadership," i.e., the relationship between an individual leader and one or more followers based on strongly internalized ideological values espoused by the leader, is a most effective form of employee motivation. In fact, motivation based on strongly internalized values is stronger, more pervasive, and more enduring than motivation based on tangible rewards or motivation based on threat and avoidance of punishment (House, Delbecq, and Travis 1997; Kouzes and Posner 1993).

Furthermore, researchers posit that the appropriation of self-transcendent values by the executive leader is crucial to the task of successful corporate management and to the communication and sustenance of the corporate vision and the organizational culture. "Visionary companies"—premier institutions in their industries that demonstrate extraordinary, long-term financial performance and are highly respected by their peers—are those organizations that demonstrate consistent commitment to their founding core values, share a sense of purpose beyond making profit or the maximization of shareholder value, and foster an environment of employee creativity and ongoing organizational critique (Collins and Porras 1994). Companies that place "people first" have demonstrated remarkable competitive advantage in their industries (Pfeffer 1994, 1998). And among many of these same companies is a clear and sustained commitment to social and environmental consciousness (Makeower 1994, 1995; Waddock 1998).

Thus, the critical task of executive leadership is to "convert the contractual employees of an economic entity into committed members of a purposeful organization. Purpose—not strategy—is the reason an organization exists. Its definition and articulation must be management's first responsibility" (Bartlett and Goshal 1998). This is a concern of vocational discernment and mission.

Leadership as a Career: Current Developments

Compounding the leader's task as one who discerns, communicates, and sustains the organizational vision are radical changes in organizational leadership as an organizational career. The explosion of informational technology, the burgeoning of globalization and deregulation, and the rapid rate of product and service innovation are having profound effects on management leadership careers. The so-called boundaryless organization has resulted in the "boundaryless career" (Arthur and Rousseau 1996). Once defined by corporate needs and nurtured by senior leaders in the organization, the management leadership career is now seen as a series of individual identity changes and continuous skills development, often designed and managed by the individual alone. The individually managed "protean career" has emerged as the dominant career paradigm (see Weiss 1996). Thus, challenged by the need for greater adaptability, individuals seek more consciously to ground their ever changing leadership careers in an abiding sense of personal meaning and purpose.

The advent of interest in spirituality and management and its attention to values of ultimate concern in relation to one's work life has accented this personal development. A new time has emerged for new efforts to understand the experience of leadership careers and the refinement of education for management leaders.

Yet, personal fulfillment is not regarded merely in isolated personal terms, but in a growing awareness of and responsibility toward the integration of diverse cultures, customs, and needs among organizational members. New terminology in business leadership literature reflects the shift in social consciousness regarding personal fulfillment and social relatedness: self-leadership, superleadership, transformational leadership, charismatic leadership, leadership and followership, and servant leadership (see Weiss 1996). Now leaders are master organizational change and transformation agents. Leaders are coaches, cheerleaders, and mentors. Leaders are stewards and servants. Leaders are strategists who spearhead alliance-building activities, and leaders are also followers.

With such diversity of expressed images the competencies of contemporary CEOs and other management leaders now appear almost endless. A new study by Andersen Consulting included fourteen leadership attributes and eight-two subcharacteristics, almost all of which reflect traditional competencies. However, several new attributes of executive leadership were revealed in the study: self-confidence, vision, and personal excellence. In addition, the ability to listen and to inspire people to commit to the organization's vision were also noted.

Such attributes reflect the quest for meaningful personal development and underscore the need for integrating the hopes and needs of both the individual leader and the organizational members into a common purpose. The concept of vocation may be the key concept to bridging the realms of management and spirituality in the quest for personal meaning. The model and embodiment of leader as someone who chooses and is "called" to authentically serve a group, an organization, an enterprise, a community, the customers, and a society is more relevant and more likely to succeed (see Vaill 1998; Novak 1996; and Conger and Associates 1994).

Although the language of "vocation" and "calling" may be foreign to many executive leaders, there is evidence in current executive research that a moral and spiritual dimension plays a part in the success of CEOs. For example, current research based on extensive interviews with several dozen highly successful CEOs, funded by the John Templeton Foundation and now being carried out by William Damon of Stanford, Howard Gardner of Harvard, and Mihaly Csikszentmihalyi of Claremont, suggests strongly that a self-transcendent purpose was and is the basis for executive risk taking. Thus, contrary to what is commonly assumed, the moral dimension of their careers was not accounted for merely as a preemptive strategy to avoid noncompliance legal action. Rather, success seemed to hinge on an interest in and commitment to values not concerned with wealth accumulation but with a larger sense of purpose, such as service or creativity. For example, Sir John Templeton viewed his pioneering global investing as an expression of his lifelong sense of a call to serve all humanity. Ted Turner envisioned the twenty-four-hour global news reporting as a way to break down conflicts internationally. Anita Roddick's highly successful venture into environmentally sensitive cosmetic processes grew out of her desire for ecological sustainability and the promotion of local Third-World economic development. In addition, many of the executives mentioned the importance of prayer and contemplative practice. They believe that prayer positively affects their business enterprises by keeping their mental and emotional facilities optimal and their decision-making acumen sharp.

Christian Perspectives on Vocation and Calling and Their Implications for Contemporary Leadership

Context: Spirituality in the Marketplace

For many centuries the nonordained members of the Christian tradition felt hard-pressed to find guidance in their journey of discovering the divine within the context of their work, particularly those engaged in the business enterprise. They were confused because much of the Christian spiritual tradition emphatically counsels withdrawal from outer activity, detachment from creatures, and flight from the "world." Even when one turned from the monastery to the parish church, one found a similar problem—"the wall of the parish church shut out the noise of the world"

(Cousins 1988, 5). Thus, the commonly accepted norm for spiritual maturity was referred to as the *via negativa*—the way of negation of sense experience and concepts, the apophatic way, which espouses an inner discipline of meditation that leads one not through the experience of creatures but beyond it.

In recent years, however, theological scholarship has begun to reclaim voices from the Christian tradition that espouse the *via affirmativa*—the way of holiness through full engagement with the world and all its creatures. Through one's awakening to the beauty, creativity, and goodness of creatures one awakens to the love of the Transcendent. Thus, an intrinsic connection exists between human experience and the ultimate mystery that Christians call God (Rahner 1978). The conversation between spirituality and work, particularly the current dialogue between spirituality and business, has furthered this exploration. The tension between the two paths to holiness, *via negativa* and *via affirmativa,* exists in many of the classic spiritual traditions—Buddhism, Confucianism, Hinduism, Islam, Judaism, and others. Yet they, too, speak of the holiness of one's engagement with the marketplace. This belief is wonderfully captured in a saying of a Sufi master: I went into the marketplace and only God I saw.

The Meaning of Work

In light of the contemporary experience of management leaders' growing concern for an abiding sense of personal meaning and purpose amidst an ever changing career in leadership, management scholars and organizational leaders themselves have begun to reexamine not only the purpose of the business enterprise but also the nature of work itself. Common among definitions of work, in philosophical, psychological, sociological, and management literature is a sense of self-transcendence or "otherness" within the actual activity of work (Applebaum 1995; Berg 1995; Fox and Hesse-Biber 1984, 2; Hall 1986, 11). This sense of self-transcendence in the activity of work opens the door for conversation with the discipline of spirituality, whose focus is the lived experience of engagement with the "other"—other humans, nature, and the divine (Delbecq 1999, 345; Schneiders 1998, 1). Thus, the concept of vocation, or calling, as the entryway into understanding the moral purpose and spiritual dimension of executive leadership is grounded in a larger framework: the spirituality of work itself.

The Christian sense of transcendence in the activity of work is rooted in the Judeo-Christian Scriptures most profoundly as participation in the work of God's ongoing creation of the world. The Hebrew Scriptures display a high regard for the worker, even the wage earner, whose lifestyle was despised in the dominant Greco-Roman world. Many of the esteemed Jewish leaders are portrayed in the Scriptures as performing commonplace work.

The Christian Scriptures continued this belief, and the subsequent philosophical-theological tradition embellished such a view. The great Augustine of Hippo, in awe of the "genius of man and his astonishing arts," referred to work as the result of the exuberant invention and remarkable vigor of the human mind (Applebaum 1995, 52). In Augustine—"the first Christian theologian of technology" (Benz 1966, 128)—one finds work as a means of moral perfection, a "calling" (vocation) from God as a pathway to humility and as a means of offering charity to others while continuing the work of God's Creation.

This esteemed view of work continued despite the monastic retrieval from the cities in the early–Middle Ages. The predominant monastic way of life, expressed in the Benedictine communities, cherished work as a medium for engagement with the divine, thus engendering the well-known monastic call for a life of balance: *Ora et labore* (Pray and work). Some sociology and management scholars even see in the order and structure of the Benedictine monastic life the seeds of the modern corporation (Cavanagh, 1998, 35).

A resurgence of interest in the meaning of work arose with the Reformation challenge to the growing distinction between laity and ordained. What emerged is of significance not only to contemporary religious debates regarding "vocation" but also to the dilemma in contemporary management leadership careers. Led by Martin Luther, the German Augustinian cleric, the sense of vocation was extended once again to the commonplace world of daily work. Work is seen as participation in God's providential care for his Creation. Each "station in life" was seen as particular context for the expression of God's call to service and contains particular tasks that promote the welfare and development of the community (Kolden 1989; Wingren 1957).

Whereas Luther considered the division of labor and the resulting class distinctions as part of the divinely created order, the reformer John Calvin extended the meaning of "calling" to include social transformation. This nuance on vocation was grounded in Calvin's belief that one's vocation arose not from one's station in life but from the gifts that arose from within the individual. Calvin also saw the role of institutions to be facilitators of the individual's skills. Consequently, he also believed that any social structure that impeded the development and use of those gifts must be reformed.

Unlike Luther, Calvin freed work from the hampering ideas of caste: work became mobile, fluid, and self-designed, even while skills and talents were God-given. And unlike Luther, Calvin praised trade, profits, and finance and considered them deserving of the same honor as the earnings of the common worker when based on diligence, honesty, and industry. Yet, both believed that the skills and talents employed in the fulfillment of one's vocation were God-given, imparted to bring about the incarnation of God's social order.

Calvin also believed that profit was a sign of God's blessing, and much has been made of Calvin's views by Max Weber regarding the connection between Protestantism and the rise of capitalism. Although much debate exists about Weber's thesis, the connection between Protestantism—Calvinism in particular—and the American work ethic is quite clear. Although unintended by the Reformation actors, eventually the notion of a religious calling (*Beruf*) became the devoted commitment to commercial endeavors, a commitment to the accumulation of wealth and the efficient use of time and effort (Krieger 1996, x).

Both Luther and Calvin ground the meaning of work in service to a self-transcendent good. Luther's sense of vocation, as dutiful response to the needs and expectations of the social order, seem to echo the traditional, organizationally driven experience of the leadership career, while Calvin's views seem to echo the emerging fluidity of the individually designed paradigm. Yet together both understandings illustrate the tension that marks the experience of contemporary leaders—the tension between one's self-realization and one's responsiveness to the needs of the community.

Like the monastic tradition and the reform tradition, contemporary theologians concerned with the meaning of work struggle with the notion of self-fulfillment on one hand and the responsibility to a larger community on the other. Contemporary management research likewise seems to struggle with such tension, because similar language regarding the dignity of work, self-realization, and the importance of community appears throughout leadership and organizational theory. A number of management scholars even contend that balanced attention to worker self-realization and the promotion of social relatedness is critical for long-term business success (e.g., Mirvis 1993; and Pfeffer 1994, 1998).

The Challenge

At the beginning of the new century, business stands as a dominant societal institution, in many cases more powerful than the nation-state. In light of the Second Vatican Council's reminder that "all Christians in any state or walk of life are called to the fullness of Christian life and to the perfection of charity" (*Lumen gentium*, no. 40, 2), an essential task of the church's mission in the new millennium will be the education and formation of the laity in forging a spirituality reflective of the lived experience of the business context. To do so is foundational to the story of salvation as expressed in the words of Monsignor Joseph Gremillion in his commentary on *Gaudium et spes*: "Indeed the salvation of the Church can only be worked out in the context of the world."

This challenge celebrates and honors the central mission of the laity to recognize God's activity in the world and to cooperate in the embodiment of the reign of God in all aspects of life. The observation asserted at the Second Vatican Council underscores the importance of bridging the gap between the work of business and leadership and the spiritual quest:

> The split between the faith which many profess and their daily lives deserves to be counted among the more serious errors of our age . . . Let there be no false opposition between professional and social activities on the one hand, and religious life on the other. (*Gaudium et spes*, para. 43)

The challenge is not trivial. While spirituality, including the spirituality of work, has emerged as a major interest in academic, professional, and popular literature, Christian spirituality in the context of the business enterprise has often been ignored. Likewise, while spirituality and business has received enormous attention in academic and professional business literature in recent years, it is often weakly linked to the great religious traditions, including the Catholic Christian tradition. For example, in the academic sphere, business scholars inspired to address spirituality are predominantly trained in business disciplines and lacking in formal studies in spirituality. In the same measure, spirituality and theology scholars are rarely familiar with recent business literature. Yet both fields encompass new and insightful contemporary scholarship bearing on an appropriate spirituality for business.

The challenge and hope is to further the emerging dialogue between business and spirituality, in particular to engage the rich wisdom of the Christian tradition and the other classic wisdom traditions in such a dialogue. In doing so, such a multivoiced, interdisciplinary conversation will reflect the rich and complex experience of diversity in cultures and faith traditions in the workplace itself. Moreover, the assertion that a career in business can be a true expression of Christian discipleship and vocation will further the transformation of business organizations as mediators of a transcendent presence in the world. As Pope Paul VI asserted, "[E]very man is called upon to develop and fulfill himself, for every life is a vocation. Endowed with intelligence and freedom, he is responsible for his fulfillment as he is for his salvation" (*Populorum progressio*, no. 15). Hence, "the ultimate vocation of man is in fact one, and divine" (*Gaudium et spes*, no. 22). Thus, the challenge of bridging the gap between spirituality and business management is grounded in a twofold renewal: the personal renewal of the executive leader and the transformation of the organization as a whole.

The Role of Contemplative Practice

Echoing the emerging results of the Templeton Foundation study of the moral underpinnings of enduring CEO success, the executives who have participated in the Santa Clara programs in spirituality and business leadership overwhelmingly see contemplative practice as essential to maintaining their commitment to their "calling" as organizational leaders. They believe that a contemplative practice is important for two reasons. First, they express an awareness of a reality not immediately present in their personal lives and in the life of their organizations. Second, they find that consciousness of "the present moment" and ever deepening self-knowledge are critical factors in sustaining their commitment because they discern not only the good from the bad but also, much more frequently, the best from among the good. The words of the Christian mystic Catherine of Siena (1309–1380) seem to echo their experience. In her own quest to discover God's path of compassion and truth, she hears these words in her prayer of repose:

Here is the way, if you would come to perfect knowledge and enjoyment of me, eternal Life: Never leave the knowledge of yourself.
Then put down as you are in the valley of humility you will know me
[God] in yourself, and from this knowledge you will draw all that
you need. ("Dialogue" 1980, 29)

You cannot arrive at virtue except through knowing yourself and
knowing me. ("Dialogue" 1980, 88)

"What one values depends on what one pays attention to and how
we pay attention to it"; however, the Santa Clara ethicist William Spohn
argues, the critical question is, "How does one acquire the virtues that
foster moral discernment and clarity?" (Spohn 1997, 115). In all religious
traditions spiritual practices are essential to train moral perception and to
sustain commitment. For theistic traditions, such practices are quite varied,
but all honor the need for a contemplative life stance, of focused attention.
Beldon Lane, a Christian spirituality scholar, believes that people today are
so stimulated by the "endless onslaught of consumer culture" that they "are
plagued by a highly diffused attention" and give themselves to everything
lightly. In saying yes to everything, they attend to nothing (Spohn 1997,
115; Lane 1994, 197). The focused attention that comprises prayer and the
self-emptying that arises from service, particularly with the suffering, are
the antidotes to confusion and overstimulation—even amidst the frenzy of
hypergrowth, rapid change, and almost constant innovation evident in
contemporary social and corporate culture.

Focused moral attention can also arise from nontheistic spirituality.
Spohn cites the argument put forth by Iris Murdoch, "prolific novelist
and occasional philosopher." She argues that often moral vision "can be
egocentric and needs transformation by getting connected with a transcendent source of beauty and goodness." Contemplative prayer, she believes, is essential to "connecting morality with its mystical background"
(Spohn 1997, 116).

The importance of contemplative practice and self-knowledge in the
discernment of and ongoing commitment to a "calling" is derived from
the belief that "vocation" is first and foremost a calling from within. For
the humanist it is a matter of self-identity and integrity. So too for the
Christian, who understands vocation as a continual process of unveiling

"that of God" that exists in every person, as the Quakers say. It is the discovery of and ongoing dedication to the particular image of God in which one is created, for as Teresa of Avila asserts, our true ancestry is in God (*Interior Castle* 1979, I.1.2)

Thus, "vocation" comes from listening, "quite apart from what I would like it to be about" or what others may suggest it to be, though one's desires and the community can concur with what is discovered in listening. Parker Palmer captures this essence of vocation well.

> This insight is hidden in the word 'vocation' itself, which is rooted in the Latin for 'voice.' Vocation does not mean a goal that I pursue. It means a calling that I hear. Before I can tell my life what I want to do with it, I must listen to my life telling me who I am. I must listen for truths and values at the heart of my own identity, not the standards by which I must live—but the standards by which I cannot help but live if I am living my own life. (Palmer 2000, 4–5)

Contemplative practice unveils the particular paths and expressions of vocation as it unmasks lesser values and illusion. Solitude is often the character of such practices, yet it is not simply physical isolation or a preferred stance of permanent removal from the activity of the world. Rather, the solitude of the contemplative stance "means being in possession of one's heart, one's identity, one's integrity" (Palmer 1991).

Conclusion

The focus of calling, then, is on each individual's journey in the holistic fullness of all aspects of life, encompassing personality, family history, religious tradition, but also occupation and work role. In this perspective, spiritual calling is connected to the day-to-day experience of organizational leadership. It eliminates any dichotomy between spirituality as part of one's private life but not of one's organizational life; or spirituality as part of one's family life but not connected to one's day-to-day work role. The mature organizational leader embodies the esteemed path of holiness: the contemplative in action.

Thus, executive leaders find professional fulfillment and grow into spiritual maturity through bringing their special gifts to the particular challenges and tasks in organizational life. For spiritually aware leaders the primary challenge is the transformation of their own organization into an "oasis of goodness," modeling not only the best practices of contemporary management but also going beyond these practices so that the just and loving presence of the Transcendent is transparent. The fully aware leader does so by developing

- empowering structures in which all employees reach toward personal potential,
- decision and governance processes that are inclusive and just,
- processes that facilitate change of management and entrepreneurship that allows for creative expression,
- just and inclusive gain reward systems,
- models of sustainable development and environmental support,
- high quality/cost performance.

It will be exactly through this leadership that management executives will express their spiritual destiny and witness to the loving presence of God. To be sure, as leaders struggle with the imperfection of their own personal leadership skills and the imperfections of organizational structures, there will be much to learn about humility and need for God's assistance. Indeed, these imperfections are part of learning the need for dependence on God and the transcendent character of work and organizational life and leadership along the spiritual journey.

> God, most vitally active and most incarnate, is not remote from us, wholly apart from the sphere of the tangible; on the contrary, at every moment [God] awaits us in activity, the work to be done, which every moment brings.

> [God] is, in a sense, the point of my pen, my pick, my paintbrush, my needle—and my heart and my thought. It is by carrying to completion the stroke, the line, the stitch I am working on that I shall lay hold on the ultimate end towards which my will at its deepest levels tends. (Teilhard de Chardin, S.J., *Hymn of the Universe*)

REFERENCES

Applebaum, H. 1995. "The Concept of Work in Western Thought." In *Meanings of Work: Considerations for the Twenty-First Century*, ed. F. C. Gamst, 46–78. Albany: State University of New York Press.

Arthur, M. B., and D. M. Rousseau, eds. 1996. *The Boundaryless Career: A New Employment Principle for a New Organizational Era.*New York: Oxford University Press.

Benz, E. 1966. "The Christian Expectation of the End of Time and the Idea of Technical Progress." In Benz, *Evolution and Christian Hope*, 121–42. Garden City, N.Y.: Doubleday.

Berg, I. 1995. "Theories and Meanings of Work: Toward Syntheses." In *Meanings of Work: Considerations for the Twenty-First Century*, ed. F. C. Gamst, 90–119. Albany: State University of New York Press.

Catherine of Siena. 1980. "The Dialogue." In *The Classics in Western Spirituality*, trans. Suzanne Noffke, O.P. Mahwah, N.J.: Paulist Press.

Cavanagh, G. F. 1998. *American Business Values: With International Perspectives*. 4th ed. Upper Saddle River, N.J.: Prentice Hall.

Conger, J. A., and Associates. 1994. *Spirit at Work: Discovering the Spirituality in Leadership*. San Francisco: Jossey-Bass Publishers.

Cousins, E. 1989. "Experiencing God in the Marketplace." *New Theology Review* 2, no. 2 (May).

Damon, W., H. Gardner, and M. Csikszentmihalyi. *The Moral Underpinnings of Enduring Success: How Are the Laws of Life Learned and Used*. John Templeton Foundation Press. Forthcoming.

Delbecq, A. L. 1999. "Christian Spirituality and Contemporary Business Leadership." *Journal of Organizational Change Management* 12, no. 4: 345–49.

Dreyer, E. A. 1994. *Earth Crammed with Heaven*. Mahwah, N.J.: Paulist Press.

Fox, M. F., and S. Hesse-Biber. 1984. *Women at Work*. Palo Alto, Calif.: Mayfield Publishing.

Hall, D. T., ed. 1996. "Careers in the Twenty-First Century." *Academy of Management Executive* 10, no. 4 (November).

Hall, D. T., and Associates. 1996. *The Career Is Dead—Long Live the Career*. San Francisco: Jossey-Bass Publishers.

Hall, R. H. 1986. *Dimensions of Work*. Beverly Hills, Calif.: Sage Publications.

Hawley, J. 1993. *Reawakening the Spirit in Work*. San Francisco: Barrett-Koehler.

Kegan, R. 1994. *In over Our Heads: The Mental Demands of Modern Life*. Cambridge, Mass.: Harvard University Press.

Kolden, M. 1989. "Luther on Vocation." *Word and World* 3, no. 4: 382–90.

Kram, K. 1988. *Mentoring at Work: Developing Relationships in Organizational Life*. Lanham, Md.: University Press of America.

Krieger, Martin H. 1996. *Entrepreneurial Vocations: Learning from the Callings of Augustine, Moses, Mothers, Antigone, Oedipus, and Prospero*. Atlanta, Ga.: Scholars Press.

Mirvis, P. H., ed. 1993. *Building the Competitive Workforce: Investing in Human Capital for Business Success*. New York: John Wiley Press.

Mitroff, I., and Denton, E. 1999. *A Spiritual Audit of Corporate America*. San Francisco: Jossey-Bass Publishers.

Novak, M. 1996. *Business as a Calling: Work and the Examined Life*. New York: Free Press.

Palmer, P. J. 1991. *The Active Life*. San Francisco: Jossey-Bass Publishers.

————. 2000. *Let Your Life Speak: Listening for the Voice of Vocation*. San Francisco: Jossey-Bass Publishers.

Pfeffer, J. 1994. *Competitive Advantage through People*. Boston: Harvard Business School Press.

————. 1998. *The Human Equation: Building Profit by Putting People First*. Boston: Harvard Business School Press.

Rahner, K. 1978. *Foundations of Christian Faith: An Introduction to the Idea of Christianity*. New York: Seabury Press.

Schneiders, S. M. 1998. "The Study of Christian Spirituality: Contours and Dynamics of a Discipline." *Christian Spirituality Bulletin* 6 (March 1998): 1, 3–12.

Soelle, D. 1995. *To Work and to Love*. Philadelphia: Fortress Press.

Spears, L. C. 1995. *Reflections on Leadership: How Robert K. Greenleaf's Theory of Servant-Leadership Influenced Today's Top Management Thinkers*. New York: John Wiley and Sons.

Spohn, W. 1997. "Spirituality and Ethics: Exploring the Connections." *Theological Studies* 58, no. 1 (March 1997): 109–23.

Stewart, T. 1999. "Leaders of the Future: Have You Got What It Takes?" *Fortune*, 11 October, 318–22.

Teresa of Avila, 1979. *The Interior Castle*. The Classics in Western Spirituality, trans. Kieran Kavanaugh, O.C.D., and Otilio Rodriguez, O.C.D. New York: Paulist Press.

Vaill, P. B. 1998. *Spirited Leading and Learning: Process Wisdom for a New Age*. San Francisco: Jossey-Bass Publishers.

Weiss, J. W. 1996. "Careers and Socialization." Chap. 13 in *Organizational Behavior and Change*. ITP/South-Western College Publishing.

————. 1996. "Leadership and Followership." Chap. 8 in *Organizational Behavior and Change*. ITP/South-Western College Publishing.

Wingren, G. 1957. *Luther on Vocation*. Philadelphia: Muhlenberg.

PART III

Some Traditional Resources for Spirituality

Judaism's Contribution to Our Understanding of Business, Religion, and Spirituality

Reflections during a Jubilee Year

EDWIN M. EPSTEIN

The theme of this volume, "business, religion, and spirituality," is particularly apt after the Catholic celebration of the Jubilee year of 2000. From a Jewish perspective, the concept of "jubilee" encompasses and intermingles all three aspects of this theme: business, or, more broadly conceived, economic activity; religion, the nexus of faith and action, belief and behavior; and spirituality, defined in broad terms as "the desire to find ultimate purpose in life and to live accordingly."

Let us review the nature of jubilee[1] as presented in Hebrew Scripture in Leviticus 25:10–14 and 39–43.[2]

> And ye shall hallow the fiftieth year, and proclaim liberty throughout the land unto all the inhabitants thereof; it shall be a jubilee unto you; and ye shall return every man unto his possession, and ye shall return every man unto his family. A jubilee shall that fiftieth year be unto you; and ye shall not sow; neither reap that which groweth of itself in it, nor gather the grapes in it of the undressed vines. For it is a jubilee, it shall be holy unto you; ye shall eat the increase thereof out of the field. In this year of jubilee ye shall return every man unto his possessions. And if thou sell ought unto thy neighbor, or buy of thy neighbor's hand, ye shall not wrong one another.

And if thy brother be waxen poor with thee, and sell himself unto thee, thou shall not make him serve as a bondservant. As a hired servant, and as a settler, he shall be with thee; he shall serve with thee unto the year of jubilee. Then shall he go out from thee, lead his children with him, and shall return unto his own family, and unto the possession of his father shall he return. For they are my servants, whom I brought forth out of the land of Egypt; they shall not be sold as bondsmen. Thou shall not rule over him with rigor; but shall fear thy God.

About the Jubilee year, Dr. J. H. Hertz, CH, the late Chief Rabbi of the British Empire, observes:

In the fiftieth year, the Hebrew slaves with their families are emancipated and property, except house property in a walled city, reverts to its original owner. The Jubilee institution was a marvelous safeguard against deadening poverty. By it, houses and lands were kept from accumulating in the hands of the few, pauperism was prevented, and a race of independent freeholders assured. It represented such a rare and striking introduction of morals into economics that many have been inclined to question whether this wonderful institution was ever in actual force. (Hertz 1966, 532)

Rabbinic sources indicate that the law of the Jubilee was observed for centuries as long as the entire territory of the Holy Land was inhabited by Israelites. When a portion of the tribes went into exile, the law lapsed. David Novak points out that the Jubilee system is based on the following premise:

Every native born Israelite has an ancestral portion of the land within the patrimony of his own Tribe, an inviolable allotment from the time of the conquest of Canaan under Joshua. . . . [A]ll wealth is ultimately inherited land wealth. Furthermore, landed wealth is part of a complete system whereby the entire land of Israel is under the total control of all twelve original tribes of Israel. The system is an economically closed one. The people of Israel are seen as being totally dependent on God's grace and the justice they are to practice with one another among themselves. (Novak 1992, 215)

Indeed, Prophetic tradition holds that it was nonobservance of the Jubilee law that was a prime reason for Israel's divinely ordained exile from the land into captivity.

The fundamental assumption underlying the Jubilee and, indeed, all of Jewish ethical thought regarding economy and society is expressed beautifully in the Twenty-fourth Psalm wherein it is said:

> The earth is the Lord's and the fullness thereof,
> The world and they that dwell therein. (Psalm 24:1)

Functionally, the Jubilee was intended to maintain an even distribution of wealth. Spiritually, the Jubilee legislation was "designed to counter man's natural acquisitive instinct" and to remind Israelites of the ultimate sovereignty of the Almighty over the land. Just as the weekly Sabbath was given to facilitate the holiness of the individual, the Jubilee and sabbatical year were designed to promote the moral elevation of the Nation of Israel by investing it with a "spiritual forgiveness and repentance and remedying the injustices of the past" (Leibowitz 1988, 260–63).

It is the Jewish view that what in traditional economic-speak we designate as productive factors—land, labor, and capital—or, in more modem parlance, as physical, human, financial, technological, and organizational resources emanate from God. Humankind, collectively and historically, and individually and contemporaneously, merely exercise stewardship with regard to these resources. Although individuals may derive benefit from their use, the community must be the ultimate beneficiary of that use and the derivative wealth. As Meir Tamari so cogently observes in his influential study of Jewish ethics and economic life, *With All Your Possessions*,

> The economic life of the Jew, then—his attitude to material assets, his conduct in buying and selling—is a reflection of the ethical and moral principles of Judaism. . . . There does indeed exist, as a result of the Jewish value system, a separate and distinct "Jewish economic man, molded by religious law and communal practice." (Tamari 1987, 1)

This all-encompassing system is *Halakhah* (literally, "road", "path," or "way"), which may be thought of, in Tamari's terminology, as "codified ethics" or "legislated morality," which was revealed to Moses by a just and merciful God and recorded in the Torah. As Yeshiva University's Aaron Levine points out:

> What Halakhah has to say for the marketplace *defines the very rules of economic participation* and is designed to promote harmonious social relations and generosity of spirit (Levine's emphasis). (Levine 2000, xvii)

Accordingly, business activity, as are all aspects of human endeavor, is an inherently religious undertaking.

The specific injunctions concerning the Jubilee year found in Leviticus may appear to moderns as archaic, even irrelevant. It is not, however, on the details of the jubilee—emancipation of Hebrew slaves and their families and the reversion of property to the original owner—that we should focus our attention. Rather it is upon the ethical lessons that underlie these injunctions—acknowledgement of the dignity, better still, the divinity of each individual ("And God created man in His own image" [Genesis 1:27]); the preservation of a just and humane community; recognition that wealth, in all of its manifestation, derives from and belongs to God; and, finally, the prevention of the misuse of power, more particularly economic power, which undermines both the dignity of the individual and "harmonious social relations." All of these are essential to the solidarity and well-being of a faith community. These principles are as germane in this century as they were when first enunciated over three millennia ago. The contemporary challenge is the interpretation and application of these fundamental teachings in a world vastly different from the agrarian, self-contained society that was ancient Israel.

As Elliot N. Dorff and Louis E. Newman reiterate in *Contemporary Jewish Ethics and Morality: A Reader*, it is the responsibility of Jewish ethicists "to engage in the process of creative interpretation, making the tradition live and demonstrating its capacity to enlighten and inform our moral choices" (Dorff and Newman 1995, 5). Taking this injunction to heart, in recent years a number of Jewish scholars have sought to make available to the lay public, Jewish and non-Jewish, Jewish ethical teachings in a contemporary and practical business and economic context. In the words of Moses Pava, another Yeshiva University scholar:

> Jewish business ethics can be treated as a practical enterprise . . . the initial question is not a hypothetical one about how business would be conducted in an ideal halakhic world, but rather, how Jewish sources can inform the business ethics debate given the realities of the modern situation. (Pava 1997, 178)

Ideally, for Pava, Jewish business ethics will provide useful models for both individual behavior and that of business organizations and establish a foundation for evaluating the justice of national and international economic systems. He offers a useful summary of essential aspects of the specifically Jewish approach to business ethics: God is the ultimate source of value; the community is central; all human life is sacred and its preservation paramount over other (including economic) considerations; there is no distinction between religious and secular values and duties; *Tikkun Olam*, the obligation to repair and perfect the world, must underlie all human endeavor; and human beings living within a community have the potential to transform themselves and to live moral lives. Given these core principles, Jewish business ethics in addition to specifying modes of moral behavior can "more importantly . . . reveal a vision encouraging us to incorporate the highest human and spiritual ideals into the ordinary world of business" (Pava 1997, 2).

It is not my purpose in this paper to provide a primer of contemporary Jewish ethical teachings concerning the myriad issues spawned by our highly complex, globally connected, technologically dynamic postindustrial twenty-first century business environment. Fortunately, works published in the past decade by scholars cited in this paper and others have provided an easily accessible corpus of pertinent materials for both business ethicists and business practitioners concerning such subjects as competitive behavior, financial transactions, employment relationships, environmental issues, marketing practices, prices and profits, property rights and distributive justice. (These sources are listed in the reference section and in Epstein [2000, 539–41].) Rather, it is my objective here to delineate fundamental principles that underlie Jewish ethical teachings and relate them to business, or, more broadly, economic activity, with specific reference to lessons inherent in the concept of a Jubilee year.

Thus far, my focus has been on two of the three themes of this conference, business and religion. Although I believe my discussion of these two dimensions suggests their profound spiritual implications, let us now turn specifically to the third aspect of the volume triad—spirituality.

In common with virtually all religions, in Judaism prayer is an important path to spirituality—to "knowing God" and aspiring toward holiness (Dorff 1992, 156–74). For Jews, however, praxis, or "holy living," constitutes an even higher road to the Almighty. As pointed out above, Judaism makes "no distinction between sacred and secular moments—everything could and should be infused with holiness." Everything, in other words, is "religious" (Holtz 1990, 40). It is significant that in the liturgy of Yom Kippur, the Day of Atonement, the holiest day of the Jewish year, the threefold path the Jew is instructed to follow is *Teshuvah*, repentance, or return to righteous ways; *Tefillah*, prayer; and *Tzedakah*, charity—deeds of loving kindness. What is significant, is that prayer as an important means of "knowing God" is positioned between two acts directed primarily toward humankind, repentance, and charity. It is to righteous behavior, the performance of *Mitzvoth*, rather than to contemplation or supplication, that Judaism attaches the highest value.

It is significant that the section of the Prophets read on the morning of Yom Kippur is drawn from Isaiah 58. The prophet excoriates the people for engaging in hypocritical ritualistic observances of fasts and worship while at the same time dealing unrighteously with their fellow human beings. He admonishes:

> Is not this the fasts that I have chosen?
> To loose the fetters of wickedness,
> To undo the bonds of the yoke,
> And to let the oppressed go free,
> And that ye break every yoke . . .
> Then shall thy light break forth as the morning,
> And thy healing shall spring forth speedily. (Isaiah 58:6, 8)

The prophet's injunction derives directly from the divine commandment:

> Ye shall be holy; for I the Lord your God am holy. (Leviticus 19:2)

Explicit in the Jewish concept of holiness is righteous action. Paraphrasing Micah 6:2, Rabbi Hertz observes:

Thus on the most solemn Day in the year, the Jew is reminded that fasting alone is not enough; *doing justice* and *loving mercy* must go hand in hand with *walking humbly with thy God* (Hertz's emphasis). (Hertz 1966, 960)

In a very thoughtful, recently published book, *Spiritual Judaism: Restoring Heart and Soul to Jewish Life*, David S. Ariel poses the question: "How can we recapture the spiritual dimensions of Judaism in a way that is appropriate to modern Jews?" and offers the answer: "We can begin by rediscovering the spiritual teachings of Judaism and by asking, *what do we believe?*" (Ariel 1998, 8, emphasis mine). Key beliefs are that Judaism is:

- a compelling system of belief and practice that leads to reaching God in the everyday world;
- a spiritual discipline that guides us to create a heaven on earth and teaches us that the Jewish ideal is not left to the future but is the imperative of today.

Ariel concludes:

> There is no greater purpose for a Jew than to recognize the possibilities within the present moment, to raise the holy sparks in the everyday world around us, and to bring the divine ideal into the world. Our spirituality is not about transcending or rising above the everyday. Rather, it leads us to dignify and sanctify the everyday by bringing God into our world. We do not seek heaven; we seek to create heaven on earth without ever leaving home. (Ariel 1998, 9)

Ariel's notion of seeking to "create heaven on earth" brings us full circle. It is not a stretch to consider the Jubilee year, which was to be proclaimed with the "blast of the horn" on the Day of Atonement of the fiftieth year and during which Hebrew slaves were emancipated and property reverted to its original owner, a very practical manifestation of the Jewish impulse to dignify and sanctify the everyday by bringing God into the world. As such, the Jubilee year has powerful lessons to teach us, Jews and Christians alike, indeed, all persons, irrespective of faith tradition, who believe in the transcendent presence of the Almighty in charting a just and humane course for humankind.

Postscript

In the January 2000 issue of *Business Ethics Quarterly* (Epstein 2000, 538), I suggest that the recent contributions to the business ethics literature based upon Jewish sources have posed, for me, a fascinating question. To what extent are these Jewish perspectives today *truly, exclusively Jewish?* Or, to put the matter somewhat differently, which aspects of Jewish business ethics have remained uniquely Jewish and which have been incorporated into a shared corpus of religiously based ethical thought regarding economic life? Conversely, what aspects of Jewish ethics concerning economic life have been "borrowed" from non-Jewish sources? To answer these questions, collaborative work by scholars steeped in various faith traditions and equipped with the requisite linguistic skills is necessary. I believe that a comparative inquiry into religion-based business and economic ethics presents an exciting, albeit challenging, opportunity for scholars in the field.

I share the hope expressed by Ronald Green (a Jew) in his 1999 presidential address at the annual meeting of the Society of Christian Ethics:

> The Jewish and Christian ethical traditions, though similar in many ways, differ from each other in several key respects. In each instance, they represent polar choices on some central issues of ethics. Neither one of these choices seems adequate by itself. Thus I conclude that these two sibling traditions are deeply complementary and must learn from one another in order to form a more complete picture of moral life. (Green 1999, 3)

I firmly believe that future multifaith scholarly collaboration can contribute to the process of mutual learning and to a "more complete picture of moral life"—a picture that demonstrates clearly the interconnectedness of business, religion, and spirituality.

NOTES

1. This paper will not discuss the Sabbatical Year during which the Israelites were instructed to rest the lands after every six years of cultivation and to leave whatever grew for the needy and wild beasts (Exodus 23:10–11). Also during

this sabbatical or seventh year all debts between Israelites were to be cancelled (Deuteronomy 15:1–3). Jubilee, the fiftieth year, completed the cycle of seven sabbatical years.

2. All biblical references can be found in any standard version of Hebrew Scripture.

REFERENCES

Ariel, David S. 1998. *Spiritual Judaism: Restoring Heart and Soul to Jewish Life*. New York: Hyperion.

Dorff, Elliot N. 1992. *Knowing God: Jewish Journeys to the Unknowable*. Northvale, N.J.: Jason Aronson.

Dorff, Elliot N., and Louis E. Newman. 1995. *Contemporary Jewish Ethics and Morality: A Reader.* New York: Oxford University Press.

Epstein, Edwin M. 2000. "Contemporary Jewish Perspectives on Business Ethics: The Contributions of Meir Tamari and Moses L. Pava—A Review Essay." *Business Ethics Quarterly* 10, no. 2 (January): 523–41.

Green, Ronald M. 1999. "Jewish and Christian Ethics: What Can We Learn from One Another?" Presidential address at the annual meeting of the Society of Christian Ethics, Burlingame, Calif., 8 January.

Hertz, J. H., ed. 1966. *The Pentateuch and Haftorahs*. 2d ed. London: Soncino Press.

Holtz, Barry W. 1990. *Finding Our Way: Jewish Texts and the Lives We Lead Today*. New York: Schocken Books.

Leibowitz, Nechama. 1988. *Studies in Leviticus*. Jerusalem: World Zionist Organization/Ahva Press.

Levine, Aaron. 2000. *Case Studies in Jewish Business Ethics*. Hoboken, N.J.: Ktav Publishing House.

Novak, David. 1992. *Jewish Social Ethics*. New York: Oxford University Press.

Pava, Moses L. 1997. *Business Ethics: A Jewish Perspective*. Hoboken, N.J.: Ktav Publishing House.

Tamari, Meir. 1987. *With All Your Possessions: Jewish Ethics and Economic Life*. New York: Free Press.

SIX

The Corporate Executive's *Dharma*

Insights from the Indian Epic *Mahabharata*

KRISHNA S. DHIR

Corporations clearly have obligations to their stockholders, and, by and large, these are fiduciary responsibilities that arise from ownership by persons or institutions. However, the separation of ownership from control has produced a set of enigmatic problems labeled collectively the "corporation problem." The corporation problem relates to the corporate executive's decision-making behavior and includes issues of (a) *efficiency* in corporate management (i.e., whether the decision-making behavior yields the greatest return to the organization or to the owners), (b) the vitiating effects of corporate *bureaucracy*, and (c) the legitimacy of corporate hierarchy. In this chapter, I will discuss insights offered by the great Indian epic, the *Mahabharata*, in regard to such decision-making behavior. First, I briefly trace the evolution of the factors that resulted in the separation of corporate ownership and corporate control and then introduce the theory of *dharma* or virtuous and righteous conduct, offered by Hindu religious and philosophical literature. In the *Mahabharata*, the "corporation problem" is described in the context of "a husband's supremacy over his wife" or the lack thereof, rather than the corporate executive's supremacy over stockholders, employees, creditors, and so on. This description provides an analogue to how Indian philosophic thought would treat the corporate executive's corporation problem.

Separation of Ownership and Control

The late-nineteenth century saw many dramatic developments in the conduct of economic activity in the United States. Perhaps the most spectacular was the emergence of large-scale manufacturing. After the severe depression of 1873, the nature of business was transformed from light to heavy industry. Mass production generated economies of large scale and, to realize such economies, business organizations had to be large. Mass production also required mass consumption. Firms that previously were engaged only in manufacturing also took on marketing and other functions. With growth in size and complexity of the vertically integrated firm, the need for expert advice and administrative structure became evident.

The firm became too large for one person, the owner, to manage and soon had to be managed by a group of executives. The organization was highly centralized, with a number of departments. Firms also underwent legal transformation; the use of corporate charter increasingly replaced partnerships. The corporation offered limited liability to individual owners, who could sell or transfer their shares to others without disturbing the business operation. More importantly, the corporate structure allowed access to a larger pool of capital funds through the sale of stocks and bonds.

Firms began to buy stocks in other firms. Mergers and acquisitions followed. Single-product, single-function firms evolved into multiproduct, multifunction businesses. The diversification movement led electric machinery manufacturing companies into appliance markets, meat packers into the manufacture of soap, and automobile manufacturers into producing refrigerators. The managers soon realized that diversified organizations required a different managerial approach. During the 1920s, DuPont, General Motors, Sears Roebuck, and Standard Oil were among the first to decentralize their organizations.[1]

Ownership was separated from control as soon as ownership became distributed through shares that could be bought and sold on the stock market. Even if the shareholders were inclined and able to tackle the many intricate decisions involved in running the multiproduct, multifunction, mass production-based business operation, they could not do so. The practical considerations of the logistics involved were forbidding.

Similarly, one person could not manage the complexities and decision-making challenges of a large-scale enterprise. Specialists were sought who could deal with capital budgeting, marketing, labor and personnel relations, production, engineering, and other sectors. This division of labor resulted in the decision-making authority being vested more and more in a group of career executives, who had little ownership stake in the company they managed. The owners were no longer in control. The professional executive's role was to act as an arbitrator for a collective enterprise in which the management, owners, creditors, vendors, employees, competitors, consumers, and government had interests; this called for a broadening of motives and objectives of the business enterprise.

The Issue of Legitimacy

There are those who are critical of the power of the modern corporate executive, who exercises control over other people's resources. The critics insist that the executive has no legitimacy, having been neither elected nor appointed, he or she is not responsible to anyone. The implication is that, in the nineteenth century, the question of legitimacy did not arise because the executive was also the owner. A major source of dissatisfaction is the compensation paid out to corporate executives. The managers of the most successful corporations are not necessarily the most highly paid, and generous stock options and salaries have not necessarily produced stellar corporate performances in terms of sales and earnings.

According to some critics, the modern corporate management is motivated by a desire to perpetuate itself as a bureaucratic oligarchy. To back their claim, the critics point to corporate response to takeover attempts: the strategies adopted to prevent hostile takeovers are not necessarily in the stockholders' interests. Administration of poison pills, deliberate acquisition of liability, and other actions intended to make the takeover target unattractive to a raider generally protect the management's job at the expense of lowering the stockholders' value. Such strategic moves by a corporate executive prevent the stockholders from maximizing their gains.

On the other hand, the raiders also come under fire. Takeovers are supposed to function in the interest of the stockholders. They are supposed to shake up overly complacent managers and bring about useful organizational restructuring and efficient resource deployment. Instead, hundreds of deals are made for the sake of profits on paper and for the fees and stock payoffs they generate, distracting corporate America from its real work of improving products and services. Today, corporate America is heavily debt ridden. In 1986 alone, 3,973 takeovers, mergers, and buyouts were completed at a record total cost of $236 billion.[2]

Alfred P. Sloan Jr. wrote in October 1927:

> There is a point beyond which diffusion of stock ownership must enfeeble the corporation by depriving it of virile interest in management upon the part of some one man or group of men to whom its success is a matter of personal and vital interest. And conversely at that same point the public interest becomes involved when the public can no longer locate some tangible personality within the ownership which it may hold responsible for the corporation's conduct.[3]

Although the modern executive may be freer from the owner's control, he or she does, in fact, have constraints such as competition, customers, rival products, labor unions, public opinions, government regulators, and other executives within the corporate world. As the Telephone Company's Theodore N. Vail, a proponent of government regulation and an opponent of government ownership, said in 1912:

> There are few big captains of industry who can run a great corporation, but there are any quantity of men who could review their acts and who . . . could say whether or not the men who were doing things were doing them right.[4]

Nevertheless, public opinion is against corporate America today. In a *Time*/CNN poll taken in February 1990, 68 percent of those polled regarded mergers and takeovers as "not a good thing" for the U.S. economy, and 74 percent regarded the corporate debt piled up in the 1980s to be a "serious" or "very serious" problem for the 1990s.[5]

Moral Dilemma and the Corporate Executive

Contemporary discussion on the ethics and moral obligation of corporate decision making has been "dominated by the two major theories of principle, the deontological and the utilitarian." The deontological approach studies the corporate decision-making behavior in terms of binding obligations, as in duty. The utilitarian approach studies this behavior in the tradition of Bentham, stressing the importance of utility over beauty or other considerations. Decision-making behavior, demonstrated in the *courage* to act in protecting human welfare even in the midst of incomplete information and in the *integrity* and *humility* in communicating with consumers about possible difficulties with a product, is not explained by these approaches. These theories fall short of explaining behavior emanating from considerations of virtue.

An alternative theory, one which may well be regarded as the universal theory of virtue, is offered in Hindu religious and philosophical literature. Central to this theory is the concept of *dharma* or virtuous and righteous conduct. This concept enables us to reexamine the nature of corporate morality and moral dilemma. The problem is particularly interesting because morality is not an Indian concept. Its Sanskrit equivalent is not easy to discover. One finds "only a strict status compartmentalization of private and social ethics."[6] In Hindu philosophic literature, closest to the concept of morality is the ubiquitous and enigmatic concept of *dharma*.

Stories in classical and contemporary Hindu religious literature, however, are rich in accounts of moral dilemmas, most of which remain unresolved. In essence, these dilemmas arise when the agent faces two or more obligations but circumstances are such that fulfillment of one violates one, some, or all the other obligations. The decision maker is faced with irreconcilable alternatives. The actual choice among the alternatives becomes either irrational or is based on grounds other than morals. Moral philosophers usually have denied that such dilemmas are possible. An adequate moral theory is supposed to eliminate them; that is to say, such dilemmas are not genuine. Kant, for instance, states:

> Because . . . duty and obligations are, in general, concepts that express the objective practical necessity of certain actions, and because two mutually opposing rules cannot be necessary at the same time, then it is a duty to act according to one of them, it is not only a duty but contrary to duty to act according to the other.[7]

Indian thought takes issue with Kant's claim, as illustrated in the *Bhagavad-Gita*. This is an account of Arjuna's moral dilemma and

Krishna's analysis of Arjuna's dilemma. The keeping of a promise, for instance, is a strong obligation, regarded as equivalent to being truthful or even protecting the truth. Plato has described an instance of dilemma "in which the return of a cache of weapons has been promised to a man who, intent on mayhem, comes to claim them."[8] Here, a conflict is created between two opposing principles: that of keeping a promise and that of benevolence; that of truth and that of nonviolence. In Kantian ethics, truth telling gets the highest priority. In the *Bhagavad-Gita*, however, Krishna argued that promise keeping or even truthfulness cannot be an unconditional obligation when it is in conflict with the avoidance of grossly unjust and criminal acts such as patricide and fratricide. Saving an innocent life is also a strong obligation. Thus, two almost equally strong obligations or duties (*dharmas*) are in conflict here, generating a genuine moral dilemma.[9] According to Hindu thought, genuine dilemmas are paradoxical and are seldom solved. They may be resolved or dissolved, but not solved.

The concept of *dharma* can be useful in the examination of many of the moral dilemmas of the corporate executive, including the issue of the correctness of corporate decisions. As stated by Herbert A. Simon:

Decisions are something more than factual propositions. To be sure, they are descriptive of a future state of affairs . . . but they possess, in addition, an imperative quality—they select one future state of affairs in preference to another and direct behavior toward the chosen alternative. In short, they have an ethical as well as a factual content.[10]

If genuine dilemmas are paradoxical and are seldom solved, what is the corporate executive to do? He or she has to be virtuous in decision making. The focus is on the obligations and on the conflict between individual obligations and social responsibility. The goal has to be not so much to solve moral dilemmas as to *recognize* them.

An example would be helpful. There have been a number of instances where corporations have recalled products from the marketplace in the interests of the consumer and society. The recall of Tylenol by Johnson and Johnson or the Rely product by Procter and Gamble are examples of corporate decisions exhibiting uncommon virtue. In these instances, the executives decided on actions that did not necessarily fulfill their obligations to the stockholders, employees, and other parties.

However, they acted to protect human welfare and save lives. They knew they faced a genuine moral dilemma. They did not solve the dilemma. They did not fulfill all their obligations. They opted to fulfill the obligation of social responsibility. They made this choice through enlightened wisdom, and they resolved the moral dilemma effectively.

The set of other familiar questions to which the concept of *dharma* could be applied for analysis includes: What is the management's authority over corporate assets owned jointly by all stockholders? What is the validity of any act or transaction of the corporate executive? Is the corporate executive's preoccupation with playing the stock market akin to an addiction? When is gambling not gambling? Is the stock market similar to the gambling hall? What is the validity of any act fraudulently and deceitfully performed by cunning persons? Is corporate strategy, as we understand it, cunning? Is industrial espionage deceitful? What is the corporate executive's *dharma*? It would be helpful to examine further the concept of *dharma*.

What is *Dharma*?

According to Indian thought, *dharma* is one of the four major goals of human life, the others being *artha* (wealth), *kama* (enjoyment), and *moksa* (spiritual freedom). The term *dharma* is complex and has many meanings in the various Hindu writings. It deals with law and custom governing the development of individuals and with the proper relationship between different groups of society. In the context of this chapter, *dharma* refers to the basic principles of virtuous and righteous conduct. According to Manu, the author of *Manusmriti*, the term *dharma* includes the concepts of (1) law, usage, custom; (2) moral merit, virtue; (3) duty, prescribed code of conduct, obligation; (4) right, justice; (5) piety; (6) morality, ethics; (7) nature, character; and (8) an essential quality, a characteristic property, an attribute.[11] With so many meanings, the precise meaning of *dharma* is derived from the context of its usage. *Adharma* is the opposite of *dharma*, or devoid of *dharma*.

Professor K. Motwani of Jabalpur University states:

> *Dharma* is the cohesive element, and on the human plane, it is the principle of organization. From the standpoint of the individual, it is the implementing of the intellectual perception of his proper place

and duties in the social cosmos; from the standpoint of the group, it is reason or intelligence . . . the basis of social life. . . . It is here that the modernity of Manu's teachings comes in.[12]

Thus, Professor Motwani supports the earlier assertion that corporate executives must be able to recognize the conflict between individual obligations and social responsibilities. The emphasis is clearly on knowledge, or enlightened wisdom, as a prerequisite for being virtuous.

In *Vaisheshika Sutra*, written by Kanada after 300 B.C., *dharma* is described as a prerequisite for and cause of prosperity. According to the *vaisheshika* (particularity) system, *dharma* results in accomplishment of exaltation and the supreme good. *Dharma* is a property belonging to the person. It is particular in that it depends to a large extent on the person's proper place and duties in the social system. "It is not a potency residing in the action performed." The *dharma* of the eldest brother relative to his younger brother is not entirely the same as that of the younger brother relative to his elder brother. The *dharma* of the *Brahman* (member of the priesthood) is different from that of the *Kshatriya* (member of the warrior class).

The means of *dharma* consist of various substances, qualities and actions . . . some belonging in common to all men, and some as pertaining specially to distinct castes and conditions. Among the common ones we have the following: faith in *dharma*, harmlessness, benevolence, truthfulness, freedom from desire for undue possession, freedom from lust, purity of intentions, absence of anger, . . . and non-neglect (of duties). *Dharma* is the direct cause of happiness, of the means of happiness and also of final deliverance. . . . *Dharma* is destructible. . . . In as much as *dharma* is an effect, it must come to an end . . . it is an absolutely impartite entity. . . . *Dharma* is also destroyed by true knowledge. Some people hold *dharma* to be absolutely indestructible; but for these people there could be no final deliverance; as there would be no end of *dharma* and *adharma* (and hence of the results of these in the shape of worldly experiences).

True knowledge leads people to become free from all affections, aversions, and other such feelings. The absence of these sentiments causes cessation of *dharma,* or *adharma,* tending toward "peace" and finally *moksa* (deliverance), emancipation, or liberation.[13]

Thus, it is *dharma* that leads to the behavior that promotes harmony in groups, in associations, in society and, indeed, in corporations; it facilitates growth and prosperity in all these. *Dharma* is related closely to *karma* (action or work) and *bhoga* (experience). This interconnection stands out clearly in the *Mahabharata*. We will examine now the "corporation problem" described in the *Mahabharata*, beginning with a description of the *Mahabharata* itself.

The *Mahabharata*

Sometime between 2000 and 1000 B.C., the Vedaic scriptures were introduced into India and gave the first framework to the Hindu religion. The period between 600 and 200 B.C. saw the emergence of philosophical doctrines through the medium of nontechnical literature, specially the great epics, the *Ramayana* and the *Mahabharata* (including the *Bhagavad-Gita*, which is part of the *Mahabharata*). This period includes the rise and early development of Buddhism, Vaishnavism, Shaivism, and Jainism. It was during this period also that many of the *dharmashastras*, or treatises on ethical and social philosophy, describing the ethical and religious obligations of the Aryans, were compiled. *Manusmriti* (the *Code of Manu*) was one such treatise. The *Mahabharata* is a *kavya* (an epic poem), a *dharmashashtra* (a treatise on ethics and righteous conduct), and an *itihasa* (a book of history). It discloses a rich civilization in a highly evolved society. India was divided into a number of independent kingdoms, yet there was a unified concept of culture and *dharma*. There was an accepted code of warfare; deviations from the code were met with reproof among *Kshatriyas*. The population lived in cities and villages. There was trade in the cities, and the mass of people was agriculturist. In addition to urban and rural life, there was a highly cultured life in the seclusion of forests, "ashrams," presided over by respected and revered ascetic teachers. The caste system prevailed, but intercaste marriages did take place, and Brahmans did take arms in war. Women were honored and played important roles in the lives of their husbands and children. As stated before, and as we shall see, in the *Mahabharata* the "corporation problem" is described in the context of "a husband's supremacy over his wife" or the lack thereof. It would be helpful, therefore, to review briefly the status of women in that culture.

The Status of Women

According to the *Manusmriti*, women are precious, to be "honoured and adorned" by their fathers, brothers, husbands, and brothers-in-law, who desire her welfare. Life and the continued existence of family and society depend on women. "Where women are honoured, there the gods are pleased. . . . Where the female relations live in grief, the family soon wholly perishes; but that family where they are not unhappy ever prospers." A woman usually is physically weaker than a man and has qualities that make her likely to be usurped by other persons against her wish. For this reason, she is to be protected at all times, by her father in childhood, her husband in adulthood, and her son in old age:

> By a girl, by a young woman, or even by an aged one, nothing must be done independently, even in her own house. . . . In childhood a female must be subject to her father, in youth to her husband, when [he] is dead to her sons; a woman must never be independent.[14]

Dyuta: A Game of Chance

The *Mahabharata* gives an account of the feud between two families, the Kauravas and the Pandavas, whose ancestries could both be traced to Vichitravirya and Santanu. The Kaurava family was large and included Duryodhana, Karna, Bhishma, Duhshashna, Vikarna, and many others. The Pandavas consisted of five brothers—Yudhishthira, Nakula, Sahadeva, Arjuna, and Bhimsena; all five were husbands to Draupadi, the daughter of Drupada, king of the Panchalas. The account of Draupadi's marriage to the five Pandava brothers is the sole instance of polyandrous marriage in the *Mahabharata*.

The first event of the series that resulted in the carnage at the battlefield of Kurukshetra was a gambling match into which Yudhishthira, the Pandava emperor, was trapped by Sakuni, the evil genius and advisor to Duryodhana. Sakuni's goal was to assist Duryodhana in acquiring Yudhishthira's kingdom. At Sakuni's insistence, Duryodhana persuaded his father, Dhritarashtra, the blind Kaurava king, to invite Yudhishthira to *dyuta* (a game of dice). Even though Dhritarashtra protested, "Your suggestion does not seem proper," being weak-witted and overpersuaded, he yielded to his son's desire. Yudhishthira, on receiving the invitation through Vidura, Dhritarashtra's chief counselor and emissary, responded, "O King! gambling is bad. It is not through heroism or merit that one succeeds in a game of chance. Asita, Devala and other wise *rishis* who were well versed in worldly affairs have declared that gambling should be avoided since it offers scope for deceit. They have also said that conquest in battle is the proper path for the *Kshatriyas.*"[15] Yet, Yudhishthira was fond of gambling and the Kshatriya tradition made it a matter of etiquette and honor not to refuse an invitation to a game of dice. On an earlier occasion, the sage Vyasa had warned Yudhishthira of the quarrels to come between the two families that would lead to the destruction of their race. Yudhishthira had promised Vyasa that he would not give the Kauravas cause for displeasure. Yudhishthira accepted the invitation and, with his Pandava brothers, arrived in the Kaurava capital of Hastinapura.

When *dyuta* began, Yudhishthira played against Sakuni. At first they wagered jewels, gold, and silver, then chariots and horses. Yudhishthira lost continuously, and Sakuni played tricks. Stakes increased. Yudhishthira lost cities, villages, his brothers' ornaments and his own, as well as the clothes they wore. Yudhishthira's response to the unbroken string of losses was a stubborn commitment to the game. He wagered his brothers. He lost them, one by one. They became Kaurava slaves. Then he wagered himself and lost.

When it was clear that Sakuni had won Yudhishthira, thus making him a slave as well, he said to Yudhishthira, "O King! That you lost yourself is no good; because losing oneself is a sin when some wealth is left there." It must be noted that Sakuni acknowledged that Yudhishthira had lost himself. He even announced to all the kings present in the gambling hall that the Pandavas had been lost. Then Sakuni said to Yudhishthira, "O King! There is one jewel still in your possession by staking which you can yet free yourself. Can you not continue the game offering your wife Draupadi as wager?"[16] Here again, Sakuni acknowledged that Yudhishthira had been conquered. Yudhishthira staked Draupadi. There were cries of "Shame! Shame!" from spectators, but none prevented Yudhishthira from betting Draupadi in this manner. Sakuni won this round as well. Duryodhana ordered Vidura to fetch Draupadi and to bring her to the Kaurava *sabha* (assembly). It was his contention that Draupadi, having been lost by Yudhishthira, was henceforth a Kaurava *dasi* (slave), and he announced that Draupadi from then on would "sweep and clean our house." Vidura refused to do so. He turned to the assembly and said, "Yudhishthira had no right to stake Draupadi as by then he had himself already lost his freedom and lost all rights." According to Vidura, Draupadi could not become a slave because Yudhishthira had no authority to bet her, having lost himself to Sakuni. Thus, Vidura was the first in the *Mahabharata* to raise the issue of "the corporation problem" by pointing to the separation of ownership and control. It is not clear whether Sakuni had recognized this subtle point. He had acknowledged repeatedly that Yudhishthira had lost his independence, but had never alluded to the complications that followed.

Duryodhana rebuked the virtuous and wise Vidura and sent his own charioteer, Prathikami, to bring Draupadi to the assembly. Draupadi was dumbfounded at the strange message conveyed to her by the charioteer. "Which prince would pledge his wife?" she asked, "Had he nothing else to pawn?" Prathikami narrated how Yudhishthira already had lost all his possessions, his brothers and himself, and then her. Draupadi asked Prathikami to return to the Kaurava assembly and "ask of him who played the game whether in it he first lost himself, or his wife." She added, "Ask this question in the open assembly; bring me his answer and then you can take me."[17] The issue of the separation of ownership and control was not lost on Draupadi. Ultimately, Draupadi was dragged to the assembly by Duhshashna. Again she asked whether the members of the assembly thought that, according to law, she was enslaved.

The situation greatly troubled the wise, virtuous, and righteous Bhishma. He spoke thus: "*Dharma* being subtle, I cannot quite properly analyze your question; no one who is not master can stake another's wealth; but a wife is always under the supremacy of her husband." Bhishma thus indicated that Yudhishthira had lost authority over Draupadi by first losing himself and, therefore, could not bet her. He indicated also that a husband's authority over his wife was never lost. Therefore, Bhishma admitted that he was unable to answer Draupadi's question.[18]

Bhishma made another point. He told Draupadi that Sakuni was an expert in the game of dice and had induced Yudhishthira to put her at stake. He noted that Yudhishthira never gave up *dharma* or accused Sakuni of deceit, "Hence I cannot answer your question." The point is that if one is induced fraudulently to act in a particular way, then that transaction becomes invalid. However, the complaint must come from the person affected. Yudhishthira probably did not complain for the same reasons that impelled him to accept the invitation to the *dyuta* in the first place.

Draupadi stressed the fraudulent nature of the transaction and its invalidity. She accused the fraudulent and cunning gamblers, expert in the game of dice, of impure intentions. She accused them of cheating and asked the assembly to state clearly and properly why Yudhishthira was induced to play a game of dice. No one answered. Duryodhana's brother, Vikarna, was astonished to see his elders, Dhritarashtra, Bhishma, Dronacharya, and others who were known for their judgment and wisdom, unable to restrain Duryodhana. Finally, he rose and made this statement: "O *Kshatriya* heroes, why are you silent? I am a mere youth, I know, but your silence compels me to speak." Vikarna first pointed out that Yudhishthira was enticed to this game by a deeply plotted invitation. This invitation took advantage of Yudhishthira's weakness for the vice of gambling. He pointed out that Draupadi was wife to all five Pandavas; therefore, Yudhishthira had pledged Draupadi when he had no right to do so because she did not belong only to him. For that reason alone, Vikarna asserted, the wager was illegal. Besides, Yudhishthira already had lost his freedom and, therefore, had no right to offer her as a stake. Vikarna continued, "And there is this further objection. It was Sakuni who suggested [Draupadi] as a pledge, which is against the rules of the game, under which neither player must demand a specific bet. If we consider all these points, we must admit that Draupadi has not been legally won by us. This is my opinion."

After Vikarna's speech, Duryodhana said to Draupadi that if all other four Pandavas stated clearly that Yudhishthira had no authority to put Draupadi as a bet, she would be freed. Bhimsena spoke, but did not meet Duryodhana's condition. Others kept quiet. When Duryodhana repeated his offer, Arjuna said that Yudhishthira had full authority to put each brother at stake before he lost himself. But when he himself was conquered, he could not bet Draupadi. At this point there were some ugly scenes in the gambling hall, and Dhritarashtra intervened at last. He stopped all further proceedings, chided Duryodhana and, with due sympathy and respect, granted boons to Draupadi. She asked for the release of Yudhishthira from bondage and secured the release of the other four Pandavas. Dhritarashtra then ordered the return of all wealth and the kingdom to Yudhishthira. The Pandavas returned to Indraprastha with full honor and authority. Here the first *dyuta* ended. Another one was to follow but that is not the concern of this chapter.

Discussion

Now let us discuss the main problems emerging from the *dyuta* described above. Such a discussion will provide insights as to how the concept of *dharma* was applied by the various characters in the first *dyuta* incident of the *Mahabharata*. Vidura pointed out that Yudhishthira had lost himself first and so had no further authority to bet Draupadi. Bhishma and Arjuna also considered this to be a valid point, although Bhishma seemed confounded by the consideration of a husband's supremacy over a wife. Bhishma was inclined to think that a husband's supremacy over his wife remained unchanged. This principle implied that the supremacy of the other four Pandavas over Draupadi also remained unchanged. But Bhishma did not take his analysis that far. If he had, he would have had to conclude that Draupadi could not be bet unilaterally by Yudhishthira. Another line of argument could be pursued: The four Pandava brothers did not object to Yudhishthira's staking them at the *dyuta*. This implies that the Pandava brothers accepted Yudhishthira's supremacy over them as the eldest brother. This, in fact, was consistent with their *dharma*. One's eldest brother was to be held in the same regard as one's father. The four Pandava brothers also did not object to Yudhishthira's staking Draupadi at the *dyuta*. If, like Bhishma, they believed that a husband's supremacy over his wife remained unchanged, they would have indicated this when Yudhishthira staked Draupadi, unless they regarded Yudhishthira's supremacy over them as superseding theirs over Draupadi. Perhaps, having been enslaved themselves they saw themselves as having lost supremacy over Draupadi and, therefore, Yudhishthira's supremacy over them remained intact.

Vikarna supported the view that Yudhishthira could not exercise unilateral supremacy over Draupadi because she was wife to all Pandavas. Since all Pandavas had been enslaved before Draupadi was staked, Vikarna rejected the notion that Draupadi had been enslaved. However, the Pandavas did not press this issue and accepted the authority of Yudhishthira; therefore, this point could not be tested. The argument that a fraudulent and deceitful transaction is invalid is a persuasive one, but, here too, Yudhishthira did not press this issue nor complain.[19]

Draupadi, it appears, did not consider herself to be enslaved. She had asked the assembly to give its verdict as to whether or not she had been enslaved, but received no answer. However, when Dhritarashtra bestowed boons upon her, she asked for the freedom of the Pandavas; she did not ask for her own freedom, which suggests that she did not consider herself enslaved, because Yudhishthira had lost authority over her as her husband after he lost himself to Sakuni.

Vikarna raised another interesting issue concerning the validity of an addict's act. According to Vikarna, Draupadi did not constitute a valid stake because Yudhishthira was engrossed in gambling at the time. This argument does not hold well because Yudhishthira could not rightly be regarded as an addict. Finally, there is the question of authority of the husband over his wife; does it cease in certain circumstances or is it limitless? Only Bhishma considered this point, but he did not express a clear opinion. Others did not discuss this issue explicitly either; however, it can be inferred that they considered that the husband's authority was not limitless—it ceased under certain circumstances.

As stated, in Hindu thought genuine dilemmas are regarded as unsolvable. Bhishma and Duryodhana make for an interesting contrast in character. They were Kaurava brothers, yet Bhishma was committed to *dharma* and experienced anguish at the plight of the Pandava brothers. He told Yudhishthira that man is the slave of wealth, whereas wealth has no slave. He said he was bound to the Kaurava's wealth and, therefore, felt helpless about Yudhishthira's plight even though he believed the Pandavas were just. Thus he requested that Yudhishthira excuse him from taking a stand, and Yudhishthira complied, freeing Bhishma from his dilemma. Duryodhana, on the other hand, lacking virtue, devoid of *dharma* and practicing *adharma*, was blinded by greed and hatred for the Pandavas; he experienced no moral dilemma.

In the context of corporate ownership and control, three points of consideration are suggested by the story:

1. What is the nature of management's authority over corporate assets owned jointly by all stockholders?
2. What is the validity of any act or transaction of an addict (irrespective of evidence of addiction or its absence in this case)?

3. What is the validity of any act fraudulently and deceitfully performed by cunning persons?

Yudhishthira, on receiving the invitation through Vidura, had responded by stating that gambling was bad because dice was a game of chance and, therefore, it was not through merit that one succeeded; success was accidental.

Would the modern-day financial system, centered around Wall Street, be a game of chance? And what of the issue raised earlier regarding addiction? Yudhishthira was accused of being addicted to gambling. Modern corporations are "addicted" to playing the financial markets, as evidenced by the importance of stock exchanges all over the world. When is gambling not gambling any more but a prudent, even virtuous, act? And is industrial espionage and corporate strategy cunning and deceitful? Is it appropriate for a corporation to raid other corporations for scientists, strategists, and employees to learn about their firms' strategies and plans? Would such actions be consistent with the corporate executive's *dharma*?

Conclusion

The concept of *dharma* does not insist on solving a moral dilemma. It does, however, insist and expects that the individual *recognize* a moral dilemma when confronted with one, which is why Bhishma is regarded as superior to Duryodhana. Bhishma recognized his dilemma and its subtlety. Duryodhana was oblivious to his own dilemma and so acted irresponsibly. The focus of the corporate executive's *dharma* is on the conflict between individual duty and social responsibility. Virtue is a necessary prerequisite for moral choice. And enlightenment is necessary for virtue.

NOTES

This chapter appeared in an earlier volume, *A Virtuous Life in Business*, ed. O. F. Williams and J. W. Houck (Lanham, Md.: Rowman and Littlefield, 1992), 91–107, and is reprinted by permission of the publisher.

1. A. D. Chandler, *Strategy and Structure: Chapters in the History of the Industrial Enterprise* (Cambridge, Mass.: MIT Press, 1962).

2. J. Greenwald, "Predator's Fall," *Time,* 26 February 1990, 46–52.

3. H. E. Krooss and C. Gilbert, *American Business History* (Englewood Cliffs, N.J.: Prentice-Hall, 1972), 264.

4. Ibid., 247.

5. Greenwald, "Predator's Fall," 47–48.

6. M. Weber, *Wirtschaft und Gesellschaft: Grundriss der verstehenden Soziologie* (Cologne: Kiepenheuer und Witsch, 1964), 366.

7. I. Kant, *The Metaphysics of Morals,* trans. J. Ladd, vol. 1 (Indianapolis, Ind.: Bobbs-Merrill, 1965), in *Moral Dilemmas in the Mahabharata,* ed. B. K. Matilal (Shimla, India: Indian Institute of Advanced Study, 1989), 8.

8. R. B. Marcus, "Moral Dilemma and Consistency," *Journal of Philosophy* 77 (1980): 121–36.

9. B. K. Matilal, "Moral Dilemmas: Insights from Indian Epics," in *Moral Dilemmas in the Mahabharata,* 8–9.

10. H. A. Simon, *Administrative Behavior,* 2d ed. (New York: Free Press, 1965), 46.

11. M. V. Patwardhan, *Manusmriti: The Ideal Democratic Republic of Manu* (Delhi, India: Motilal Banarsidass, 1968), 80.

12. Ibid., vii.

13. S. Radhakrishnan and C. A. Moore, eds., *A Source Book in Indian Philosophy,* 2d ed. (Princeton, N.J.: Princeton University Press, 1960), 416–18.

14. Ibid., 189–92.

15. C. Rajagopalachari, *Mahabharata,* 8th ed. (Bombay, India: Bharatiya Vidya Bhavan, 1966), 87–88.

16. Ibid., 90.

17. Ibid., 91.

18. S. M. Kulkarni, "An Unresolved Dilemma in *Dyuta-Parvan:* A Question Raised by Draupadi," in *Moral Dilemmas in the Mahabharata,* 152.

19. Ibid., 154.

SEVEN

Islamic Teaching and Business

JAMAL A. BADAWI

There are nearly 1.3 billion Muslims worldwide; about one-fifth of the total world population. As is the case with any universal religion, a great cultural diversity does exist among them. Similarly, the extent of religious commitment and practice varies considerably between individuals and cultures. This poses a major challenge in attempting to deal with business ethics from a religious perspective. While culture-specific or country-specific studies are needed, a "linking pin" connecting them may be helpful. That linking pin is normative Islam, based on its universally accepted sources and teachings. An implicit assumption here is that such teachings are likely to influence the mind-set and actions of their adherents in some degree. As most readers may not be fully familiar with Islam, a brief introduction may be in order.

The term "Islam" is derived from the Arabic root *slm*, which means peace, submission, and acceptance. In the Islamic religion, the term means to achieve peace with Allah (God); with oneself (inner peace), and with the Creation of Allah through submission to Allah, putting one's trust in him and accepting his guidance and injunctions.[1] This broad definition explains why Islam is more than a religion in the general, limited sense, that concerns itself mainly with the spiritual and ritual aspects of life. In fact, the term "religion" is an imperfect translation of the Arabic term *deen*, which means, literally, a way of living. This way of living embraces the creedal, spiritual, moral, social, educational, economic, and political aspects of life. An issue like business ethics is an integral part of normative religious practice. If so, then it is essential to be clear about the sources of such normative practices.

There are two primary sources of normative Islamic teaching. The first and most important source is the Qur'an (in transliteration, commonly misspelled "Koran"). Muslims accept the Qur'an as the verbatim word of Allah, revealed to the prophet Muhammad (P)[2] over a period of

139

twenty-two years (610–632 C.E.)[3] and dictated word for word by the archangel Gabriel. The second primary source is called Sunnah, or Hadith, which means the words, actions, and approvals of the prophet Muhammad (P). Although the words of Hadith are not those of Allah (verbatim), they are believed to be another form of revelation to the Prophet, in meaning only. Both primary sources provide broad principles and guidelines in conducting a normative Islamic life. These broad principles and precepts, such as social justice, *shura* (mutual consultation), or moral conduct are not subject to nullification or change. They are presumed to be valid for all times and places. The human endeavor is limited to understanding and implementing them in a manner that is suited to the needs of time, place, and circumstances. While these two sources focus on broader guiding principles, they also contain injunctions that are more specific due to their importance. Both, broad principles and specific injunctions, constitute the normative teachings of Islam, which may or may not coincide with the actions of Muslims.

Given the growing complexity and diversity of business dealings and of life in general, a legitimate question is: what defines a normative Islamic position in respect to a new issue or problem that is not directly addressed in the two primary sources of Islam? A built-in mechanism to deal with this is called *ijtihad,* or the exertion of effort by a learned scholar to find answers to new questions or solutions to new problems. In the process of ijtihad, the principles and spirit of Islamic law guide the scholar in forming his opinion. As ijtihad is a human endeavor, influenced by the needs of time, place, and circumstances, such opinions may vary as well. They may vary even under the same circumstances. However, a cardinal rule is that if there is a clear and conclusive text in the Qur'an or Hadith on any issue, it cannot be replaced or supplanted by any scholar's opinion.[4]

This article focuses mainly on widely accepted principles and norms relating to business ethics as stipulated in the two primary sources of Islam. These principles and norms, however, do not exist in a vacuum, apart from the Islamic worldview (about Allah, humans, the universe) and the role of ethics in such a worldview. At the center of this worldview is belief in and devotion to Allah, who is the source of all bounties and the ultimate authority in defining what is ethical and what is not and whose guidance and injunctions are the source of justice in all dealings, business or otherwise. This belief is examined in the next section.

Allah: Source of all Bounties

Humans are born into this world owning nothing that they have earned and depart from earthly life with no assets that they have saved. Between one's birth and physical death, the human is utterly dependent on Allah's bounties. Allah is the only creator, sustainer, and cherisher of the universe. As such, it is useful to begin with an exposition of Islam's conception of Allah. This conception may be summed up in the key term *tawheed*, the cornerstone of Islam, the foundation of its ethics and approach to life, the basis of its systems and institutions, and the primary determinant of one's relationship to the natural and social order. It may be helpful to begin with an explanation of the meaning of tawheed before examining its implications.

The Meaning of Tawheed

Tawheed is an Arabic term, which has often been translated into English as "monotheism," the belief in one God, as opposed to dualism, polytheism, or atheism. Such a definition does not fully capture the deeper meaning of tawheed. As a theological term, it means the oneness, uniqueness, and incomparability of Allah (God) to any of his creatures. Based on the Qur'an, there are three crucial requirements of tawheed: (1) to believe in the one and only true God (Allah) as the sole creator, sustainer, and cherisher of the universe; (2) to believe that Allah alone is worthy of worship and of unshared divine authority; and (3) to believe in the unity of the essence and attributes of Allah, which are all attributes of absolute perfection.

This comprehensive meaning of the unity of Allah implies other types of unity. The first unity is that of the basic divine message to mankind, as it is communicated in various revelatory forms. For adherents of the Qur'an it is mandatory to believe in, love, and honor all prophets and messengers of Allah. They are viewed as one brotherhood and as links in the revelatory chain throughout human history. This chain, according to the Qur'an, was completed by and culminated in the advent of the last messenger, Muhammad (P). The Prophet is presented in the Qur'an not only as the seal and last of all prophets, but also as the only messenger whose mandate and mission embrace the whole world. His teachings represent the completion and culmination of all earlier forms of revelation.[5] The second unity is that of the human race, created by Allah and descended from the same parents, which depicts humanity as a large family characterized by unity in diversity. This concept shapes one's attitude toward other humans, Muslims and non-Muslims alike.[6] The third unity is that of all aspects of human life on earth, as they all come under the jurisdiction of Allah.[7] To compartmentalize life into the religious and the secular, the spiritual and the mundane, is contrary to the essence of tawheed. The fourth unity is that of the present life and the life to come; both fall under the same divine jurisdiction.[8] As such, individual and collective decision making is guided by a time scale that is not limited by one's life span, the life span of one or more generations, or even the life span of all generations. Every action has consequences both in this life and in the life to come.

The Human: Beneficiary of Allah's Bounties

The bounties of Allah embrace all creation. Yet the main beneficiaries of these bounties are humans. What is the nature of human beings and why are they here on earth? The following passage from the Qur'an sums up human nature:

> Such is He, the Knower of all things, hidden and open, the Exalted [in power], the Merciful; He who has made everything which He has created most good. He began the creation of the human with clay. And made his progeny from a quintessence of the nature of fluid despised. Then He fashioned him in due proportion, and breathed into him something of His Spirit. And He gave you [the faculties of] hearing, sight and understanding [and feeling]. Little thanks do you give.[9]

In this passage, humans are described as physical-intellectual-spiritual beings. The "clay" represents the earthly, carnal elements of human nature. Urges and instincts, in themselves, act as mechanisms that ensure the physical survival and perpetuation of the human race. Humans are also endowed with intellect and the power of reasoning. It is true that reason alone is insufficient to understand all the mysteries of Creation. Nonetheless, reason is neither irrelevant to the strengthening of one's faith, nor is it the antithesis of faith. Indeed, the use of intellect and reason is not only accepted, but also urged.[10] The physical component of human nature is shared by other living beings. Animals possess intelligence in varying degrees. Yet only in the case of humans does the Qur'an say that Allah breathed into them something of his spirit. It is that breath that endows humans with their innate spiritual and moral qualities. It also establishes the unique position of the human as the crown of Creation. This position of honor is closely tied to the fulfillment of one's role as "trustee" of Allah and as a free agent. It is a heavy responsibility, one that requires making the right choice. Failing to make such a choice leads to the loss of that position of honor and distinction. Humans may even descend to a position that is less than that of animals. A person may become one of those who

> have hearts [minds] wherewith they understand not, eyes wherewith they see not, and ears wherewith they hear not. They are like cattle, nay more misguided; for they are heedless [of warning].[11]

The physical, intellectual, and spiritual elements in human existence are not regarded as three different compartments. They are not necessarily irreconcilable either. A human being is regarded as neither a fallen angel nor a higher animal, but rather as a responsible being with the potential of ascending to a position that is higher than that of the angels or descending to a position that is lower than that of cattle. The "forbidden tree," from an Islamic perspective, symbolizes the universal ethical experience of every human being.[12] It eloquently and effectively sums up the concepts of freedom of choice, temptation, decision making, erring, realization of error, repentance, forgiveness, and reconciliation. It represents the main ethical challenges of humankind: first, rising above the purely physical element and ruling over it instead of being ruled by it; second, developing the spiritual and intellectual elements and bringing them into harmony with the divine will through conscious and committed submission to Allah; third, realizing the consequences of obedience and disobedience to Allah; fourth, striving to succeed in the "test" of earthly life, in order not merely to return to an even greater "garden" after physical death, but to enjoy the ultimate bliss of nearness to Allah and the company of the pure.[13] These challenges relate directly to one's conception of the purpose of Creation.

The Qur'an teaches that humanity was created to worship Allah.[14] Worship of Allah, however, is not mere formalism. It is not restricted to the performance of certain rites or other devotional acts. Rites and devotional acts have their place. Yet, the concept of worship in Islam is much more comprehensive than the common meaning of the term. Any act is a potential act of worship if it meets two fundamental conditions: first, it has to be done with pure intention; second, it has to be done within the limits prescribed by Allah. Even customary and mundane activities such as eating, sleeping, and innocent recreation may be regarded as acts of worship if they meet those two conditions. An extension of this broad concept of worship is the absence in Islam of any artificial compartmentalization of the various aspects of human life. Life is seen as an integrated and interrelated whole. It includes individual and collective pursuits—moral, social, economic, and political. Indeed, one of the main challenges to humanity is to relate and harmonize such activities under divine guidance.

It is that challenge that qualifies the human race as the *khalifah* (trustee) of Allah on earth. It also makes earthly life a test, or trial, for humans.[15] Their conception of human nature and their understanding and acceptance of the purpose of Creation and their role of khalifah determine how they see their relationship to the natural and social order.

The World: Sharing Allah's Bounties

The Qur'an lays the foundation of understanding and harnessing the Allah-given resources in numerous areas of economic pursuits. In so doing, humans act as the trustees of Allah and are subject to the conditions of that trust. As humans are the trustees of Allah on earth, it follows that their actions in the social order must be in accordance with the conditions of that trust. Tawheed upholds the exclusive sovereignty of Allah as the real owner of the universe and his full right to determine how his property should be used. Resources made available to humans in the universe are to be regarded as tools to fulfill the responsibilities of their trusteeship. The Qur'an makes it clear that all things on earth are made to be subservient to human use (not abuse). It goes beyond that to remove any notion that exploration of the universe outside the earth is an encroachment on Allah's domain.[16]

The attribution of property in the Qur'an varies depending on the context. On one level all property is attributed to Allah alone. This attribution is in relation to Allah's ultimate "ownership" of, or dominion over, the universe.[17] On another level, property is attributed to persons, individually or collectively. This is a recognition of the innate desire to own property, a common desire among all humans. Such ownership, however, is not seen as an absolute ownership, but rather as a transitory ownership by way of a trust given by Allah. Exercise of such ownership rights is permissible if it meets the conditions of the trust. This is clearly expressed in the Qur'an when it commands its adherents to give "out of the means which He has given to you" and "spend out of the sustenance whereof He has made you trustees."[18]

The conditions of the trust include (a) that the method of acquisition of property exclude theft, extortion, cheating, or other illegitimate dealings; (b) that the enjoyment of one's property not infringe on the property rights of others, such as establishing a factory in a residential area or preventing access to natural resources such as beaches or rivers; (c) that public interest be taken into account as in the case of necessary expropriation of property deemed to be in the public interest, such as the construction of highways or other public facilities, provided that a just compensation is paid to the owner; (d) that owners be mentally capable of looking after their property or else have a guardian who acts on their behalf (e.g., in the case of a minor); (e) that owners pay whatever is due on property (*zakah*)[19] as determined by the ultimate owner (Allah). Zakah is neither a tithe nor a tax. It is above all a highly rewardable act of worship and an application of tawheed as it relates to property. It is intended to achieve a fairer distribution of wealth and to promote an attitude of material security, sympathy, and love in society.[20]

In addition to the minimum prescribed by Zakah, open general charity is strongly encouraged. Charity may be announced without boasting only if the purpose is to encourage others to donate. It is better, however, to give in secret.[21] As avoidance of boastfulness and advertising is a fruit of sincerity and love of Allah, it is a common virtue taught by all prophets to their followers. If the amount of zakah is insufficient to meet social needs, additional levies may be imposed to fulfill those needs. The prophet Muhammad (P) taught that "in (one's) wealth there are claims other than zakah."[22]

To fulfill the function of trustee, humans must understand, explore, and harness the tools and means of that trusteeship. This issue is examined next.

Qur'anic Inducements to Study and Explore

The Qur'an does not present the universe as an adversary of mankind. It is presented, rather, as a friend and means of human endeavors on earth. Following are a few examples from the Qur'an that clearly stimulate research, discovery, development, and improvement of the quality of life. The Qur'an lays down the foundations for the understanding and harnessing of agricultural resources, seafaring and international trade, fisheries, and animal resources.[23] It exhorts humankind to reflect on the creation of the heavens and the earth and to understand the natural laws created by Allah. Examples of this include the rotation of day and night, the condensation of clouds by the force of winds so as to produce rainfall, the spherical shape of the earth, the nature of the sun as source of light and the moon as reflection of that light, and other astronomical phenomena unknown at the time of the revelation of the Qur'an and for many centuries later.[24]

The key to such understanding is to seek knowledge, a highly valued pursuit according to the Qur'an. In fact, the very first revealed word of the Qur'an was *iqra'*, which means read or recite. The first revealed passage speaks about teaching and the use of the pen.[25] The Qur'an gives those endowed with knowledge a higher status in the sight of Allah and considers the pursuit of knowledge as a source of deeper faith in Allah.[26] Failure to use the Allah-given faculty of reason is condemned.[27] The scientific method, founded on evidence instead of conjecture and speculation, is rooted in the Qur'an as well.[28] More specifically, one can find exhortations in the Qur'an to use the "experimental method" to discover the medicinal qualities of certain substances such as honey and the properties of metals and to study anatomy, anthropology, biology, embryology, geography, and other disciplines.[29]

This brief review shows that, at the normative level, the mind-set of a committed Muslim is quite favorable to productivity and its requisite motivation and learning. The attitude toward learning is reiterated in numerous sayings of the prophet Muhammad (P).[30] These exhortations, when heeded by Muslims, contributed immensely to productivity and human civilization.[31]

This analysis of the Islamic worldview makes it possible to understand the place and role of ethics in Islam, one manifestation of which is in the sphere of business.

Role and Nature of Ethics in Islam

I indicated earlier that Islam is more than a religion in the common, restricted sense. Rather, it is a complete way of living. As such, ethics is not one of its compartments, but something at its very core. This may explain why the prophet Muhammad (P) summed up his mission in the following words: "I was not sent except to perfect moral characters."[32] The Qur'an does not speak of *iman* (faith) as an abstract concept or a quality that is independent of action. It ties faith and righteous deeds together as inseparable components of what constitutes a true believer. The prophet Muhammad (P) was even more explicit when he negated the quality of faith in dishonest persons even if they claim to be believers. "Anyone who lacks honesty is devoid of faith, and anyone who does not keep his commitment is devoid of religiosity."[33]

Conversely, he tied faith to acts of kindness to others.

> Whoever believes in Allah and the [life] hereafter, let him be hospitable to his guest, and whoever believes in Allah and the [life] hereafter, let him not hurt his neighbor, and whoever believes in Allah and the [life] hereafter, let him say something beneficial or remain quiet.[34]

Although acts of pure worship constitute essential pillars of Islam, the Qur'an and Hadith indicate that they are not always meant as mere rituals. The five mandatory daily prayers are described in the Qur'an as acts to help restrain the believer from immorality and wrongdoing.[35] Zakah is described as a means of purification: of the giver from greed, stinginess, ungratefulness, and apathy; of the receiver from envy and hate of uncaring well-to-do persons; and of society from injustice, oppression, and social instability.[36] Fasting is described as a means of attaining righteousness.[37] Even the highly structured rituals of pilgrimage to Makkah (Mecca) are tied to good moral behavior.[38] The pilgrim is instructed not to hunt an animal for food or even pluck a tree leaf as a form of training on how to live in harmony with all the creation of Allah. This may explain why the prophet Muhammad (P) said: "There may be someone who gains nothing from his fasting except for hunger and there may be someone who gains nothing from his night prayers except for staying up late" and, "Anyone who does not desist from falsehood in words and deeds, Allah has no need for him to abstain from food and drink."[39] Such explanation of the nature and purpose of the essential acts of worship in Islam might have led the noted scholar Muhammad Al-Ghazali to describe acts of worship as practical drills in moral behavior.[40]

Inasmuch as the broader Islamic ethics are anchored in the Islamic worldview, they are also the foundation of specific applications in the economic sphere of life. These applications are examined in a framework that is familiar to most readers—especially those with a background in economics and business—production, consumption, and distribution.[41]

Islamic Ethics in Production

It was previously indicated that the Qur'an clearly and explicitly stimulates research, development, and improvement of the quality of life through the wise use and harnessing of the resources that Allah created for the benefit and comfort of humankind. Harnessing these resources, however, requires the exertion of effort, or labor. The Qur'an exhorts people to "go about in the spacious sides of the earth and to eat of His provisions."[42] It affirms that Allah has established the human race on earth and provided for it the means of livelihood.[43] Devotional acts are not meant to restrict one's pursuit of livelihood. Even on Fridays, after the mandatory congregational midday prayer is performed, Muslims may "disperse in the land and seek of the bounties of Allah."[44]

Work Is Worship
From an Islamic perspective, labor is a potential act of worship. In fact, all legitimate activities and efforts exerted with pure intentions are potential acts of worship in the broader Islamic meaning. They are seen as part of the fulfillment of one's role as a trustee of Allah on earth. That role, in turn, is called worship in the Qur'an.[45] It follows that work is not only a means of survival but also a rewardable act of worship. Properly understood, this concept can be instrumental in motivating productivity, but

its religious significance is even greater. The time scale, the reward expected, and the need to please the Ultimate One by productive work go far beyond any finite concept or person.

The Qur'an affirms that the reward should be commensurate with effort.[46] This rule applies to the immediate reward in this life as well as the deferred reward in the hereafter. The pursuit of excellence in work should be motivated not only by material reward but also by the pursuit of Allah's pleasure. Performance evaluation of one's work is not only done and rewarded by other humans, but is also done, appreciated, and rewarded by Allah.[47] The prophet Muhammad (P) taught: "Allah has ordained excellence in everything."[48] And, "Allah loves, when one of you is doing something, that he [or she] do it in the most excellent manner."[49]

The Arabic term for "excellence" used here is *ihsan*, which was defined in another saying of the Prophet as "worshipping Allah as if you see Him, but if you can't see Him [you realize that] He sees you."[50] I explained earlier that the concept of worship in Islam includes any constructive endeavor or work. This implies that committed Muslims should perform their work with the realization that Allah is watching their performance, even if the boss is not around.

The broader scope of rewards, which includes divine reward, is however, no justification to accept unfair or exploitative wages. This is especially true in the cases of sweatshops and child labor. Both are based on exploiting the vulnerable in society. When sweatshops are situated in economically developed countries, their operations are largely underground so the owners can avoid and evade legal requirements pertaining to pay, benefits, employment policies, health and safety requirements, and child labor. The problem of child labor relates not only to the question of exploitation, but also to the Prophet's emphasis on education as the mandatory duty of every Muslim. The most opportune time to begin acquiring knowledge is the childhood years. The child should neither be deprived of the opportunity to seek knowledge, nor be robbed of his playful childhood. From an Islamic perspective, the right to education is a legitimate right of the child on religious and moral grounds.[51]

While Islamic teachings safeguard the rights of the vulnerable, they also encourage hard work and productivity. One way of inducing productivity on the macrolevel is to discourage a welfare mentality, not welfare itself. Islamic law recognizes the entitlement of the weak, young, and poor to a minimum level of a decent life, but it discourages the abuse of welfare systems or the exploitation of people's kindness if the person is able to seek work and earn a living. The following Hadith illustrates this aspect of work ethics.

> It is better for one of you to take his rope, go to the forest and bring some firewood to sell so as to safeguard his face [dignity] than asking people [for charity], whether they give [it to] him or decline to do so.[52]

And again:

> Charity is not permissible for [someone who is] rich [has enough to decently] or [someone who is] able-bodied.[53]

Restrictions on the Production Process

As the production of goods and services or any value added is part of one's trusteeship role, it has to abide by the conditions of that trust. Hence, production is restricted by the following conditions:

1. The product or service must be lawful and must not trespass the limits set by Allah. For example, the production of wines or other intoxicants is prohibited in Islam. Wines are not regarded as a commodity of value. Likewise, any activity connected with gambling, prostitution, or other indecent occupations is restricted.
2. Productive resources are not to be left idle in the name of private ownership, especially resources that are crucial to the lives of people. The following Hadith provides an illustration of this concept: "If one of you possesses a piece of [arable] land, let him cultivate it. And if he is not able to cultivate it himself, let him give it to his brother."[54] The message of this Hadith is clear: Do not let productive assets sit idle. This makes ownership of resources a social function, rather than an absolute, individual right.
3. The production process should not cause harm to others (e.g., building a noisy factory in the middle of a residential area), as restricted currently by zoning regulations. This is based on the instruction of the Prophet: "One should not harm oneself or others."[55] In situations

where some harm is inevitable, a careful weighing of relative harms and benefits should be made. Furthermore, a party that has been harmed must be compensated, based on the cardinal rule in Islamic law that harm must be removed (or compensated for if inevitable).

4. The method of production should not cause undue and excessive harm to Allah-given resources and bounties for the benefit of all mankind. The Qur'an speaks repeatedly against spreading mischief or corruption in the land.[56] The prophet Muhammad (P) spoke of the punishment of anyone who kills a sparrow without a legitimate reason (e.g., for food), or one who cuts a tree for no good reason. The Prophet was keenly aware of the ecology and the preservation of resources for the benefit of future generations. He taught that if the Day of Judgment begins while one is planting a tree, one should complete the task first if possible.[57] One may wonder what the point is of planting something that cannot immediately benefit the planter and of planting a tree whose fruits may never be reaped. It probably derives from the inculcation of the attitude of working within a larger time frame, consideration of future generations, and, above all, anticipation of divine reward. He also taught that those who plant a tree of which a human or animal or bird eats will get a perpetual reward for all who benefit from it.[58] Sustainment and prudent use of natural resources are exemplified by the Prophet's critical reaction to a companion who was using an excessive amount of water for his ablutions in preparation for prayers. When the companion responded, "Is there excess in the use of water?", the Prophet replied, "Yes, even if you're [making ablutions] in a running river."[59] The Prophet also forbade his followers to pollute rivers, stagnant water, roads, and areas used for shade.[60] Based on the Islamic legal principle of *qiyas* (analogy), reasonable restrictions on methods of production may be legitimately imposed in the interest of environmental protection. Contemporary examples of these restrictions include the requirement of exhaust control devices in automobiles, sewage treatment regulations, and restrictions on dumping waste, especially chemical and nuclear waste. The latter issue has become a global one not only because of the interdependence of all nations, but also because of the attempt by some technologically advanced nations to dump dangerous waste in other, less developed countries. Whatever payments are made in return for accessibility to dumping sites in these countries are far outweighed

by the human costs, especially those relating to health problems. What makes it even worse is that such countries are the least capable and the least resourceful to manage hazardous waste or deal with the resulting health problems.

A more complex environmental issue is the use of genetic modification in animal and agricultural production. It was shown previously, in the section on inducements to study and explore, that the Qur'an encourages research, experimentation, and discovery so as to improve the quality of life. However, the fruits of such research are used sometimes to maximize profits irrespective of the potential long-term damage to ecology or even public health. A particularly disturbing practice is the production of genetically modified, hybrid seeds in such a way as to make it impossible for farmers to use their crops as seeds for the following season, as has been the long-standing natural renewal method. This makes farmers highly dependent on seed producers. As a result, seed producers gain considerable power to dictate the price of their products. Should the use of these genetically modified seeds become global, it would be difficult to predict its damaging impact on ecology. Any potential future monopoly on seeds may be equivalent to monopolistic control of foodstuffs, which is forbidden in Islam, as will be shown in the next section.

Lawful Consumption, Moderate Spending, Lawful Financing

The basic principle is that the consumption of everything is deemed lawful unless there is evidence to the contrary. "O mankind, eat from whatever is on earth [that I] should read [that is] lawful and wholesome and do not follow in the footsteps of Satan. Indeed, he is to you a clear enemy."[61] This passage puts lawfulness before wholesomeness. Allah-determined lawfulness defines what is good, or wholesome. Market forces such as supply and demand do not determine exclusively the definition and value of goods in Islam. For example, intoxicants do not fall within the scope of goods as an economist would consider them. Since the production of intoxicants is forbidden by Islam, there should be no supply produced in the first place. Nor should there be demand for them in a community that accepts such injunctions. Failure to observe the divinely defined lawfulness means "following in the footsteps of Satan."

As it is forbidden to consume the unlawful, it is also forbidden to restrict the consumption of the lawful without a valid reason.[62] In order to partake of the lawful, *infaaq* (spending) is a must. The Qur'an encourages spending (as opposed to hoarding), whether for one's own needs, those of one's dependents and close relatives, and charity at large. The prophet Muhammad (P) included several categories of spending in one Hadith: to spend in the way of Allah (for the defense and security of the community), to help set free a slave, to give to the needy, and to support one's own family. In fact, failure to spend to support one's family is regarded as sin: "Suffice as sin for anyone to be unsupportive of his dependents."[63] Both consumption and spending are qualified, however, by the ethical rule of moderation and avoidance of extravagance. "And eat and drink, but be not excessive. Indeed, He [Allah] likes not those who commit excesses."[64]

Spending has economic implications. Moderate spending is necessary to generate jobs and contribute to economic activities and development. That moderation allows for some savings, which, in turn, can be invested and hence contribute to further development. Capital investment is likely to be more productive than extravagant spending, particularly in the long run. Aside from reducing wasteful use of resources, it may help rationalize the use of scarce resources to cater to the needs of society at large, especially crucial needs. The issue here is not to forbid the production of luxury items, which is not unlawful. The real issue pertains to the macroeconomic implications of the manner of utilizing resources in the context of social and economic needs.

Another issue relating to consumption is credit financing, particularly the modern system of charge cards. It is not unlawful in Islam to borrow so long as no interest is involved. This is hardly the case in credit financing, whether for the purpose of production or consumption. It is lawful, in the opinion of many contemporary Muslim scholars, to use charge cards. This is conditional, however, on the payment of the entire balance by the due date so as to avoid the payment of any interest. Commonly, however, credit cards are used as a form of borrowing with interest added to the principal. The problem is not only with interest, but also the violation of the Prophet's exhortation to avoid unnecessary debt. He used to "seek refuge in Allah" from the burden of debt.

Permissible Marketing

A link between production and consumption is distribution and marketing in a competitive setting. That link is also subject to an ethical
framework founded on the two primary sources of Islam. Its framework
is centered on lawfulness and fair play. To begin with, trade in itself is
lawful. However, items of trade must be lawful in Islam. One basic rule
in Islamic law is that if an item is unlawful, then buying or selling that
item is also unlawful. Examples of this include trading in intoxicants,
living off prostitution or other "immoral" activities, and trading in stolen
goods. "Allah has made wine and its price unlawful, and made the dead
animal and its price unlawful, and made the swine and its price unlawful."[65] Even if the item of trade is lawful in itself, the process of trade
must be lawful as well. A merchant, therefore, must refrain from hiding
any known defect in an item offered for sale. Buyers should be informed
about any defects, and it is up to them to buy it or not, and at what price.
The prophet Muhammad (P) taught:

> The buyer and the seller have the option [to cancel or confirm the
> bargain]. And if they spoke the truth and made clear [the defects of
> the goods], then they would be blessed in their bargain. And if they
> told lies and hid some defects, their bargain would be deprived of
> Allah's blessing.[66]

Furthermore, honesty in all dealing is an ethical requirement. This includes the honoring of all contracts, commitments, and promises[67] and re-
fraining from any form of cheating such as failure "to give the full weight
and measure."[68] The Qur'an warns those who violate this injunction:

> Woe to those who give less [than due]. Who, when they take a mea-
> sure from people [as buyers], they take in full. But if they give by
> measure or by weight [as sellers], they cause loss [to others by giving
> less than due]. Do they not think that they will be resurrected? For a
> momentous Day (the Day of Judgment). The Day when mankind will
> stand before the Lord of the worlds?[69]

The Prophet addressed the problem of cheating in more than one Hadith;
as in the following example: "Anyone who cheats us is not of us."[70] Ex-

ploitation of the ignorance or desperate needs of others is prohibited as well, such as paying a person less than a fair price (or wage). The Qur'an enjoins Muslims to "not deprive people of their due."[71]

One form of that exploitation that the Prophet forbade is *tanajush*. This refers to deceptive practices at auctions where persons who do not intend to buy keep bidding the price up, often in conspiracy with the seller, so others "get stuck" with the deal.[72] Another form of exploitation is to interfere with the free flow of information about markets and going prices so as to acquire goods at an artificially low price. At the time of the Prophet, some middlemen would go to the outskirts of towns where they intercepted out-of-town merchants or farmers who were bringing their products to sell in the town's market. These middlemen would then offer to buy such products at a price that was commonly less than the going market price. The Prophet forbade that practice and gave instructions that the sellers be allowed to get to the market first to find out the going price for their products before an offer was made to them.[73] From an economist's perspective, it is a case of promoting the exchange of information between buyers and sellers. This improves the competitive nature of the market and thus helps determine an equitable price.

In order to avoid unfair risks to buyers, the sale of an item that is not available and whose delivery is doubtful is prohibited. This is known as *bay'ul-gharar*.[74] Examples include selling fish that are still in the river or selling agricultural products before the plant becomes viable and takes root. Exceptions are made in cases of necessity in which fairness can be preserved. Contemporary examples of this are contracts to supply an item like oil that may not be readily available in storage but is abundantly available in the market. The intent behind that restriction in earlier times was apparently to prevent the sale of the produce of a farm, for example, before the plant was viable enough to make it likely to be productive.

Another measure to achieve justice was to restrict unfair monopoly. Today it could be argued that some monopolies may be more efficient and beneficial to society at large, such as of utilities, provided that proper controls and regulations are in place to prevent abuses. What the Prophet condemned were monopolies designed to create an artificially higher price or to create artificial shortages, especially in respect to foodstuffs. According to the Hadith,

He who monopolizes is sinful.[75]

And again:

Whoever monopolizes foodstuff for forty days, he has dissociated himself from Allah and Allah has dissociated Himself from him.[76]

The Prophet also forbade the practice whereby a town dweller withholds and hoards foodstuff that belongs to a desert dweller, waiting until the price goes up (possibly due to this artificial shortage) and then selling it, thus receiving a higher commission for his services.[77]

As to competition, it is lawful for sellers to compete in order to attract buyers. However, attempting to "snatch" a customer who had already negotiated a deal with another seller was regarded as unethical, unless the earlier negotiation broke down or was cancelled for some other reason.[78] A contemporary form of "snatching" contracts is to bribe employees or officials who have the power to decide on tenders or suppliers. (Some like to use a different name for bribes, such as BFP, or business facilitation payments.) Both primary sources of Islam forbid bribery.[79] This prohibition is especially strict when the payment of a bribe is intended to provide a privilege to which the person is not entitled, usually at the expense of others. There are instances, however, in which prompt securing of necessary clearances or papers relating to a legitimate and ethical deal are almost impossible without the payment of a bribe. This is especially true when corruption is so rampant that it permeates all government and organizational levels. In many instances, the bosses themselves are part of the bribery scheme and receive their share of what is paid at a lower level. Some Muslim countries are not free from such a practice, especially among those who are not practicing Muslims. In some instances such a practice may be induced or sustained by a combination of poverty, social injustice, low pay, rising prices, and secularization with its resulting emphasis on materialism.

Related Issues in Islamic Business Ethics

There are other issues of concern to the student or practitioner that are related to Islamic business ethics—the prohibition of interest and the role of women in business. Following is brief discussion of these two issues.

The Prohibition of Interest

Does Islam prohibit usury or interest? The English term "usury" refers to excessive interest. This implies a difference between the two terms and the sanction of charging "reasonable" and nonexcessive interest. But this distinction is totally irrelevant to Islam since the Qur'an was not revealed in English and thus is not subject to its lexical meanings. The Qur'an was revealed in Arabic, and the term used is *riba*, which means, literally, an increase, no matter how large or small. In financial dealings it means the additional income derived from lending, beyond the original amount of the loan. This basic definition applies to both consumer and business loans. Such a prohibition may be understandable in the cases of some consumer loans necessitated by personal or family emergencies and relates to basic human needs (not wants, as with many consumer loans). Does the same prohibition apply to business loans, which the borrower uses to generate profits? Shouldn't the interest paid on such loans be regarded as a share in profit? These questions are not new, and neither is the Qur'anic answer: "[T]his is because they say: 'trade is like riba' but Allah has permitted trade and forbidden riba."[80]

The line between trade and riba sums up the tension between permissible Islamic financial dealings and the dominant interest-based financial system. In the latter case, capital is regarded as a commodity in itself, sold and bought at a risk-adjusted price. The return for capital providers is fixed. Even if variable interest rates are used, the price of capital is independent of actual performance.

In an Islamic system, capital is not seen as a commodity. It is seen, rather, as a means of measuring value. As such it does not have a price like other real commodities or physical products. Return on contributed capital is based not on assumed profit, but on actual profit. In other words, sharing in the risk of profit and loss is a cardinal principle in Islamic finance. A businessperson dealing with practicing Muslims may find it helpful to explore various forms of partnership that are in harmony with this principle. While the interest-based financial system is global, there are signs of a growing segment that is based on this Islamic premise. In some cases, it takes the form of Islamic banks and financial institutions. In addition, some commercial banks both in the Muslim world and elsewhere are opening "Islamic windows" in order to accommodate the religious requirements of Muslim investors and businesspersons while making a profit as well."[81]

Women in Business

This article would not be complete without addressing the role of women in business from a normative Islamic perspective. The topic of women in Islam is a significant one, partly because there are discrepancies between the normative teachings of Islam and local cultural traditions and practices in various parts of the Muslim world. Such traditions are not necessarily uniform or monolithic. It is also important because of the many stereotypes and misconceptions about it.

The role of Muslim women in business or in society at large varies considerably between conservative cultures, where women are not commonly seen in public life, to more open cultures, where women occupy public offices and are involved in business. No attempt is made in this article to survey this mosaic of cultures of the 1.3 billion Muslims worldwide. It may be helpful, however, to examine what the primary sources of Islam state about women's position and role in society.

The Qur'an depicts women as spiritually equal to men.[82] Central worldview concepts such as trusteeship, human dignity, and responsibility are presented in a gender-neutral manner.[83] The only basis for superiority in the Qur'an is piety and righteousness, not gender.[84] Justice for children is required regardless of gender.[85] The marital relationship is described as dwelling in peace, love, and compassion.[86] Perhaps the most relevant aspect of the position of women in normative Islam is that she is entitled to her own legal identity, independent of her husband or others. She may own, invest, or dispose of her private property according to her own wishes.[87] In the meantime, she is guaranteed full financial security and is not required to spend anything on the household even if she is richer than her husband. In fact, the prophet Muhammad's (P) first (and only) wife for twenty-five years was herself a merchant, with the Prophet acting as her business manager. Are such normative teachings followed in the Muslim world?

As indicated earlier, the Muslim world is far from monolithic. In more open and less conservative Muslim cultures like Egypt, Malaysia, and Indonesia, one would expect to see relatively more women engaged in business and in public life in general. In other more conservative and closed cultures, women may not be as visible in public, even though they do exert influence on society. In such cultures, there is a strong emphasis on modesty and aversion to the unrestricted mixing between the genders that is common in Western or Westernized cultures. Even if women in those cultures are engaged in business, some transactions may be done through a male member of the family or through a business manager.

These cultural norms may be so strict that they may place those who are doing business in such cultures in difficult situations. For example, although expatriate female physicians, nurses, and teachers are welcome, some government agencies or other organizations may frown on the arrival of expatriate women engineers. Although such cases are rare, they place business practitioners in a dilemma. On the one hand, they are competing for profitable contracts in the marketplace. On the other hand, they are bound by their country's laws, which prohibit gender discrimination, including discrimination in the hiring, assignment, and deployment of employees. The situation is further complicated when the businessperson's own values and business ethics are considered. It should be noted that the nondiscrimination issue is compatible not only with a Western businessperson's values, but also with normative Islam, as well as the practices of many Muslim business partners.

Awareness of such cultural practices may necessitate the inclusion of a nondiscrimination clause in the business contract. Alternatively, an attempt should be made to understand the concerns of the host culture and the reasons behind them and, whenever possible, to find solutions that may alleviate such concerns to the satisfaction of all parties involved. In time, the evolution, promulgation, and implementation of global business ethics may overcome such problems. However, for business ethics to be truly global, it is necessary to understand, without preconceived stereotypes, diverse cultural practices and even accommodate those that are reasonable and fair. The question of the exact meaning, even desirability, of globalization has not been fully resolved, whether in the area of human rights, women's issues, or business ethics. Readers of this article who do not have a Muslim background may find a considerable area of common ground between Islamic teachings and their own religious or philosophical convictions. Such a common ground is a good start, both for understanding business ethics and for interfaith dialogue in general.

Enforcement Mechanisms

Enforcement mechanisms of Islamic business ethics begin with the individual. They operate through the appeal to the person's conscious fear of Allah and the desire for his blessings in this life and in the life hereafter. These mechanisms are founded on the person's realization that Allah knows the manifest and the hidden and will hold all accountable for their deeds. These are perhaps the most powerful enforcement mechanisms, more so than any government control. The sense of ultimate responsibility is exemplified in the Qur'anic warning: "And fear a Day when you will be returned to Allah. Then every soul will be compensated for what it earned, and they will not be wronged [treated unjustly]."[88]

Islam teaches responsibility before Allah and the belief in resurrection and eternal life, whose nature depends upon one's actions while on earth. Tawheed also means belief in the absolute perfection of divine attributes, one of which is perfect knowledge, even of the most secret thoughts of the heart. The result of such belief is that self-policing becomes the primary motive to avoid evil or wrong. Mere social controls are incapable of policing everything. Properly implemented, one's sense of responsibility before Allah avoids the attitude of "getting away with whatever you can so long as you don't get caught," or even the attitude of taking advantage of legal or administrative gaps or flaws to maximize one's gains at the expense of society. That sense of fairness is greatly enhanced both by the infinite time scale and by the keen sense of *taqwa* (being Allah-conscious), the realization that nothing can be hidden from Allah, who will hold each person responsible for his or her deeds.

As individuals vary in the extent of their fear of Allah and their motivation for righteousness, other sanctions are necessary. One such mechanism is social values, norms, and rewards, which are considered legitimate insofar as they are consistent with Islamic teachings and injunctions. Another inevitable enforcement mechanism, in any organized society composed of less than angels, is government control, through monitoring and policing. In normative Islam, however, the proper role of government is no excuse for totalitarianism. The Prophet was once asked by his companions, "Why don't you set prices [of goods] for us?" His answer was, "Allah is the One who sets prices."[89] He seems to be referring to the natural laws of supply and demand that Allah created, which, under normal circumstances, should be more valid than decisions made by a given bureaucracy. This does not rule out, however, limited government intervention when necessary for the protection of public interest and within the Islamic process of *shura* (mutual consultation).

Conclusion

This article outlines business ethics from an Islamic perspective. In light of the most important pillars of Islamic teachings—belief in and devotion to Allah—the concept of tawheed was explained and its implications explored. The concept of humankind—its nature and the purpose of its existence—was specifically related to human pursuits on earth, whether in economic or other spheres. To fulfill their trusteeship of Allah on earth, humans were granted access to various bounties in the world in order to harness resources, subject to certain conditions of that trust. This harnessing in turn requires the acquisition of knowledge and the understanding of Allah's creation and bounties, a matter that is highly commended by the Qur'an.

In order to apply the worldview discussed in the first five sections of this article to specific areas of business ethics, I explained the nature of ethics in Islam, paving the way for an exposition of Islamic ethics in the traditional areas of production, consumption, and distribution.

The article examined the subject from a foundational, normative perspective. It would be interesting to see the extent to which such ideal norms are implemented in various parts of the Muslim world today, and how present realities affect international business, international management, management of diversity, and the broader process of globalization. The reader will likely be able to see a significant common ground, in the area of business ethics, between Islam and other major world religions. This may be especially true in relation to Judaism and Christianity. "Secular" business ethics, in turn, may share many aspects with "religious" business ethics. Such common ground may contribute to the evolution of some form of global business ethics. Should all parties involved abide by such ethics, the enforcement mechanisms will be facilitated, though not guaranteed. Further dialogue and research are both needed and helpful as the topic of business ethics is taking its rightful place both in the areas of religious studies and business management.

NOTES

1. The Arabic term "Allah" is more correctly the proper name of God. In any case, it refers to the one and only creator, sustainer, and cherisher of the universe. The same term is used by Christian Arabs and in Arabic Bibles. It is strikingly similar to the Aramaic *Alaha*, which also refers to God. From a Muslim perspective, the term "Allah" is preferable to the term "God," not only because it is the proper name of God, but also because linguistically the term "Allah" is not subject to gender or plurality. The term will be used throughout this article.

2. (P) is an abbreviation of "Peace be upon him," an honorific formula that Muslims use when the name of a prophet is mentioned. This abbreviation will be used throughout this article.

3. C.E. stands for Common Era and is equivalent to A.D.

4. The primacy of the Qur'an and Hadith in the interpretation of Islam has been a universal rule followed by Muslim scholars from all schools of jurisprudence. The universal acceptance of this rule is due to the fact that it is rooted in Muslim belief and the revelatory nature of these two sources. This means that any attempt to overrule them implies claiming more knowledge and wisdom than Allah; it is the antithesis of faith in him. Shortly before passing away, the prophet Muhammad (P) said, "I have left amongst you that which, if you hold fast to, shall preserve you from error, a clear indication, the Book of God and the word of His Prophet." (Quoted in Martin, Lings, *Muhammad: His Life Based on the Earliest Sources*, Islamic Texts Society [London: George Allen and Unwin, 1983], 334.) Two other widely accepted sources are *ijma'* (consensus of scholars) and *qiyaas* (analogy). These sources, however, are themselves derived from the Qur'an and Hadith. It is difficult to see how a broad consensus on any issue can be attained among scholars throughout the centuries unless that issue is clearly stated in one of the primary sources of Islam or both. Examples include the pillars of Islam, prohibition of injustice, and the imperative of *Shura* (consultation) in the political process. Analogy (or analogical deduction), by definition, means the derivation of a ruling concerning a new situation or problem by analogy with a similar situation dealt with in the Qur'an or Hadith. Thus, both sources—ijma' and qiyaas—are themselves derived from the primary sources, the Qur'an and Hadith. There are, in addition to these sources, other, debatable secondary sources that are beyond the scope of this article. For more details on these issues of methodology, see Abdur Rahaman Doi, *Shari'ah: The Islamic Law* (London: Ta Ha Publishers, 1984), and Abdul Wahhab Khallaaf, *'Ilm Usool Al-Filth* (Al-Dar Al-Kuwait-iyyah, 1968).

5. See for example the Qur'an 21:107, 34:28. The following translations of the Qur'an were used: *The Holy Qur'an*, trans. Abdullah Y. Ali (Washington, D.C.:

Khalil Al-Rawaf, 1946); *The Qur'an* (Jeddah: Saheeh International, 1997). Some modifications were made for greater clarity.

6. "O mankind! We created you from a single [pair] of a male and a female, and made you into nations and tribes, that you may know each other. Verily the most honored of you in the sight of Allah is the most righteous of you. And Allah has full knowledge and is well acquainted [with all things]" (Qur'an 49:13). "And among His Signs is the creation of the heavens and the earth, and the variations in your languages and your colors; verily in that are signs for those who know" (Qur'an 30:22).

7. "O you who believe! Enter into Islam wholeheartedly; and follow not the footsteps of the Evil One; for he is to you an avowed enemy" (Qur'an 2:208).

8. "But seek with the [wealth] which Allah has bestowed on you, the Home of the Hereafter, nor forget your portion in this world; but do you good as Allah has been good to you and seek not [occasions for] mischief in the land: for Allah loves not those who do mischief" (Qur'an 28:77).

9. Qur'an 32:6–9. To articulate the privileged position of humans the Qur'an states: "We have honored the children of Adam; provided them with transport on land and sea; given them for sustenance things good and pure; and conferred on them special favors above a great part of our creation" (Qur'an 17:70). A significant symbol of this honor was the command of Allah to the angels to bow down to Adam: "Behold! We said to the angels, bow down to Adam. They bowed down except Iblis. He was one of the Jinn, and he broke the Command of his Lord" (Qur'an 18:50). For further readings on this issue, see Jamal Badawi, "The Application of Tawheed in the Natural and Social Order" *Humanomics* 7, no. 1 (1991); and Jamal A. Badawi, "The Earth and Humanity," in John Hick and Edmund Meltzer, eds., *Three Faiths: One God* (London: Macmillan, 1989).

10. "Do they not reflect in their own minds? Not but for just end, and for a term appointed, did Allah create the heavens and the earth, and all between them. Yet, are there truly many among people who deny the meeting with their Lord [and resurrection]?" (Qur'an 30:8). "Do they see nothing in the domain of heavens and the earth and all that Allah has created?" (Qur'an 7:185).

11. Qur'an 7:179.

12. The story of the forbidden tree appears in both the Bible (Genesis 3) and in the Qur'an (e.g., 2:35–37, 7:19–25, 20:120–22). While both versions of the story are similar, there are significant differences concerning what happened after "eating from the forbidden tree." According to the Qur'an, Adam and Eve acknowledged their mistake, prayed for forgiveness, and were forgiven. Thus, the Qur'an does not provide a basis for the notion of original sin, founded on the biblical version of the story. For more details refer to Jamal A. Badawi, *Islamic*

Teachings, album 2 (Halifax, Islamic Information Foundation, 1982), audio cassette. Also available at the following web site: www://islamicity.org./Radio Islam.

13. "All who obey Allah and the Messenger are in the company of those on whom is the Grace of Allah, of the Prophets, the sincere [Lovers of Truth], the martyrs and the righteous. Ah! What a beautiful fellowship" (Qur'an 4:69).

14. "I have only created Jinns and humankind that they may worship [serve] me" (Qur'an 51:56).

15. Qur'an 67:2.

16. Qur'an 45:13.

17. Qur'an 5:123.

18. Qur'an 51:19, 70:24–25.

19. Qur'an 51:19, 70:24–25.

20. The Qur'an speaks against the circulation of wealth among the wealthy only (Qur'an 59:7).

21. Qur'an 2:271. Among the seven categories of the pious the prophet Muhammad (P) included "a person who gave a charity in secret so that his left [hand] would not know what his right [hand] spent" (narrated by Bukhari and Muslim), quoted in A. Al-Nawawi, *Riyadh Al-Saliheen* (Riyadh Dar Al-Warraq, 1991), Hadith no. 376, p. 155. Translated by author.

22. Abdul-Bagi, *Sunan Al-Tirmidhi*, vol. 3 (Mecca: Al-Maktabah Al-Tijariyyah, n.d.), Hadith no. 659, p. 39. Translated by author.

23. Qur'an 13:4, 45:12, 16:14, 16:5–8.

24. Qur'an 3:190, 24:44, 24:43, 39:5, 22:61, 10:5, 36:40.

25. Qur'an 96:1–5.

26. Qur'an 58:11, 35:28.

27. Qur'an 8:22, 7:179.

28. Qur'an 6:148, 4:174, 23:117, 21:24, 27:64, 28:75, 53:28.

29. Qur'an 16:69, 57:25; and 23:12–14, 3:137, 6:11, 16:66.

30. Among the Prophet's sayings on learning are: "Seeking knowledge is a mandatory duty of every Muslim"; "Whoever pursues a way in search for knowledge, Allah will make an easy way for him to paradise"; "The priority of a scholar over a worshipper [without understanding] is like the superiority of the moon over other stars"; "Scholars are the heirs of prophets." See Birnamij Silsilat Kunuz Al-Sunnah, *Al-Jami' Al-Sagheer Waziyadatih*, 1st ed., Hadith nos. 3914, 6298, 4212, and 6297; 1410 A.H., computer software. Translated by author.

31. For a summary of such contributions, refer to Badawi, *Islamic Teachings*, album 5.

32. Muhammad Al-Albani, comp., *Silsilat Al-Ahadeeth Al-Saheehah*, vol. 1 (Beirut: Al-Maktab Al-Islaami, 1985), Hadith no. 45, p. 75. Translated by author.

33. Quoted in Muhammad Al-Ghazali, *Khuluq Al-Muslim* (Kuwait: Dar Al-Bayaan, 1970), 51. Translated by author.

34. Muhammad M. Khan, trans., *Translation of the Meaning of Sahih Al-Bukhari*, vol. 8 (Riyadh: Maktabat Al-Riyadh Al-Hadeethah, 1981), Hadith no. 47, p. 29.

35. Qur'an 29:45.

36. Qur'an 9:103.

37. Qur'an 2:183.

38. Qur'an 2:197.

39. Muhammad F. Abdul-Bagi, ed., *Sunan Ibn Majah*, Al-Maktabah Al-'ilmiyyah, vol. 1 (Beirut, n.d.), Hadith nos. 1690, no. 1689, p. 539. Translated by author.

40. Ibid.; 52; Al-Ghazali, op. cit., 6. Translated by author.

41. For an excellent and detailed treatment of this topic following the same classification, see Yusuf Al-Qaradawi, *Dawr Al-Qiyam Wal-Akhlaaq Fi Al-Igtisaad Al-Islaami* (Cairo: Maktabat Wahbah, 1995).

42. Qur'an 67:15.

43. Qur'an 7:10.

44. Qur'an 62:10. The concept of "Sabbath" in the biblical sense has no parallel in Islam. This implies that business deals can be negotiated on Friday, except during the Friday congregational prayers at midday.

45. Qur'an 51:56.

46. Qur'an 3:136, 99:7, 48:19.

47. The Qur'an promises: "Indeed, Allah will not allow to be lost the reward of any who does a good work" (18:30); "and say, do [as you will], for Allah will see your deeds, and [so will] His Messenger and the believers. And you will be returned to the knower of the unseen and the witnessed, and He will inform you of what you used to do" (9:105).

48. Abdul Hamid Siddiqi, trans., *Sahih Muslim*, vol. 3 (Beirut: Dar Al-Arabia, n.d.), Hadith no. 4810, p. 1078.

49. Quoted in Al-Qaradawi, op. cit., 152. Translated by author.

50. Abdul-Fattah Abu-Ghoddah, ed., *Sunan Al-Nasaa'i*, vol. 8 (Aleppo, Syria: Maktab Al-Matboo'aat Al-Islaamiyyah, 1994), Hadith no. 4990, pp. 97–100. Translated by author.

51. In a summary of the financial rights of the child in Islamic law, Al-Salih explains that the child is entitled to financial support without being required to earn a living, at least until he reaches puberty, if a male. If the child is female, support continues until she gets married, in which case the responsibility for her support shifts to her husband. If the child is successful in his education, he is entitled to financial support so as to be able to complete his education. See Muhammad Ben Ahmad Al-Salih, *Al-Tiff Fi Al-Shari'ah Al-Islaamiyyah*, 2d printing (Riyadh, n.d.), 213–25.

52. Khan, op. cit., vol. 2, Hadith no. 549, p. 319.

53. Abdul-Bagi, *Sunan Al-Tirmidhi,* vol. 3, Hadith no. 652, p. 33. Translated by author.

54. Abu-Ghoddah, op. cit., vol. 7, Hadith no. 3874, p. 36. Translated by author.

55. Abdul-Bagi, *Sunan Ibn Majah,* vol. 2, Hadith no. 2341, p. 784. Translated by author.

56. Qur'an, 2:60, 2:205, 7:56, 28:83.

57. Al-Albani, op. cit., vol. 1, Hadith no. 9, p. 11. Translated by author.

58. Khan, op. cit., vol. 8, Hadith no. 41, p. 26.

59. Abdul-Bagi, *Sunan Ibn-Majah,* vol. 1, Hadith no. 425, p. 147. Translated by author.

60. Muhammad M. Abdul-Hameed, *Sunan Abi-Dawood,* vol. 1 (Beirut: Al-Maktabah Al-Asriyyah, n.d.), Hadith nos. 25, 26, p. 7; Sayyid Sabiq, *Fughus-Sunnah,* vol. 1 (Beirut: Dar al-Kitab Al-Arabi, 1969), 35; and Siddiqi, op. cit., Hadith no. 553, p. 167.

61. Qur'an 2:168.

62. Qur'an 7:32.

63. Abdul-Hameed, op. cit., vol. 2, Hadith no. 1692, p. 132. Translated by author.

64. Qur'an 7:31. The Qur'an also states: "O believers, do not prohibit the good things that Allah has made lawful to you and do not transgress. Indeed, Allah does not like transgressors" (5:87). Describing true believers, the Qur'an states: "And those who, when they spend, they do so not excessively or sparingly but are ever, between that, [justly] moderate" (Qur'an 25:67).

65. Abdul-Hameed, op. cit., vol. 3, Hadith no. 3485, p. 279. Translated by author.

66. Khan, op. cit., vol. 3, Hadith no. 323, p. 183.

67. Qur'an 23:8.

68. In the Qur'an we read: "Give full measure and do not be of those who cause loss [to others]. And weigh with an even [honest] balance" (26:181–83): And again: "And give full measure when you measure, and weigh with an even balance. That is good and the better at the end" (17:35).

69. Qur'an 83:1–6.

70. Abdul-Bagi, *Sunan Ibn Majah,* vol. 2, Hadith no. 2225, p. 749. Translated by author.

71. Qur'an 7:85.

72. Abdul-Bagi, *Sunan Ibn Majah,* vol. 2, Hadith no. 2174, p. 734. Translated by author.

73. Ibid., Hadeeth no. 2179, p. 735.

74. Ibid., Hadith no. 2195, p. 739.

75. Ibid., Hadith no. 2154, p. 728.

76. Al-Qaradawi, op. cit., p. 293.

77. Abdul-Bagi, *Sunan Ibn Majah*, Hadith nos. 2175, 2176, p. 734.

78. Khan, op. cit., vol. 3, Hadith no. 350, pp. 197–98.

79. Bribery is forbidden in the Qur'an (2:188). The same prohibition is also mentioned in the Hadith.

80. Qur'an 2:275.

81. For examples of alternative financial dealings that are acceptable in Islam, see Imtiazuddin Ahmad, *Islamic Banking and Finance: The Concept, the Practice, and the Challenge* (Plainfield, Ind.: Islamic Society of North America, 1999). See also Jamal A. Badawi, "Is There Halal Mortgage?" *Islamic Horizons* 2 (May–June 1996): 26–28.

82. Qur'an 4:1, 7:189, 3:195, 4:124, 33:35, 57:12.

83. Qur'an 32:9, 15:29, 2:30.

84. Qur'an 49:13.

85. Al-Nawawi, op. cit., Hadith no. 1773, p. 517.

86. Qur'an 30:21.

87. For more details, see Jamal A. Badawi, *Gender Equity in Islam* (Plainfield, Ind.: American Trust Publications, 1999), 15–19.

88. Qur'an 2:281.

89. Abdul-Hameed, op. cit., vol. 3, Hadith no. 3451, p. 272.

EIGHT

Spirituality and Religion

Some Reflections

LAWRENCE S. CUNNINGHAM

One often hears both in casual conversation and in the media a sharp distinction made between "spirituality" and "religion," as in the assertion, "I no longer attend church, but I do think developing a spirituality is important," or, "I have my own spirituality even though I am not religious." A recent Gallup poll conducted for Cable News Network and *USA Today* reported that on the cusp of the year 2000 fully 30 percent of the American public described itself as "spiritual" but not "religious." [1] The subtext of such statements is, of course, that there is some connection between the word "religion" and "spirituality," but the latter is more self-constructed and self-satisfying than "religion," which is seen as too institutional and too far removed from the concerns of the individual. In that reading, "religion" seems like a restriction and spirituality seems like a liberation. In essence, what such sentiments express is something like an aversion to primary identification with an institution like a church or synagogue but a desire to be—however one defines the term—a spiritual person. [2]

I will make no attempt at the offset of these reflections to actually define the words "spirituality" or "religion" since those who have attempted to do that have learned quickly what a difficult task it is. For my purposes I will assume the common-sense understanding of spirituality as having something to do with a part of human life that is beyond the mundane and the obligatory and can be subsumed under a phrase like "having to do with one's deeper life" or something of the sort. If that sounds a bit vague, please note that Webster's *New Collegiate Dictionary* offers "sensitivity to religious values" and "the quality or state of being spiritual" as its two stabs at definition.

In actual practice what counts for spirituality covers a wide range in American culture. Athletics and exercise are touted as having spiritual

168

benefit, as does meditation, using crystals, sitting under pyramidal shapes, or doing yoga. Perhaps two phenomena, one rather functional and eclectic, the other more like a well-thought-out system, will help us see what the common meaning of spirituality is so that we can ask what religion adds to the phenomena. We might then be ready to advance to the final part of this paper to speak a bit about *Christian* spirituality which is the area of discussion where my intellectual comfort zone is highest. I am setting forth the argument here that when one speaks of Christian spirituality (or, mutatis mutandis, Jewish or Islamic spirituality) the words "spirituality" and "religious faith" meet.

Spirituality: Two Examples

Soul Tenders

I recently happened on an article about "Micro Softies" by James Atlas.[3] For those not familiar with the expression, "Micro Softies" refers to those lucky young people who first went to work with Microsoft, got in on the ground floor by having stock options or by actually purchasing stocks, and, possessed of varying degrees of wealth, for a variety of reasons, retired in their twenties or early thirties. Atlas traces their subsequent career choices, which ranged from starting up their own businesses in one or the other area of information technology to West Coast enterprises like opening schools of paragliding or stores to sell recyclable goods and organically produced or environmentally conscious wares.

One pair of (female) former investment bankers, however, badly burned out from their days of financial labors, opened a consulting firm called "Soul Tenders." For $250 heavily burdened overachievers in the world of business can take a series of seminars and workshops that utilize a number of strategies gleaned, as far as I can judge, largely from New Age sources in order to create in themselves a better sense of self-consciousness, a more meditative way of working, a purging of bad personal and social habits, and a larger feeling of purposefulness about their lives and their work. The actual tools utilized in this enterprise (meditation, soft music, symbolic gestures, exercises, and so on) will come as no news to those who have even superficially scanned the advertisements found in the back of airline magazines.

The goals that drive the agenda of Soul Tenders are, quite patently, functional and targeted: their aim is to help people find a way to live amid the stress of a culture that prizes high achievement, full dedication to the task at hand, and a kind of secular asceticism in which one puts aside present pleasures (sleep, leisure, time with the family, and so on) for long-term goals such as advancement, prestige, more money, and status. In other words, Soul Tenders hopes to provide strategies to enlarge a person's perspective while allowing that same person to live in and be a productive member of the organization within which he or she has already chosen to live. As its official literature puts it, the aim of Soul Tenders is "reconciling spiritual life with corporate culture."[4] It is easy to see that this functional aim is not far removed from (indeed, bears striking similarities to) the various popular forms of psychotherapy that promise reduction of stress, adjustment, and the like. This kind of "soul" science has deep roots in American culture, going back at least to nineteenth-century movements like Christian Science, Mind Science, Theosophy, or the health cults touted by the Kellogs of Battle Creek, Michigan.

Alcoholics Anonymous
Alcoholics Anonymous (AA), founded in 1935, by contrast, is a far more systematic form of nonreligious spirituality. AA also bears more than a family resemblance (I borrow the term from Ludwig Wittgenstein) to traditional schools of Christian spirituality. To join AA one must make a confession of one's actual state (i.e., "I am an alcoholic") freely and voluntarily. Such a confession carries with it the intention of changing or, to borrow traditional formulations, "convert" from one form of living to another one. That confession is the first of the famous "twelve steps" that form the heart of the AA program. The second step provides the first glimpse into the "spiritual" matrix out of which AA operates: "[We] came to believe that a Power greater than ourselves could restore us to sanity." That power is next described as "God as we understand Him" (step 3).[5]

Two further characteristics of AA must be noted. First, the successful fulfillment of the passage through the twelve steps does not mean a graduation in the sense of exit from the program. Those who internalize the steps are then expected to spread the message to others and to apply the steps in every area of their lives. Second, the journey through the twelve steps is not typically done in isolation; AA has a strong communitarian thrust in which members are expected to come to meetings and, at the same time, to be partners and interventionists for others who are in need and who call upon the help of AA.

What is striking about this movement (and those cognate groups who use the twelve steps for mastering a whole range of addictions whether they be to gambling or eating or narcotics or sex) is the degree to which it borrows, either consciously or unconsciously, from traits found in the traditional Christian schools of spirituality. The salient characteristics are clear: the emphasis on conversion, the demands for a particular form of asceticism, the reliance on a faith commitment, the insight that the converted person learns by steps or gradual levels of attainment, the requirement for self-examination and further repentance (step 10), and the insistence that part of this process calls for awareness of the presence of God (however one understands that term) through prayer and meditation (step 11). Finally, and this is striking, not only is the commitment to the principles of AA analogous to paths of spiritual maturity, but in both instances the paths demand a lifelong commitment. In other words, the usages and the goals of AA are not merely instrumental (a technique to change a person who drinks to one who does not drink) but envision a radically new way of being in the world—what Saint Paul, in a different context, called creating the New Person (in Christ).

Involvement with the twelve-step program is not only a personal process but it has within its framework an implied evangelizing task, which is "to carry this message to alcoholics" once one has come to a state of "spiritual awakening" (step 12). It is also striking that the twelve-step approach bears a similarity to those formulations of the spiritual life in which a person is invited to pass by stages into a greater life of perfection. Christian schools of spirituality, for instance, often describe spiritual growth in terms of stages; the most famous of these (with roots in the late-third century) envision the Christian life as the passage from sin (purgation) to openness to prayer and instruction (illumination) to a close identification with God by a palpable sense of God's presence (union).

Open meetings of AA—the only ones I have ever attended because the closed meetings are only for members in recovery—have about them the character of a sedate revival with a period for public confession ("Hi. I am Bill. I am an alcoholic"), a time for community support, and a final period of fellowship. The tenor of these meetings leave no doubt at all that AA is an intensely communitarian enterprise.

Spirituality and Religion

To stay with the example of AA, we can pursue a further question: if AA shows a family resemblance to schools of traditional Christian spirituality, in what sense is that movement not simply to be called a "religion"? Could one not say, "I am a member of AA," the way one would say "I am a Christian or a Muslim or an observant Jew or whatever"? One could, at a certain level, argue that AA is a religion or, to go back to Wittgenstein's phrase, that AA bears a strong family resemblance to religion. One empirical proof of its religious character is that there has been, in recent times, an attempt to reconfigure AA in such a manner as not to offend the sensibilities of nonbelievers, whether they be agnostics or atheists, since these persons bristle at the religious language and practice of the original AA philosophy.

The one obvious difference between religions, traditionally understood, and AA is that, although AA is concerned with a radical makeover or conversion of the person, the ethos of the movement does not celebrate or sacralize a person's life in anything like a holistic fashion. Unlike forms of spirituality, even those which are as comprehensive as AA surely is, religious traditions hew more closely to the whole person by making sacred life's journey in the full sense of human development at both the personal and social level. Traditional religions, for example, play a central role in what anthropologists since Arnold van Gennep (who coined the word in 1909) have called "rites of passage." Rites of passage are those (usually) once-in-a-lifetime rituals that mark off the stages of a person's life. Birth and naming rituals are followed by those that mark the transition from childhood to the childbearing years. Marriage rituals and those connected with births in the family are followed by rituals that aid in time of sickness or impending death. Finally, traditional religion provides appropriate gestures and formulas for death as well as commemorative rites for the deceased. Traditional religions, in short, provide a kind of symbolic scaffolding for the person as he or she enters the world, matures, takes on new social responsibilities, and, finally, goes through the transition to life's end.

Within that large framework of ritual activity traditional religions also possess what I will call a "grammar" of meaning that can be called on and instantiated as need and opportunity arise. That grammar and its attendant vocabulary serve a spectrum of purposes. For Christians, the articulation of the creed—"I believe" or "We believe"—helps constitute a community. That community, in turn, has a hallowed repertoire of incantatory language (The Lord's Prayer or the Ave Maria or the familiar language of the liturgy for Christians; the *Sh'ma* for Jews; the *Shahada* in Islam, and so forth) that evokes responses available only to those who have made that language their own. In addition, there are formal and informal strata of language, gesture, and so on that can be called up in times of crisis or need or mourning or exaltation.

This grammar carries with it not only the language of the sacred but both positive injunctions (do this or that) and negative admonitions (do not do this or that) in either an explicit or implicit fashion. Traditional religion differs from, say, mere systems of ethics, however, in that injunctions, prohibitions, and so on flow out of the more fundamental grammar of observance, faith, and practice. Jesus, to cite an obvious example, does not preach mere social amelioration; his commands to serve the poor or to preach freedom for the captive derive from his urgent plea to bring in the reign of God promised by the prophets or mirror his own love for the least in the world. For Jesus, the correct moral calculus by which one measures the goodness of action derives directly from the command in Deuteronomy that makes up the Jewish act of faith called the *Sh'ma*, namely, to love God above all things and one's neighbor as oneself (Deut. 6:4). The order of love of God, then self, and then neighbor is not casual but imperative.

Up to this point we have sketched out, with broad strokes, the ways in which religion, traditionally conceived, constitutes the broader frame within which spirituality may be subsumed; one can be a good Christian, for example, and a diligent member of AA, but one cannot subsume all of the Christian religion under the aegis of AA. I observe this fact not to be contentious and certainly not to be critical of movements like AA, but to establish some real relationships between spirituality understood in its most loosely defined fashion and the broader category of religion. As a coda to these observations I will also hazard the observation that one can inject spirituality into one's life as a businessperson ("reconciling spiritual life with corporate culture"), but one cannot subsume one's religious life under the rubric of business unless one sees—there may well be people who do so—business as the final frame for one's existence. In other words, one must first be a Jew or Christian or Muslim and then a businessperson, but not vice versa. I shall return to this point later.

Christian Spirituality

This section will focus on Christian spirituality in obedience to the principle that one should speak about what one knows. It should be noted, however, that, all things being equal, what is said here about Christianity could be said, for example, of Judaism or Islam. After all, to be a practicing Jew is to shape one's life in concord with the Torah, just as a Muslim lives his or her life in the submission to God, which is implied in the very word "Islam." Islam and Judaism are, after all, ways of life and not mere additions to one's value system.

Being a Christian does not mean, in the first instance, giving assent to formulations of the creed or undertaking to observe the moral norms of the Christian tradition, even though both exercises are laudatory in themselves. Being a Christian is to enter into a way of life. It is useful to remember that in the "Acts of the Apostles" the first Christians were known as Followers of the Way (see, for example, Acts 9:2). The concept of "the Way" is a very rich one in the books of the New Testament. In Mark, for example, the following of the Way was a mark of discipleship, whereas in John Christ calls himself the Way. Since it is not possible to disentangle the various nuances of this usage in this brief work,[6] we will simply stipulate that a "way of life" encompasses a broad fashion in which one relates to others and to the larger world that impinges on and makes contact with a given person. To undertake the Christian life, in other words, is to be inserted in the world in a certain fashion, to react to the world by an instinct developed by this way of life, and to see the frame of one's existence from birth to death under the rubric of the Christian way of living.

Obviously, most people do not live this way of life with explicit consciousness at all times. Even the great saints and mystics had to go about the everyday experiences of living—getting up, getting dressed, attending to needs, responding to family and neighborhood, making a living, and so on—just the way others do who are not followers of the Way. When, however, a person undertakes a way of life, that person does react to those moments when routine confronts opportunity in a fashion that says a great deal about how that person sees himself or herself in a larger context. Such moments of opportunity can be relatively banal (Am I a person who is grateful?) or more momentous (Need I take a firm moral stand on this or that issue even at a certain cost?). While I would not agree with Alfred North Whitehead's observation that religion is what one does with one's solitude, I would agree that how, from an interior perspective, one reacts to the occasions of life when decisions become paramount does say a good deal about how one has framed one's deepest sense of values.

To adopt a way of life, of course, requires that a person has a criterion for judging what is compatible with or antagonistic to that way of life. It is here, when seeking what that criterion might be, that we need to note, albeit briefly, something peculiar about Christianity. The historic tradition of Christianity has always taught that the primary decision to be a Christian is not to follow the teachings of Jesus, but to become a disciple of the person of Jesus from whom these teachings flow. Pious Muslims follow the revelation of God given to the Prophet (the *Qu'ran*) and followers of the Buddha follow the teachings of the Buddha, but Christians follow Jesus the Christ and from that following learn what the meanings of his teachings are.

To follow Christ is to become a disciple. The word "disciple" (in Greek, *mathetes*) occurs about 250 times in the New Testament with roughly 70 of the citations linked to some form of the verb "to follow." Technically, the word "disciple" means "learner." In that sense, at least, one learns from Christ, who is the source of one's religious convictions. That learning involves not only studying of the teachings of Christ as they are found in sacred documents, but, rather, encountering the living Christ who presents himself to us in his person, in the proclamation of his word, and in the sharing of his person in what the New Testament calls the "breaking of the bread." Jesus himself stipulates the various ways in which he is present to those who take up his challenge of discipleship:

1. In the community that gathers in his name
2. Seeing him in the poor, needy, naked, imprisoned, and so forth
3. Recognizing him in the breaking of the bread
4. Affirming that he lives as Lord
5. Participating in his death and resurrection through rebirth in baptism

Conversion

I hesitate to use the word "conversion" since for many people it conjures up either dramatic interruptions in one's life (Saul on the road to

Damascus), emotional responses to preachers inviting people to repent, or the adoption of a life of piety that becomes conspicuous to one's own self and to others. By conversion, however, I mean something far more fundamental, something tightly tied to the very etymology of the word itself. In classical Greek *meta+noia* means a change of mind; in the New Testament it means to exchange one way of life for another.[7] In that sense, the word signifies a change by which one gives up an older way of life for a new one—the word implies a new direction, a new way of being, and a new way of seeing.

In that sense, every conversion carries with it, often implicitly, an aversion: to turn toward something or someone means, almost by definition, turning away from something else. In other words, there is a kind of subtle shift that goes on in the dynamics of conversion—a turning to and a turning from. In the context of our discussion of Christian spirituality it is crucial to grasp this dynamism. Conversion involves a certain way of being in the world in which one makes assertions about who one is and how one relates to others while, at the same time, this conversion to discipleship demands an affirmation of who one is not and how one may not relate to others and to the world. To put it bluntly: conversion demands both a yes and a no. Such conversions for adults, of course, are more radical and fundamental than other life-changing decisions: one chooses to marry or to change one's occupation or whatever in the context of having already chosen a way of life that is called Christian.

The practical consequences of this understanding of Christian conversion are many, but the most important of them for our topic of spirituality and the modern businessperson is this: before one can relate the Christian spiritual life to one's vocation in life, one must ask the far more radical question: "Who am I and who am I not?" That question, as we indicated above, is asked in consort with the image of the master who is the model for the disciple.

This dual question, Who am I and who am I not is not an abstract one. The question must be asked in the concrete: "Who am I in terms of my real situation as a real living person who exists in concrete circumstances with specific social obligations in quite recognizable cultural situations?" To ask that question in the concrete is the only way to avoid abstractions or build castles in the air, musing about who it would be nice to be if only factor x or condition y were not part of my exigent reality. One may ask, not to put too fine a point on it: "Who am I, this middle-aged

American with a wife and family who lives in the Midwest at the beginning of a new century with a position in this or that particular company or institution?"

Such questioning about the concrete situation in which one finds oneself is, of course, crucial for anyone who wishes to live a concrete Christian life since that life must be lived in the exigent circumstances in which one finds oneself. One cannot adopt a spirituality fitted for a Carthusian hermit if one lives in suburbia with a family. Saint Francis de Sales, a classic spiritual master, understood this four centuries ago. Writing to a young woman in a work that would become one of the great classics of Catholic spirituality, the wise bishop wrote that "the practice of devotion must differ for the gentleman and the artisan, the servant and the prince, for widow, young girl, or wife. Further, it must be accommodated to their particular strength, circumstances and duties."[8]

At the same time, when we examine ourselves in our real situation, we may also conclude that the *way* we live in that concrete situation is such that it is impossible to lead a Christian life. Our negligence or ingrained habits or boredom or sinfulness may make it impossible to advance in love of God, imitation of Christ, or love of neighbor. In other words, we may be required within our actual living situation to discern the how of our life and, with God's help, make some radical decisions about how our lives take shape. As a witty political pundit (and Notre Dame graduate) once told a commencement audience here on our campus, he had never heard of anyone on his deathbed saying to those assembled, "Gee, I wish I had spent more time at the office."

The Expanding Circle

Traditional forms of Christian spirituality have used many metaphors to describe growth in the way of Christian perfection. From the earliest patristic times we find the image of the Children of Israel described in the Book of Exodus. The Christian life, this model says, is like a journey from the fleshpots of Egypt through the experience of the desert to the revelation of God on Mount Sinai; from this image comes the classic image of the way of purification, illumination, and union. Other spiritual writers have used the ascent motif of climbing from the lowest rung of life to the highest. Spiritual writers have described this ascent in many different ways: the climbing of the ladder, the ascent of the mountain, and so on. The steps of such ascents have varied depending on the author who has used this model; the ascent model is found in writers such as John Climacus (*climacus* means "ladder"), and John of the Cross.[9] For our purposes, I would like to offer another model, or paradigm, for understanding Christian life: the expanding circle. The image envisions each one of us as living in a tight circle composed of ourselves in relation to our defining significant others (spouses, children, family members, intimate friends); that circle, in turn, expands as we mature to take in others who touch us as members of the human community: our workplace, our involvement in our neighborhood and town, our church and civic communities, and so on. These communities (intimate and larger) live in some kind of symbiotic relationship at an ideal level; they become destructive only when part of the wider circle intrudes on the more intimate circle: it is just as bad to become obsessed with local athletics or even local church to the detriment of family responsibilities as it is to make work and career all consuming. In this model we can adopt the ecological slogan of "acting locally and thinking globally" as a rule of thumb for life.

Maturity should ideally bring with it an expanding circle; that is to say, that our circle should become more "catholic" (i.e., universal) in the etymological sense of the term. In that sense, a person who enters into the Christian way of life with all the specificity discussed above becomes more Christian and more Catholic to the degree that such a person can hold on to a core identity while, at the same time, enlarging his or her life by linking the ordinary round of living with a greater sense of human solidarity. In the concrete this desired maturity means that a person is not indifferent to the ways in which he or she has a fundamental human link with every other person in the world and knows, further, that a person's ways of acting and being have consequences for others. Business people, above all others, are (or should be) cognizant of that fundamental fact about the human race.

In the concrete, a lived Christianity should sharpen three areas of our life: our perceptions, our motivations, and our identity.[10]

Our perceptions pertain, at a fundamental level, to what we turn our attention. A lived Christianity ought to be a filter and criterion that help us make sense of what we wish to direct our attention toward as concrete human beings who possess a concrete, lived situation. One other way of thinking about perception is to ask to where we should direct our most precious energies.

Our motivations (motivations are very close to what at one time was called in Catholic piety "an examination of conscience") do not judge our drives and needs; motivation coupled with perception asks us, more deeply, to inquire into the expended energies that lead us to do this or to avoid that. If we are achievement- or success-driven, then we need to inquire to what end and for what purpose. The molding we receive in a religious tradition helps us to sort out these questions by providing us with a large moral calculus to judge negatively (I am driven by greed, power, and so on) and affirmatively (I am driven to be a good bread winner, to help society through my labors, to develop a sense of self-worth, and so on). It is worthwhile to remember that almost all the negative answers deeply implicate the self at the expense of others, whereas those that are good, almost of necessity, implicate the good of others. Not without reason did the old doctors of the church describe the sinner as *incurvatus in se*—"turned in on the self."

Finally, identity. Identity, in this particular context means simply that we are shaped, almost defined, by how we look out at the world (perception) and what drives our lives, and, consequently, our activities (motivation) determine to a large extent who we are.

Let us here stipulate (but not make the argument) that a religious tradition, like the Christian faith, has both resources and means to shape perception and motivation; in so doing, it also shapes identities. This shaping of identity might come in a flash for a person who has a deep conversion experience, but most of us will find that shaping force in our lives only through a long, sometimes tedious, attempt to be faithful to what Christ teaches us and how his favor changes our lives.

Some Modest Conclusions

If this paper has anything like a polemical or argumentative thesis, it is that much writing in the area of spirituality and business—or, at least, the writing I have managed to examine—is reductionistic and instrumental in the sense that its exponents offer advice, disciplines, strategies, and resources to make one a better businessperson—or, to borrow what is now almost a cant phrase, a "highly effective person." There is not, of course, any reason why one would not wish to become effective or content in one's occupation or capable of struggling against the ennui and duplicity so brilliantly described in the comic strip *Dilbert*, but such spiritual strategies limit themselves to the a priori condition of being a corporate person (academics are not excluded from this category). It is in that sense that such spiritualities are instrumental: they intend to aid in overcoming whatever holds one back from being a good corporate citizen.

Such strategies are also reductionistic since the good they hope to achieve is conditioned by the demands that arise from the de facto situation in which a person sees improvement not in terms of life, but in terms of occupation. To say that those spiritualities (I have in mind everything from Chopra to Covey) are reductionistic or instrumental is not to damn or condemn them. They serve, after all, certain therapeutic ends that are goods in themselves. It is only to say that they are partial. What religious faith does is to provide a larger frame within which to see how one lives in the business or academic worlds; that is, religious faith, understood as a way of life, is more holistic.

This holistic way of life manifests itself in the following fashion:

1. It provides a total framework in which the human life span from birth to death can be celebrated as well as elaborated with meaning. The very language of Christian sacramentality also undergirds the conviction that the individual has intrinsic merit and worth such that he or she need not—cannot—be sacrificed for some abstract greater goal.
2. It gives a large frame within which one seeks and finds meaning prior to particular decisions about occupation, life changes, ways of living, and so on. In other words, there is an interior lens through which one views the actual acting out of one's life.
3. It should ideally provide a widening sense of linkage and obligation to others so that both personal and social decisions carry within them an ethical calculus. Such ethical or moral criteria, as a consequence, act as a brake for those kinds of actions that would be detrimental to others.
4. It provides us with a prophetic grammar for those times when it may well be imperative to resist a course of action with an explicit no and, at the same time also supplies the vocabulary to assert the reasons for that no. Such a grammar provides deep resources for those (rare) oc-

casions when one must draw a line in the sand and resist someone or
something that is destructive or immoral.

5. Finally, the way of life that we call Christian is expansive enough to
    make us realize that being a person of faith is far more than being
    only an "ethical" or "moral" person. Saint Augustine was once imper-
    tinent enough to stipulate: "Love God and do what you please," be-
    cause of his deep conviction that those imbued with the love of God
    and love of neighbor would instinctively do the right thing.

A person who embraces the Christian way of life is, of necessity, a
public person. One cannot relegate the role of faith to the personal cultivation of piety. Christian faith is, in essence, outward-looking and embracing. The orientation of the Catholic Church has been increasingly
occupied with finding ways in which people of faith can learn ways of
cooperating with all others for the betterment of our world. This cooperation is not seen as only a form of social amelioration, but as a bringing
into being what Jesus called the "reign of God." Nearly forty years ago,
dimly realizing how modern media, changing patterns of travel, and a
greater global awareness were radically remaking culture, the assembled
bishops wrote this at the Second Vatican Council:

> At the present time, when the means of communication have grown
> more rapid, the distances between people have become overcome in
> a sense, and the inhabitants of the whole world have become like
> members of a single family, these actions and works [of charity and
> social justice] have grown more urgent and extensive. Those chari-
> table enterprises can and should reach out to absolutely every person
> and every need. Wherever there are persons in need of food and
> drink, clothing, housing, medicine, employment, education; wher-
> ever people lack the facilities for living a truly human life or are tor-
> mented by hardship or poor health, or suffer exile or imprisonment,
> there Christian charity should seek them out and find them, console
> them with eager care, and relieve them with the gift of help. This ob-
> ligation is imposed above all upon every prosperous person and
> nation.[11]

It should be clear that not every person is called upon to aid directly
those who are in need as they are described in the above paragraph. The

mind of the fathers of the council, though, was to insist that all Christians had an obligation, commensurate with their state in life, to advance the reign of God—and the most significant way of doing that is to respond to those who have needs.

To be a person of faith in the world of business (or in any world—journalism, academe, sports, and so on) demands an alertness, first, to who one is and, second, how one stands in relationship to others—and all this under the gaze of God. Religious faith, in that sense, is a kind of spiritual alertness, an alertness fed by the exercises of faith and sharpened by practice. No writer that I know of in the modern world wrote more beautifully of that kind of religious attention than the French mystic Simone Weil. At the conclusion of an essay that she wrote on the relationship of school studies and the love of God she wrote some words that can serve as a coda to this essay:

> The love of our neighbor in all its fullness simply means being able to say to him: "What are you going through?" It is a recognition that the sufferer exists, not only as a unit in a collection or a specimen from a social category label "unfortunate" but as a person, exactly like us, who was one day stamped with a special mark of affliction. For this reason it is enough, but it is indispensable, to know how to look at him in a certain way. The way of looking is first of all attentive. The soul empties itself of all its own contents to receive into itself the being it is looking at, just as he is, in all his truth.
>
> Only the one who is capable of attention can do this.[12]

NOTES

1. Reported by Catholic News Service, 9 January 2000. On the frequent use of this distinction in American parlance, see Wade Roof, *A Generation of Seekers* (San Francisco: Harper, 1993).

2. On the various spiritual strategies see Robert Wuthnow, *After Heaven: Spirituality in America since the 1950s* (Berkeley: University of California, 1998).

3. James Atlas, "Cashing Out Young," *Vanity Fair*, December 1999, 214 ff. For a review of writing on this culture see James Fellows, "Billion Dollar Babies," *New York Review of Books*, 16 December 1999: 9 ff.

4. Atlas, "Cashing Out Young," 228.

5. Ernest Kurtz, *A.A.: The Story*, rev. ed. (San Francisco: Harper, 1988) is the standard history of the movement.

6. Lawrence S. Cunningham and Keith Egan, *Christian Spirituality: Themes from the Tradition* (New York: Paulist, 1995), 9–14, provides further details. Also see Gustavo Gutierrez, *We Drink from Our Own Wells* (Maryknoll, N.Y.: Orbis, 1982), 79–83, for further details.

7. I simplify here a complex evolution of the word; for details see G. Bromiley, ed., *The Theological Dictionary of the New Testament* (Grand Rapids, Mich.: Eerdmans, 1985), 636 ff.

8. Francis de Sales, *Introduction to the Devout Life*, trans. Michael Day (London: Burns and Oates, 1956), 13–14. Devotion is a technical term in Francis de Sales; it means spiritual alertness and promptness, which enable us to cooperate with the charity God gives us to love him and neighbor.

9. For a handy survey of such models see Richard Byrne's article "Journey: Growth and Development in Spiritual Life" in *The New Dictionary of Catholic Spirituality*, ed. Michael Downey (Collegeville, Minn.: Liturgical Press, 1993), 565–75.

10. I borrow here from William Spohn's essay "Spirituality and Ethics," *Theological Studies* 58 (1997): 109–23.

11. *Decree on the Laity* (chapter 2, para. 8).

12. The complete essay is in Simone Weil, *Waiting for God*, trans. Emma Cruford (New York: Putnam, 1951).

PART IV

Listening to People in Business

NINE

Business Not as Usual

Reflections on Spirituality
in the Workplace

IAN I. MITROFF

The path of a Sufi is not to communicate . . . even with God; it is to communi-cate with one's deepest, inner-most self, as if one were blowing one's inner spark into a divine fire.

Hazrat Inayat Khan, *The Heart of Sufism*

Even in our own selves there are great secrets that we don't understand.

Teresa of Avila, *The Interior Castle*

Contemporary spirituality, if it is to have any effect on our lives, cannot flourish apart from the world, in cloisters, chapels, and churches, or what-ever one's religious institution may be. It has to grow and live in the market-place; it has to be a source of meaning for all of life and relate to our daily problems, our family and community, our science, our politics, our whole world as we scientifically explore and experience it today. This spirituality which we so much need as a true leaven and "bread of life" can only become a transforming agent of our world today, a true spirit to live and grow by, if it is nourished and nurtured within our secular institutions as well as within our traditional religious ones. Otherwise it will be impossible to create a world of peace and justice.

Ursula King, *The Spirit of One Earth*

All of us—whether we work or not—have good reasons to be wary of the intrusion of spirituality into the workplace. History demonstrates repeatedly that the dangers associated with broaching sensitive and personal topics in public and semipublic settings are real. Spirituality in the workplace is not to be undertaken lightly.

And yet in spite of this—maybe even, strangely, because of it—the need and the desire to express one's spirituality will not go away. There is something deep and fundamental in all of us that demands that our innermost self, our spiritual core, be recognized and nourished daily. Something cries out for the proper recognition and treatment of our entire being, especially in the particular setting where we spend the majority of our waking hours. Something in all of us resists the countless pressures to fragment our souls into a thousand disconnected pieces. We demand continuity and wholeness, for without them we cease to be human.

If the growing number of books and articles touting the benefits of spirituality without any mention of its dangers, in addition to the inevitable appearance of quick and easy how-to-do guides, is any indication, then spirituality in the workplace is fast becoming the latest management fad and gimmick. This makes its proper treatment all the more necessary.

This chapter is based on scores of personal and in-depth interviews I have conducted with practicing managers and high-level executives regarding both the benefits and the dangers of spirituality at work. It is also based on my general background research in spirituality.[1]

I believe strongly that spirituality has a legitimate role to play in the workplace. I do not believe for one moment that organizations can make world-class products or provide world-class service with employees who are emotionally abused or spiritually impoverished. I believe even more strongly that unless spirituality is done properly, it will do more harm than good. One cannot continually raise, and then dash, the hopes ("hope" is a deeply spiritual concept if ever there was one)[2] of employees with one half-hearted "management program of the month" after another without serious repercussions.

The design of jobs and organizations that provide meaning and contribute to the deepest and the fullest development of human beings is one of the most important and, sadly, still unrealized tasks of the human condition. In this regard, work is not something apart from one's spirituality, but, rather, work is an integral expression and a fundamental part of one's spirituality.

This paper comes to a radical conclusion. Even if every single member of an organization were to become spiritually advanced, this would not necessarily ensure that the entire organization would become spiritual. An organization is much more than the sum of its individual parts or members. An organization is a far more complex entity than a single individual.

If organizations as a whole are to become spiritual, then they will have to evolve new roles, job descriptions, and governing structures that will allow them to express, maintain, and develop their spirituality. For this reason, my work emphasizes the organizational aspects of spirituality.[3] This is not because the spiritual development of individuals is unimportant or unnecessary. Quite the contrary. It is because the literature on spirituality focuses almost exclusively on the development of individuals to the virtual exclusion of organizations. My work is an attempt to correct this deficiency.

A Spiritual Audit of Corporate America

For better or for worse, work is the centerpiece of most people's lives. Whether we like it or not, work is inextricably intertwined with our perpetual search for meaning. Work is an integral part of our spirituality, our search for ultimate meaning.

Today's organizations and today's jobs are in serious need of redesign. Far too many pose a serious threat to the human soul.

The invention of organizations is one of humankind's greatest achievements. Organizations are essential in passing on the hard-won knowledge from one generation to the next. Few things long-lasting can be accomplished without them. Thus, the fundamental choice is not between having or not having organizations, but rather concerns the kind of organizations we want to bring into existence and maintain. The fundamental choice is whether we will have organizations that promote human health and development or ones that promote sickness and dysfunction.

These conclusions are the direct result of the scores of interviews I have conducted with high-level managers and executives.[4] Over the past three years, I have been privileged to participate in the most incredible series of interviews and conversations with managers and executives from all kinds of for-profit organizations, not-for-profits, government, and social service agencies. The primary purpose was to ascertain what gave people meaning in their work and lives, and the relationship between them. They were also intended to explore the much more sensitive topics of spirituality and religion and their relationship to work.

The results were published in a book, A Spiritual Audit of Corporate America.[5] To my knowledge, Spiritual Audit is unlike any other book on the topic of spirituality in the workplace because no other book is based on the actual experiences and opinions of practicing managers and executives.

Because most books on spirituality are not based on data, they are perceived by most managers and executives, at least those to whom I spoke, as "superficial and sappy." Certainly everyone with whom I spoke was turned off by "the New Age sappiness and silliness" of most books. Indeed, the label "New Age" was the veritable kiss of death. It resulted in the instant and total rejection of an article or book.

One of the most important outcomes of the interviews was the finding that people desperately want the opportunity to realize *their full potential as whole human beings* both on and off the job. Second, they want to work for ethical organizations. Third, they want to do interesting work. And while making money is certainly important, at best it is a distant fourth.

First and foremost, people want to bring their full and complete selves to work, the whole person, the "complete package," so to speak. They are extremely frustrated with and tired of having to leave significant parts of themselves at home and with pretending that one can do it. Most people report that they can only bring their brains to work and not their deepest feelings and emotions, let alone their souls. But this has the direct consequence that organizations do not reap the full creativity of their employees and employees do not get the opportunity to develop themselves as whole persons. Both seriously impact the ability of organizations to compete effectively in the global economy.

People especially want to develop and to express their soul and spirit at work, the place where they spend the majority of their waking time. They are tired of being used and abused by organizations. They have had it with all the BS, buzz-words, the endless parade of stupid fads, dumb tricks, and management gimmicks that really fool no one and accomplish nothing fundamental and long-lasting.

Another important outcome was the fact that a significant majority of those with whom I spoke differentiated strongly and sharply between religion and spirituality. Religion is seen as dividing people through dogma and its emphasis on formal structure. Religion is viewed as intolerant, close-minded, and excluding all those who do not believe in a particular point of view.

Spirituality, on the other hand, is viewed as both personal and universal. It is perceived as tolerant, open-minded, and potentially including everyone.

When asked for *their* definitions of spirituality, and especially what meaning spirituality had for their lives, *everyone* had the same definition: Spirituality is not only the intense feeling of being totally integrated as a whole person, but it is the feeling of being totally connected with everything else in the universe. Spirituality is the ultimate ground, the supreme guarantor, and the fundamental basis for ultimate meaning, purpose, and responsibility in people's lives.

Everyone felt strongly that if people and organizations were spiritual and, hence, followed a "higher set of ethical principles," then they could not disown the negative impacts of their actions, particularly those that resulted in harm to the physical and social environment. One could not be spiritual if one produced dangerous or shoddy products, abused employees, disowned the bad consequences of one's products and services for the larger society, and so forth.

Perhaps the most significant finding of all was that those organizations that were perceived as "more spiritual" or "had a greater spiritual orientation" were also perceived as being significantly more profitable. They not only allowed their employees to bring more of their total selves to work, but as a result both they and their organizations were able to "develop ethically" to a much greater degree. In short, spirituality was perceived as the only true and lasting competitive advantage. The vast majority of those I interviewed felt strongly that if organizations wanted to be successful, they had no choice but to become spiritual.

Thou Shalt Make No Company Religion

If there is a single guideline that emerges from my work and that is critical in "managing" spirituality in the workplace, it is this: Do not promote religion under the guise of spirituality.

I confess that for as long as I can remember I have shared many of my respondents' views regarding religion. Lately, however, I have had second thoughts. I have come to appreciate the positive role that religion has to play. Apparently, many of my respondents do as well. At the very same time that they rejected religion as both an appropriate topic and force in the workplace, they also admitted freely that "some of the best people I know are religious. I deeply admire their values, even though I may not agree with some of their more fundamental beliefs."

Kathleen Norris's marvelous book *Amazing Grace* has had a powerful impact on changing my views of religion and apparently those of many others as well.[6] As I read and reread her loving accounts of her rediscovery of the religion she knew as a child and then abandoned as a young adult, I was constantly moved. The following is typical of the grace she received as she rediscovered and rekindled her faith:

> The temptation to simply reject what we can't handle is always there; but it means becoming stuck in a perpetual adolescence, a perpetual seeking for something, *anything* that doesn't lead us back to where we came from (Norris's italics).
>
> When I see teenagers out in public with their families, holding back, refusing to walk with Mom and Dad, ashamed to be seen as part of the family, I have to admit that I have acted that way myself, at times, with regard to my Christian inheritance. A hapless and mortally embarrassed adolescent lurked behind the sophisticated mask I wore in my twenties: Faith was something for little kids and grandmas, not me. I lived for years in a sublimely sophisticated place, the island of Manhattan, and the thought of crossing the door of any of the thousands of churches there did not occur to me. I suspect that it is only because I so blindly and crazily embraced my inheritance—leaving the literary world of New York City for a small town, the house my Mom grew up in, the church my grandmother belonged to for nearly sixty years—that I am now glad to identify myself as an ordinary Christian, one of those people who, to the astonishment of pollsters, still totter off to church on Sunday morning. It's been a lively journey. And I am the same person who departed, so long ago, and not the same at all.[7]

I remained a sophomore for many years, feeling superior to people who still needed religion, especially "organized" religion. But now that I have been a member of an ordinary church congregation for some time, a group that gathers for worship on Sunday mornings but is far less "organized" than the average cult, I have begun to wonder what people mean, exactly, when they say they have no use for "organized" religion. They may mean that they reject Christianity in an intellectual sense or resist what they perceive is the power structures of Christendom. But as it is the ordinary church congregation that most Christians dwell in and that has defined Christian experience from the beginning, I have come to suspect that when people complain about "organized" religion, what they are really saying is they can't stand other people. At least not enough to trust them to help work out a "personal" spirituality. How can they possibly trust these unknown others, people with whom they may have little in common, to help them along on their religious journey?[8]

However much I am moved by and agree with Norris's sentiments, I still believe that formal, organized religion has only a small, if any, role to play in the workplace. This is not because I am hostile toward religion, although I must admit that I was for many years, and certainly many of the executives with whom I talked were. Instead, my opposition to religion in the workplace has more to do with the fact that particular religions serve to divide people from one another. In this sense, Norris is right. We do not trust other people when it comes to their imposing their brand of religion on us, especially in the guise of spirituality. Furthermore, I believe that we should not trust others in this regard.

One of the most prominent characteristics of higher forms of spirituality is their complete transcendence of the distinctions that govern everyday life. In everyday life, we impose hard boundaries between ourselves and others, including inanimate objects. In fact, the "self-object" distinction is one of the most important and fundamental of all human experiences. We largely define who and what we are in contrast and in opposition to who others are and to other objects. In other words, the fact that "I am I" is because "I am *not* you" or "I am *not* a tree." However, in higher forms and states of spirituality, all distinctions, all dichotomies, all boundaries, all dualities, all either-ors vanish entirely.[9] The dominant feeling is one of being totally integrated and connected with the entire universe such that there are no boundaries between where one starts and where one leaves off.

For this reason, I do not think that religion will work in most workplaces, unless of course one specifically and deliberately chooses to work for an organization that is affiliated with a particular religion, say, the Mormon Church. However, this situation is far different from that of most people, who do not choose their place of employment based on its affiliation with a religion. For those who deliberately seek such an association, their choice is to be respected. But it is not to be imposed on others.

One of the severest arguments against formal religion, especially in the workplace, is that it does impose distinctions. To worship a particular form of God and in a particular way is, consciously or not, to reject others. It is for precisely this reason that the vast majority of those with whom I spoke strongly rejected any form of religion in the workplace. At the same time, they affirmed even more strongly the appropriateness of spirituality. They were genuinely seeking forms of spirituality that were not New Age, mushy, or wishy-washy.

Some of our greatest spiritual sages have held even harsher views with regard to organized religion:

> The Divine Truth is greater than any religion or creed or scripture or idea or philosophy—so you must not tie yourself to any of these things. . . . [Y]ou say that you ask only for the Truth and yet you speak like a narrow and ignorant fanatic who refuses to believe in anything but the religion in which he was born. All fanaticism is false, because it is a contradiction of the very nature of God and of Truth. Truth cannot be shut up in a single book, Bible or Veda or Koran, or in a single religion. The Divine Being is eternal and universal and infinite and cannot be the sole property of the Mussulmans or of the Semitic religions only—those that happen to be in a line from the Bible and to have Jewish or Arabian prophets for their founders. Hindus and Confucians and Taoists and all others have as much right to enter into relation with God and find the Truth in their own way. All religions have some truth in them, but none has the whole truth. All are created in time and finally decline and perish. Mohammed himself never pretended that the Koran was the last message of God and there would be no other. God and Truth outlast these religions and manifest themselves anew in whatever way or form the Divine Wisdom chooses. You cannot shut up God in the limitations of your own narrow brain or dictate to the Divine Power and Consciousness how or where or through whom it shall manifest; you cannot put up your puny barriers against the design Omnipotence. These again are

simple truths, which are now being recognized all over the world. Only the childish in mind and those who vegetate in some form of the path deny them. [10]

Hazrat Inayat Khan has this to say:

> We come to the aspect of religion which is not the law or the ceremony or the divine ideal or God, but which is apart from all these four. It is something living in the soul, in the mind, and in the heart of man; its absence keeps man as dead, and its presence gives him life. If there is any religion, it is this. And what is it? The Hindus have called it *Dharma*, which has the ordinary meaning of the word "duty." But it is something much greater than what we regard as duty in our everyday life. It is life itself. When a person is thoughtful and considerate, when he feels his obligations towards his fellow man, towards his friend, towards his father or mother, or in whatever relation he may stand to others, it is something living, it is like water which gives the sense of living to the soul. It is this living soul which really makes a person alive. And the person who is not conscious of this, this tenderness, this sacredness of life, may be alive, but his soul is in the grave. One does not need to ask a man who is conscious of this what his religion or his belief is, for he is living it; life itself is his religion, and this is the true religion. The man conscious of honor, the man who has a sense of shame, a feeling of sincerity, whose sympathy and devotion are alive, that man is living, that man is religious [Khan's italics].[11]

But isn't the exclusion of religion from the workplace itself a fundamental distinction that divides people from one another? If we are totally honest, the answer to this question must be a firm "Yes!" It may be true that in the realm of higher states of spirituality one is beyond all distinctions that govern everyday life. Unfortunately, these states do not apply directly to the world in which we operate. In the world of everyday experience, the question is not whether one makes or has to make fundamental distinctions, because one must. Rather, the question is which distinctions one is willing to let govern one's life. This does not mean that higher states of spirituality have nothing to offer us regarding how we shall conduct ourselves in everyday life. While we may not be able to dispense with all distinctions entirely, this does not mean that we cannot relax and loosen them.

If any religion is to be tolerated in the workplace, it is a "universal religion," one that we are far from realizing.[12] And yet, it is precisely the idea of a universal religion that is synonymous with spirituality.

A Tentative, Working Definition of Spirituality

I want to close this paper with a tentative, working definition of spirituality.

When those whom I interviewed were asked, "What meaning does spirituality have for you?", certain ideas emerged repeatedly.

- Spirituality is highly individual and intensely personal. You don't have to be religious in order to be spiritual.
- Spirituality is the basic belief that there is a Supreme Power, a Being, a Force, whatever you call it, that governs the entire universe. There is a purpose for everything and everyone.
- Everything is interconnected with everything else. Everything affects and is affected by everything else.
- Spirituality is the feeling of this interconnectedness. Spirituality is being in touch with it.
- Spirituality is also the feeling that no matter how bad things get, they will always work out somehow. There is a guiding plan that governs all lives.
- We are put here to do well. One must strive to supply products and services that serve all of humankind.
- Spirituality is inextricably connected with caring, hope, kindness, love, and optimism. Spirituality is the faith in the existence of these things.

When the views of the respondents were analyzed in more detail, the following, more complete definition emerged:

Spirituality is not formal, structured, or organized.
In contrast to conventional religion, spirituality is not formal or organized. Organizations and formal structures are not critical ingredients of

spirituality. Although spirituality is often associated with a particular religion and hence realized through its rituals and dogmas, it is not inherently part of any formal, organized religion.

Spirituality is not denominational. It is both above and beyond denominations.
Spirituality is not denominational. It is not even interdenominational. If anything, it is profoundly nondenominational. Thus, spirituality is not Christian, Hindu, Jewish, Muslim, or any other particular faith. At the same time, however, spirituality *is* Christian, Hindu, Jewish, and Muslim in the sense that these are all historically important ways in which it has been experienced and celebrated.

Spirituality is broadly inclusive. It embraces everyone.
Spirituality is universal and nonproselytizing in the sense that it does not promote a particular way of being spiritual. It is inclusive in the best possible sense of the term. It embraces everyone no matter what their age, beliefs, creed, gender, race, religion, or sexual orientation. Furthermore, it does not attempt to convert everyone to a single way of believing or celebrating his or her spirituality. The essence of spirituality is the embrace of all ways of experiencing and practicing it without condemning or endorsing a particular way. Nonetheless, a clear preference is expressed toward the universal way of expressing and practicing spirituality.

Spirituality is universal and timeless.
Spirituality is both more general and universal than particular, individual values, which vary with place and time. In this sense, it is neither relative nor absolute. It is not relative in the sense that it is a general yearning on the part of most people. Furthermore, there is strong agreement between the most diverse people as to its meaning. On the other hand, it is not absolute, in the sense that there is not one—and only one—final meaning of the term. At the same time, it is an integral part of the universe. It was there prior to and subsequent to its creation.

Spirituality is the ultimate source and provider of meaning and purpose in our lives.
Spirituality satisfies a deep hunger and yearning in all of us for meaning and purpose in our lives. This is reinforced by the notion that the universe

itself is not meaningless. It is not devoid of purpose. There is a Supreme Being who is the source of all life, existence, meaning, and purpose.

Spirituality expresses the awe we feel in the presence of the Transcendent.
Spirituality recognizes the awe and the mystery that are at the core of the universe and life itself. It asserts that there is a transcendent power that is responsible for the creation and the care of the universe. Spirituality also asserts that this power, whatever it is, is beyond full human comprehension. Hence, the awe and the reverence toward all creation.

Spirituality is the sacredness of everything, the ordinariness of everyday life.
The concept of sacredness is a fundamental part of spirituality. The sacred is not only found in the starry heavens above us, but it is also present in the everyday, so-called ordinary things of life. From this perspective, everything is sacred.[13] Thus, God, or a higher power, is also imminent in the world. In other words, God is not only transcendent but everywhere present as well.

Spirituality is the deep feeling of the interconnectedness of everything.
Spirituality also expresses the fundamental belief that everything is interconnected. Everything is not only related to and affected by everything else, but, more importantly, everything is part of everything else. The universe is seamless. While our everyday lives may be compartmentalized and fragmented, the universe is not. The universe is calling out for us to undo the fragmentation and compartmentalization of our daily lives. To be spiritual is to examine the connections between one's products and services and the impacts they have on the broader environment. This recognition of interconnectedness constantly forces one to expand one's vision.

Spirituality is inner peace and calm.
Spirituality is integrally connected to inner peace and calm. One attains this inner peace and calmness by being related to the world, not separate from it. One attains peace and calmness by doing well.

Spirituality provides one with an inexhaustible source of faith and will power.
Spirituality gives one the power and the will to persist in the face of seemingly hopeless and insurmountable odds. It provides the strength to

carry on the good fight for righteous causes. It allows one to persevere no matter what. It provides an abiding sense of hope and optimism.

Definitions are always important. They are especially so when we are dealing with complex and controversial matters. At their best, definitions help us to clarify the crucial differences between acceptable and unacceptable behavior. Definitions thus help to ensure that we do not cross over the line into dangerous and forbidden territory.

However, while definitions are important, they are not a total substitute for the immense feelings and tremendous passions that are essential parts of spirituality. Definitions are too cold, too abstract, too unfeeling to do proper justice to what they are trying to elucidate. For this reason, my work has attempted to integrate reason and passion.

Finally, it is also important to understand that inappropriate forms of spirituality constitute a far greater threat than religion per se. The greatest threats arise from extreme positions—in effect, quasi-religious views—masquerading as spirituality. The following is as strong and vivid an example of personal deity worship as one could ever hope to find:

> Gurudev Nityananda was the idol of my adoration, the object of my saguna worship, my saguna meditation, and my saguna devotion. Nityananda was my saguna deity. I worshipped him as Sita and Rama, Radha and Krishna, Paravati, and Shiva, Guru Dattareya. I saw all these gods as Nityananda. I had no thoughts for any other deities. . . . I believed that all gods were contained in my Guru. I firmly believed that to worship the Guru was to worship all deities, that to meditate on the Guru was to meditate on all deities, and that to repeat the Guru's name was to repeat the seventy million mantras. I had earlier visited sixty great saints . . . and I had heard the same thing from all of them: "There is no higher path than that of meditation on, obedience and service to, the Guru!" . . . I had frequently heard that to lose oneself in the Guru was the best path of all. . . . I meditated on Nityananda; I sang of him; I repeated the mantra he gave. After he had bathed in the spring, I drank the water as holy water. No one was allowed to go into his kitchen in the afternoon. Even if you begged for his leftover food, you couldn't get any. I found out where his cooks . . . through the leavings when they washed the dishes, and would secretly go and take a few pieces of food . . . my mind was filled with joy to be able to eat some of Gurudev's leftover

food. I would rub on my body particles of dust from where he had sat. Sometimes I was given the opportunity to massage his body or his feet. While doing all these things, my saguna worship, my saguna devotion, and my saguna meditation grew deeper everyday. I never felt hatred towards my Guru, never found fault with him, never argued with other people about him, and never listened to any criticism about him. So my identification with him increased, my faith deepened, and my devotion became stronger and stronger.[14]

Shun all religion masquerading as spirituality. And shun all spirituality masquerading as religion.

NOTES

1. See Ian I. Mitroff and Elizabeth A. Denton, *A Spiritual Audit of Corporate America: A Hard Look at Spirituality, Religion, and Values in the Workplace* (San Francisco: Jossey-Bass Publishers, 1999).

2. Donald Capps, *Agents of Hope: A Pastoral Psychology* (Minneapolis, Minn.: Fortress Press, 1995).

3. Mitroff and Denton, *Spiritual Audit*, 61 ff.

4. Ibid., 31 ff.

5. Ibid.

6. Kathleen Norris, *Amazing Grace: A Vocabulary of Faith* (New York: Riverhead Books, 1998).

7. Ibid., 25.

8. Ibid., 258–59.

9. Ken Wilber, *No Boundary: Eastern and Western Approaches to Personal Growth* (Boston: Shambhala Publications, 1985).

10. Sri Aurobindo, *The Integral Yoga: Sri Aurobindo's Teaching and Method of Practice* (Twin Lakes, Wis.: Lotus Light Publications, 1993), 352–53.

11. Hazrat Inayat Khan, *The Heart of Sufism: The Essential Writings of Hazrat Inayat Khan* (Boston: Shambhala Publications, 1999), 52–53.

12. James W. Fowler, *Stages of Faith: The Psychology of Human Development and the Quest for Meaning* (San Francisco: HarperCollins, 1995).

13. For one of the most powerful expositions on this point, see the marvelous book by Lynda Sexson, *Ordinarily Sacred* (Charlottesville: University of Virginia, 1992).

14. Swami Muktananda, *Play of Consciousness: A Spiritual Autobiography* (Siddha Yoga Publication, 1971), 59–60.

A Response to Ian Mitroff

Some Reflections of
a Business Leader

JOHN T. RYAN III

I would like to challenge some comments of the respondents that Ian Mitroff interviewed concerning religion and modern life. I sense that they have an archaic image of what religion is. They give a false dichotomy between religion and spirituality when, in fact, many of the positive aspects that they attribute to spirituality fit right in with mainstream Christian belief.

I see a straw man in the image of religion that is presented by his respondents that somewhat reminds me of Father Theodore Hesburgh's definition of an atheist as someone who has rejected his or her five-year-old's view of God. The religious believer also moves beyond this concept but substitutes an adult view of God as something he or she can positively support.

The terms "dogma" and "dogmatic" are used by his respondents in a fairly universally negative way when, in fact, dogma and dogmatic are not intrinsically negative, nor are they positive, characteristics or concepts. The word dogma is actually defined as a belief, opinion, or way of thinking—a neutral concept. There are useful dogmas and dysfunctional dogmas. Additionally, who are the most dogmatic (in the negative sense) types in today's Western world? Are they mainstream Christians? Or are they politically correct, elite college professors and activists? Or are they overly committed environmentalists or Wall Street figures whose dogma glorifies profit maximization even at all costs? I agree with some aspects of all the above repositories of dogmatic concepts such as responsible environmental stewardship, but I would say in the negative sense of dogmatism that the latter three groups are far more intense in dogmatic thinking and in promulgating their dogmas and putting them into action than are the mainstream Christians in today's world. I think and I have observed that it is easier to challenge and discuss and receive a reasonable hearing, if not agreement by challenging key Christian beliefs at a university such as this than it is to challenge the canons of political correctness at an Ivy League university.

I agree with the position of both previous authors that there should not be an official workplace religion. As Ecclesiastes tells us, "There is a time and place for everything under the sun." As in the separation of church and state, things work better for both sides if corporate policies and personal religious beliefs are separate. However, a corporate culture in the workplace is positive when it is supportive and nurturing of the religious beliefs and practices and other values of its associates and when the company develops within its corporate culture a common ethic in which all sorts of religious and ethical beliefs can coexist. I see that many companies are, in contrast, not supportive of religious and personal values by their demands on and time scheduling of their people. As an example, Robert Crandall, a previous CEO of American Airlines, used to make a point of scheduling his business meetings for a very early hour of Sunday morning and then having them run all day. I find myself having to ensure, with meetings at my own company and trade associations, that we are not getting in the way of our people's worship. As an example, we had a business meeting on a Friday that was attended by our international general managers, including a gentleman originally from Egypt and working in the Arabian Gulf area who is a very observant Moslem. Word got to me that the scheduling of our closing lunch was conflicting with his desire to go to the mosque on a Friday afternoon. So I chatted with him and noted that when you receive invitations for simultaneous functions from two different people, you generally accept the invitation of the more important person. I went on to say that it appeared he had invitations from me and from Allah that were conflicting. There should be no doubt in either of our minds who was the more important inviter, so we would give him a chance to present his questions for discussions earlier so that he could leave in time for his religious service. My colleague was appreciative.

Furthermore, I think that organizations can develop a workplace ethic that goes beyond minimalist feelings and the desire to focus strictly on the avoidance of legal problems as is often seen in general discussions and as noted by one of Mitroff's respondents.

It seems to me that there is a general consensus on workplace ethical issues by reflective Christians, Jews, Moslems, and others on goals from a religious point of view. There can be considerable differences on practical applications of principle among people, but generally I find that differing personal points of view, rather than differences in religion, are the basis of variations in these issues.

I would like to comment further on an element of Mr. Mitroff's presentation. It was noted that "people desperately want the opportunity to realize their full potential as human beings, on and off the job," and that "today's organizations and today's jobs are in serious need of redesign. Far too many pose a serious threat to the human soul." (The soul, I might add, is threatened both in the secular and sometimes in the religious meaning of the concept.)

I fully agree with his statements and am equally concerned about these issues. However, based on my observations, I regret to conclude that the trend in a majority of businesses, particularly those driven by the bottom line—either by Wall Street or highly ambitious entrepreneurs—goes decidedly in the opposite direction from that which Mr. Mitroff and I desire. The concept of concern for the stakeholders and for medium- to long-term results, as contrasted with exclusively the interests of the stockholders, has been pretty much rejected in public American businesses with the exceptions of certain corporations, often those with family ties or those that are highly prosperous. I think that in our society we are retreating on work-life balance issues and the difficulties are becoming even greater, at least in terms of the ethos of most businesses and how most of them treat their employees. Yes, there are exceptions to that trend. Concern for the individual associates' personal lives and the working conditions is being modified in a positive way in a limited number of cases involving skilled people in those businesses that are having difficulty retaining such skilled people. There are also contrary examples to the trend within companies on microissues, such as the increased respect given to self-directed work teams and empowerment of associates. But my observation is that the overall trend seems to be clearly going against the goals of enhancing human potential in any area where there is conflict with job demands. I do not disagree with the basic business premise that organizations must make a solid profit and provide attractive returns to the shareholders. As a famous hospital leader, who is a nun, says, "No margins; no mission." I also know that economic growth, particularly the strong growth we have had in recent decades, is, as Shumpeter tells us, the process of "creative destruction" where much is destroyed in the process of growth of the entire economy.

However, I am concerned and would like to paraphrase the saying of a famous American that "extremism in the pursuit of virtue can become a vice." An unmitigated focus on the bottom line and on the quick buck creates improper demands on people's time, on their priorities in life, and sometimes on their ethics and can require a total commitment of all of their energy to the organization. There is a silly phrase that I heard some years ago in business circles concerning the sources of a bacon-and-eggs breakfast. It was said that the hen is a contributor to the breakfast, whereas the pig is totally committed. This was often done to praise the pig who, I think, if it had any realization of and choice in the matter, would be rather stupid. The hen is the one who cleverly deals with human breakfast needs and, in the long term, contributes to many breakfasts, whereas the pig contributes to only one.

Also, there is a predilection today for risky ventures and for regarding persons who are producing big money for the bottom line as heroes, regardless of how they do it. Good examples of how such ventures can go bad are Westinghouse Electric, which was ruined by excessive risks, and the infamous Mr. Leeson, working in Singapore, who destroyed Barings Bank.

On the subject of the disturbing lack of ethos in today's business, there are several useful examples from recent years. There was an article by Holman Jenkins in the *Wall Street Journal* of March 5, 1996. I find this writer often infuriating but more often very useful because of the clear and unambiguous way in which he presents his positions. He said, "The movement to focus management on the stock price *and to make the sum stentorian enough to drown out the clamor of the stakeholders has become one of the defining capitalist reforms in recent memory*" (my emphasis). This writer made it clear what excessive management compensation programs are all about—massive bribes to a select few to get them to ignore their sensitive feelings about their fellow associates at work and other psychological claims to make the bottom line right now. It reminds me of what has been done through the years with high salaries of people at all levels in cigarette companies, because they have to be paid to forget what they are really doing.

If you are a successful individual at a renowned, tough company, that may not even be enough. An article in the *Wall Street Journal* of March 1997 was focused on the person who had just been made the chief executive of Pepsico's global beverage division and who had doubled domestic sales and operating profits in his previous tenure as Pepsi's U.S. beverage chief. Its headline read, "Is Craig Weatherup too nice for Pepsico's own good?" The article went on to quote a Wall Street consulting firm: "What's needed at Pepsico is some basic brutality because when you're dealing with killers, that's the only way to help you prevail. Craig is a strong man but is he a brutal man?" (I see the reference to the other company, Coca-Cola, as extreme hyperbole.) The article continued, "Mr. Weatherup made no apologies and defended his style saying that Pepsi could beat Coke without a tyrant at the top and 'it staggers me that, for whatever reason, being nice is seen as being inconsistent with being tough. If you're a visionary but you're mean, employees won't follow you.'" Weatherup continues, "The winning company with the highest stock price will be the one that has humanity. If we get to $55, and the difference between our getting from $55 to $60 (in a short period) is to lose our humanity, I wouldn't want to do that." However, at least one spokesman on Wall Street, a major Pepsico shareholder, responded in the article, "That kind of talk hardly thrills Wall Street. Shareholders would love a 9% in Pepsico stock price—*humanity or inhumanity*" (my emphasis). This sometimes, I fear, is the ethos of too many elements in the investing and management community.

We cannot make out the investment community as the total villain because, after all, in today's age of broadly based mutual funds, they are often responding to the demand of individual fund shareholders for maximum rates regardless of the consequences. In this way I'm afraid we are like the famous cartoon of Pogo, "We have met the enemy and he is us." Individual mutual-fund holders, who themselves are often quite decent and humane people, can collectively push their surrogates to do things that have contrary effects.

I once read and kept an article by a well-known Fortune 100 CEO who has a highly touted business performance reputation. In the article a reporter went around with him as he traveled to locations on some typical business days, and at one location his managers expressed their concern to him that, with all of the heavy demands placed on them, it was impossible to spend very much, let alone adequate, time with their families. The article quoted the CEO responding by saying, "This is a very good question; unfortunately, I don't have a very good answer for you."

I had the good fortune of being in the audience when the same individual made a presentation and had a question-and-answer session. I quoted that article to him and asked him if he had been misquoted and how would he respond to the question if it were made again today. His response gave the impression of sensitivity. He himself has the good fortune of having a large family, undoubtedly with tremendous effort in their upbringing on his wife's part. But, in the end, he admitted that he still didn't have a good answer and said that people had to set their own priorities and manage their own lives. While being correct, this is not in my opinion a good answer on the issue of how we as leaders of business organizations sometimes push our people to a level that can be destructive.

Another famous business leader had an article written about him in a business publication that I thought was somewhat embarrassing to him. The article reported that he had demanded that one of his executives leave a house full of relatives on Christmas afternoon to go down to the office to settle some business matter. I later learned that that article had been framed and was hanging in the CEO's office reception area.

How many executives are there still around such as the one quoted in the book *Answers from Within* by the Reverend William J. Byron? This individual was talking about his factories and how he expected them all to be productive and profitable. He noted that, relatively speaking, among all his plants, the plant in East St. Louis, Illinois (a well-known area of poverty and social problems), was not among the top echelon of his factories, but that as long as they were making a profit and carrying their weight and as long as he was CEO, he would never shut down that factory because of his concern for that troubled community. Not many in my profession in public companies could get away with this.

The human effects on people we all have seen. Once, out on the West Coast, I happened to be in a group conversation and hear the story of a friend of an old army buddy of mine. This individual was among the top five executives of a well-known corporation, an established non-Silicon-Valley company, not a new "dot-com" start-up. He told us that when he was invited by his company to enter the fast track to management, it was made clear to him that he had to commit himself to work seventy hours a week or he would be out. He noted that, when working in training courses with younger people in his company who were prospects for management positions, he had to make that issue clear to them. At the end of such sessions, some people said that they would like to opt out of such a life and preferred to remain in their present areas, and some, I would suppose, looked for advancement elsewhere.

He noted that he practically had to give up parenting at the point at which he got on the fast track that got him closer to the top of the company, and that he was fortunate that his wife took up the full burden of rearing their three children. He also said that he had become rich beyond any expectations that he ever had while growing up in a small town in Colorado and made more money than he could ever spend, yet I noted that at the age of fifty-six he was burned out. He fulfilled his commitment to his wife (and, I think, to himself) to retire from the company when he was fifty-five, and he does some interesting business things now. I suspect that he is not contributing potentially as much to society as he could have done in his former position, had he been in an environment with a less demanding pace. I also noted that he is one of the few people at my socioeconomic executive level who still smokes cigarettes.

At the end of the session, I took him aside and said, "You know, having heard your story, I thought of what I would think if I were a man from Mars who had a fairly omniscient view of things on earth and was coming down to earth for a couple of hours. What I would say is that you and your colleagues received money far beyond your expectations; you received monetary rewards for your labor in quantities well beyond what you would have been willing to settle for, but you lost a lot of life experiences and the ability to contribute to your family life. Wouldn't it be better for a company like yours to be structured in such a way that everybody would earn, say, 30 percent less and still be quite rich and yet be happier in life experience? Of course, that company would have to employ 30 percent more executives so that they could get the work done in fifty-four rather than seventy hours, but it would allow you all to have a life." Such a company would have exactly the same executive compensation load as his former company had. He responded that while this was very interesting in theory, any company who did this would be hard hit by the financial community, which closely watched the total head count and management head count against sales. The fact that people might earn less wouldn't be considered relevant, as observers would compare the ratios of the company's head count to that of their peers.

I was involved in a contrary situation with an executive, Domenic O'Meara, in a company run by someone I know well. Both his boss and the CEO noted that Domenic was working extraordinarily long hours and was in the office almost every Saturday and every Sunday. This is not to say that the other two didn't put in long hours themselves, though sometimes they worked at home to have some interaction in personal and family life.

Dom was counseled that, as he had a wife and three daughters at home at decisive points in their lives, he should try to balance the company's demands on him so that he could participate in his family life and avoid future problems. His boss talked to him about practical methods of delegating his work and using his people to get the work done so that the load was not always on him. This effort had positive results and Dom is just as effective today as he was before but is able to attend to other aspects of his life.

I wonder how many companies there are that would do such a thing and how many companies there are where the boss would portray in management meetings the "old" Domenic O'Meara as the epitome of the kind of commitment (like the pig in the bacon-and-eggs breakfast) that all the other executives should emulate.

Elsewhere I heard the poignant story of another friend, who reflected that the one place he could escape from work-related calls and demands was on the golf course because he and the other influential members had put in a rule that barred pagers and cellular phones from that golf course, and therefore it was the one place he could go where he could be sure that the demands of the workplace would not get hold of him.

In this environment, how does a concerned person escape the all-encompassing personal demands but still manage to hold down a meaningful job? One way is to keep up with currently valued high-level skills so that companies will have to offer employees reasonable compensation while letting them have a decent life. Will family-sensitive people be weeded out of our leadership positions? What will be the consequences? This reminds me of how Jewish people a few generations ago, Asian people now, and others handled matters when they were not fairly treated—they became doctors or scientists or gravitated to other skilled positions in which they would be respected.

It is undoubtedly true that, as was reported, executives said that money was number four on their compensation scale, but, unfortunately, to judge by the actions of many executives, money is de facto number one, particularly when coupled with power and glory, among those in charge and among board members. This may not be so bad if it is a matter of individuals within a few organizations, but when this ethos is demanded of a large number of people, many of whom do not share in the extraordinary remuneration of executives, it has a huge impact on people and society. It was not just in the '70s that workaholic attitudes to get ahead were required at some selected organizations like ITT; today it is the general ethos of almost everyone.

I agree that "even if all people in an organization were spiritual, this would not make the organization spiritual." But even if an organization is now spiritual, one CEO, a few board members, or one senior executive can thoroughly change, in a probably irreversible manner, the ethos of an organization. As an example, note what Mark Willis of the *Los Angeles Times* did to the journalism ethic at his paper. How often do we see the words "relentless" or "hypercompetition" in the business press. Things that used to be vices have been turned into virtues.

Space does not allow me to talk about excessive management compensation, but greed is still a moral and secular evil. I think it is only the definition that is changing, and the line defining morally offensive greed is a matter that is hard to pinpoint. I reflect on the definition that Justice Potter Stewart put on pornography, "I can't define it but I know it when I see it."

To put things into perspective, I am not a "liberal." I consider myself a conservative Republican and generally vote that way. My most enjoyable presidential votes were my two votes for Ronald Reagan, though the most meaningful vote I ever cast was the opportunity to vote against Lyndon Johnson. My comments were prompted by the observation that I hear very few people in the business community or even the business-related academic community talk about the issues of people and how our activities as business leaders affect people's lives.

TEN

Can Religion
and Business Connect?

JOHN CARON

The subject of this book, "business, religion, and spirituality," challenges concerned Christians who work in business. In this chapter I want to tell the story of two groups that were formed by business executives to connect their religious values with their business lives. I want to explore some of the obstacles that hinder making this connection between religion and business and suggest ways in which these obstacles can be overcome.

The National Conference of Christian Employers and Managers

The National Conference of Christian Employers and Managers (NCCEM, pronounced Nacsem) was the first group with which I was involved. NCCEM, was founded in 1959, as stated in its brochure, "by a small group of Catholic businessmen who shared a common desire to relate their Christian convictions to their everyday business life." Originally the organization was called Catholic Employers and Managers, but in 1964 "Catholic" was changed to "Christian."

NCCEM was started in Chicago by several businessmen who had been involved with the Christian Family Movement (CFM). The CFM had developed an inquiry process of Observe, Judge, and Act and NCCEM adopted that process. The group observed a business situation, judged what was good or bad about it, and then decided what could be done to change the situation. A process book was developed, as well as special programs based upon topical issues. A chaplain played an important role in the group. These meetings took place in Vatican II days when social action was surging throughout the Catholic Church and priests wanted to be involved with the laity.

The first-year process book laid out materials for twelve meetings and set up meetings in which principles were articulated and then applied to a case study. After the first year, program extras were provided, often based on an article in a business magazine or on a book, such as *The Man in the Grey Flannel Suit*. The approach was still Observe, Judge, and Act. The groups studied the facts about a problem, discussed the ethical issues to be explored, and considered approaches to resolve the problem. Topics included: Business Gift Practices, Poverty and the Businessman's Responsibility, Middle Manager's Dilemmas, How to Resolve the Conflict between Family and Business, Mergers, Automation, and Seniority issues.

In addition to the group in Chicago, groups were started in St. Paul, Detroit, and Rockford, Ilinois. Groups did exist in other cities, but they were short-lived.

At the same time, the Catholic Employers movement was strong in Europe and Latin America. Father Joseph Gremillion, who taught at the University of Notre Dame, wrote a book on this movement, the Union Internationale des Associations Patronales Catholiques (UNIAPAC). UNIAPAC was a must-join for many Catholic businessmen, especially in France, Italy, Belgium, and Holland. Several attempts were made by UNIAPAC to persuade NCCEM to affiliate, but they were unsuccessful. The elite of U.S. business did not join NCCEM the way the European and Latin American business leaders joined UNIAPAC. UNIAPAC tended to be more political and denominational, and their discussions were often quite political, which did not appeal to most U.S. businessmen. Also, in the United States, Catholics had often felt discriminated against in business, and Catholic business people were somewhat reluctant to be identified as Catholic. They wanted to be part of the establishment.

NCCEM functioned during the sixties and then faded away during the seventies. Why did it not succeed over the long run? The principles against which situations were evaluated were built upon the papal encyclicals, that is, "The Pope says." This voice of authority gradually lost its impact. The enthusiasm of Vatican II was followed by disillusionment, and the day of emphasis on social action was over.

The Woodstock Business Conference

The Woodstock Business Conference was the second business-Christian group with which I became involved. Springing from dialogues with businessmen that were instigated by the Woodstock Theological Institute at Georgetown University, the Woodstock Business Conference participants wanted to affirm the relevance of religious faith to business practice. Woodstock began, for me, with a series of dinner meetings in New York with a speaker. The list of invitees was impressive and the turnout was respectable, but the subject matter didn't catch on.

A small group that had participated in these dinner meetings expanded the concept and started the Woodstock Business Vocation Conference. It was well funded for three years with a Chicago-based, full-time executive director with a CEO business background. The Woodstock board felt that since this was a business conference, business people should run it with little input from the clergy. A series of annual conferences was held with good attendance, but there was no fervor and little carry-over into one's own business.

Father James Connor, S.J., finally took the initiative and in 1992 launched a business discussion group in Washington, D.C., using the Jesuit process of evaluation, which is similar to NCCEM's Observe, Judge, and Act, but with more detail. The word vocation was dropped from the title, and the organization is currently known as the Woodstock Business Conference. The Chicago office was closed, and a new executive director was relocated to the Woodstock Theological Center at Georgetown. A new understanding arose of the importance of small groups and peer interactions, with an emphasis on a discussion process that stimulated thought and led to action.

The mission of the Woodstock Business Conference is threefold: (1) to assist the individual to integrate faith, family, and professional life, (2) to help the leadership of the firm to develop a corporate culture consistent with Judeo-Christian values, and (3) to aid business leaders and corporations to exercise a beneficial influence on society at large. First the individual, next the company, and eventually society itself.

The membership of the first Woodstock group, built on people interested in Georgetown University, was prestigious, and the participation was good. Participants were interacting with peers and addressing the issues that were of concern to them.

The process involved first observing the data, including not only the event that was under discussion but also the surrounding circumstances, the people, the relationships, and the communities involved, as well as the underlying desires and motivations of the participants. Different perspectives were brought into the conversation. When an understanding of the issue was attained, then a judgment was made. Is what is happening good? The final step was deliberation, discernment, and decision. Responsibility called for a response with some kind of action, to avoid unethical conduct or to capitalize on an opportunity to do better.

Today a Woodstock meeting starts with the reading of a Scripture passage that sets a moral context, followed by a five-minute silent reflection, a discussion of the Scripture passage, and a presentation and discussion of a current topical issue that relates to the moral issue. A key point of the discussion is recognition of how the issue being examined affects a member's business and how it should influence the decision-making process in that business.

A first-year formation book with twelve meeting topics and a second-year moral-decision-making book with ten meeting topics have been published. Both these books are designed to present a cumulative learning process. After the first two years, individual topical materials based upon the same format of Scripture reading, silent reflection, discussion of the passage, and discussion of a topical issue are available.

As of the year 2000 the Woodstock Business Conference had chapters in sixteen cities. The Jesuit network of colleges and universities has been important in recruiting new members. Jesuit educators have reacted positively, as they want what they have preached to their students to be put into practice by their graduates.

Why have the Woodstock chapters not grown more rapidly? Two reasons stand out. First, regular attendance means a time commitment, a monthly meeting where the process is cumulative in nature. One meeting builds on another. A person can occasionally attend a prayer breakfast or listen to a dinner speaker, but one cannot occasionally attend a Woodstock chapter meeting and contribute to or get much out of the discussion.

Second, and what is perhaps more important, attending chapter meetings also implies a life-change commitment. Woodstock asks its participants to think and analyze situations and apply moral principles to his or her own business practices. Running a business is tough enough without adding the extra dimension: Is there a moral issue involved in the decision or the action? Participating in a Woodstock chapter requires a time and life commitment and is not easy, but for those persons who have persisted the experience has been rewarding and makes the connection between business and religion meaningful.

"I think what the group has done is to enable us to sharpen our sensitivity," wrote one Woodstock participant. "I think it is amazing the amount of sharing that happens," commented another. A third wrote, "What happens in business is that you are by yourself trying to integrate your faith, family and professional lives. When you walk into this room, you realize that there are many others trying to do the same thing." And still another member said, "I've been struck by this whole idea of the relationship between the organization and the individual; that I am being shaped without my even knowing it. . . . I am molded by my organization and by the market that it is in and by the whole business and the competitive environment."

I am convinced that the occasional prayer group or lectures cannot give a person that kind of insight. There must be awareness and a learning process and a peer group for the exchange of ideas.

Obstacles to the Business-Religion Connection

I have a problem with the term business ethics. That term seems to emphasize don't rather than do, indicating that an ethical person is one who doesn't break the law, who doesn't cheat. Although that is a good first step, it is not enough. What a person does proactively is more important. He or she must constantly ask, Is there a moral issue here?—a difficult task.

I will now address the obstacles that impede the connection between business and religion.

Business is amoral.
Business ethics is considered by some to be an oxymoron. Others, like Milton Friedman, claim that you do well by being a good businessperson, period.

A number of years ago I was asked by Father Oliver Williams and Professor John Houck, the then codirectors of the Notre Dame Center for

Ethics and Religious Values in Business, to speak to their class of MBA students and undergraduate students. This was a cynical group; their assumption was that the only way to be successful in business was to be unethical. They believed that those who succeeded in business were the ones who cut corners as much as they could without getting caught. They also thought that to succeed in business one had to compete by the same unsavory rules as everyone else. This still seems to be the attitude of many young people. To get along, one must go along. So, mistrust of the ethical standards of the business community presents one obstacle.

An example from the dean of the Business School at Arizona State University is his comment that students coming back from ethics courses taught by the philosophy department believed that capitalism is the tool of the devil. Capitalism is the source of all poverty. Most people are in it for the money.

Giving to charities is sufficient.
Another obstacle is to equate being a good Christian businessperson simply with giving to charities. The predecessor of the Woodstock chapter meetings was an annual two- to three-day conference with speakers addressing what it means to be a Catholic in the world of business. One of the main speakers addressed the topic by stating that giving money to charities was what it meant to be a Catholic and a businessman. This is an easy and relatively painless way out that certainly misses the point, but may be a fairly widely held view.

What does spirituality have to do with running a company?
A third obstacle is the misunderstanding of the purpose of uniting business, religion, and spirituality. For example, when a Wall Street executive was asked to join a Woodstock chapter in Connecticut, he replied, "I don't want to join a group to go running naked in the woods." I couldn't understand his reply until I later realized he thought Woodstock was similar to Robert Bly's men's movement (the name Woodstock, a memory of the sixties, probably didn't help).

Religion has been used for unethical ends.
Sometimes religion is used as a cover for unethical objectives. For a number of years a group of top-level CEOs gathered monthly for breakfast at a private club in New York for a prayer breakfast. A friend, who

was a participant, told me that God is really present at those meetings. Yet I read, shortly after we had spoken, an article in the New York Times that exposed a member of that group who had been accused of fraud in a classic Ponzi scheme involving charitable donations. He claimed he had an anonymous donor who was willing to match other people's charitable gifts. The money would be given to him, and then at a later date double the money would be contributed to the designated charity. Six- and seven-figure contributions from members of the breakfast group were involved. The group's confidence that God was present at those meetings was probably shattered.

It is all just a gimmick.
The seventieth anniversary issue of *Newsweek* carried a cover story entitled "The Growing Presence of Spirituality in Corporate America: Religion in the Workplace." The article described a shamanic healing journey in a candle-lit room thick with the haze of incense. Toward the end of the article, the reporter wrote that perhaps the largest driver of this trend was the mounting evidence that spirituality-minded programs in the workplace not only soothed the workers' psyches but also delivered improved productivity. I am uncomfortable with this type of spiritual promotion because it seems like gimmickry to me and probably to most corporate executives.

The clergy are reluctant to talk about business.
Another obstacle in connecting religion and business life may be the lack of business experience of many members of the clergy. When I was trying to establish a Woodstock chapter in my hometown, I first discussed the project with my pastor, who had just given a homily on how one's religious values must be expressed in everyday life. He explicitly mentioned business life. When I explained to him the Woodstock conference and suggested that we start a group in our parish, he replied, "I see nothing wrong with that." This was not the reply I was looking for. I had assumed he would have seen the connection between his homily and the means to make it happen.

I decided to take a townwide, ecumenical approach and invited to my house several Protestant ministers and priests from other parishes (as well as my own) and several business people. The business people said that night was the first time they had ever discussed the relevance of religion to their business lives. The clergy said they did not know how to talk with business executives. One stated that she did not even know business vocabulary. I was not successful in overcoming this gap. I also talked with our local rabbi, who referred me to a highly regarded member of his synagogue. When I talked with him about affirming the relevance of religion to business, he queried, "Whose religion?" People can be suspicious of what the word religion really means. Pope John Paul II, with his image of authoritarianism and dogmatism, doesn't ease the concerns of non-Catholics.

The bishops don't seem to understand.
The lack of comfort when dealing with business executives can extend to bishops. I once attended a meeting in Chicago of a small group of businessmen with Cardinal Bernadin, Archbishop Weakland, and Bishop Malone, who was then president of the U.S. Bishops' Conference. We spoke of the lack of understanding between business and clergy. Bishop Malone commented that he came from a blue-collar union-affiliated family. Archbishop Weakland told of going as a young boy to soup kitchens to get food for his family. Cardinal Bernadin said that the meeting was the first time he had met with businessmen to discuss the relevance of religion to business. Attitudes are often conditioned by early life experiences.

The U.S. Bishops' pastoral letter on the economy created an uproar. Some protested that bishops should stay out of business, because they knew nothing about business. When the first draft of the bishops' letter was circulated, people were asked to read it and give their reactions to their local bishop. I live in Fairfield County, which is the home of many Fortune 500 companies. I knew some CEOs who were Catholic, so I wrote to Bishop Curtiss, offering to host a dinner, at his convenience, and invite a number of executives to give him feedback on the pastoral letter. His response was that he had assigned this task to an assistant professor at Fairfield University. I was dismayed and disappointed.

Academics Dominate the Discussion.
On the anniversary of the papal encyclical *Quadragesimo Anno*, I was invited to speak at a conference at Notre Dame. I was the only business executive on the program. All the rest were academics. Even in this book, there are relatively few executives writing chapters. I fear the gap

continues and that we have not been successful in starting a meaningful dialogue on the subject of the relevance of religion to business.

Overcoming the Obstacles

The Amoral Image of Business

What drives the dynamism of our economic system is entrepreneurial individualism. This drive can be in conflict with the Catholic concept of the common good. People need balance in their lives. The demands and excitement of business can be time consuming. What about our family and the rest of the world? There is an oft-repeated saying that no one wants on his tombstone the epitaph, "I wish I had spent more time at the office." Religion can help people focus on the meaning of life and be an influence in achieving balance.

Giving to Charities

A person must spend time thinking about what it really means to be a Christian; otherwise religion is only a cultural experience on Sunday morning. The exploration takes time and commitment and interaction with peers.

Why Spirituality?

Reading Claudia McGeary's chapter on Henri Nouwen should answer this question. Everyone has a goal of happiness. Nouwen's books *Bread for the Journey* and *From Fear to Love* describe the journey. Spiritual awareness is the means to the end.

Religion Used for Unethical Ends

History is filled with charlatans. Samuel Johnson said, "Patriotism is the last refuge of a scoundrel." The same might be said of religion. Just as scoundrels wrap themselves in the flag to cover up their real interests, unethical people can use religion to disguise their real interests. Jesus said, "By their fruits you shall know them." Judge a person by what he or she does, not by what they say.

Just a Gimmick

This relates to the above paragraph. The *Newsweek* article describes using spirituality as a management tool. That is not what spirituality is about.

The Clergy's and Bishops' Lack of Comfort with Business

Business people are advisors and friends of pastors and bishops, but there seems to be a reluctance to step on each other's turf. Religion is the pastor's and bishop's domain and business belongs to the businessperson and the twain don't seem to meet.

Our parish held a men's retreat at the New York Archdiocese seminary in Yonkers. The priest who led the retreat suggested that the participants sit with the seminarians at lunch, which I did. I talked with them about the issues we had discussed that morning, such as how church attendance had dwindled, especially among young adults and among those who did not accept certain church teachings. I asked how they were being prepared to deal with these problems. Their response was, "We have the truth. They will come back." I commented that Catholic priests had poor reputations as homilists and asked how they were being prepared. The response was, "All the Protestants have is the homily. We have the sacraments." I don't see the gap between business and religion dwindling, at least with this group of seminarians.

If the clergy is reluctant to talk about the connection between business and religion, the layperson might conclude that the connection between the two is a nonissue, not relevant.

Academics Dominating the Discussion

Academics can be influential in the formation of future business leaders. Moving religion and business life to the top of the priority list should start at Catholic universities. Every course or research project that deals in any way with issues that could effect human beings should have a built-in decision-making process that asks if a potential moral issue is involved. This process should become second nature to a mature Christian and not remain confined to an elective course on business ethics. Even the word elective indicates that the subject matter is not required and the course can be considered of peripheral importance. A small Woodstock student group does meet at Notre Dame, but it is an extracurricular activity, somewhat like a club.

In the long run, the businessperson must be the one to confront the issue of how to connect one's religious values to one's everyday business activities. Universities can and should preach, but it is the graduate from the university who must put the principles into practice. Alumni groups should become involved in this continuing education.

Summary

I am confident that people do want to discuss this connection between their religious life and their working life, but the concept is not an easy sell. Business is an influential and essential element in our society. Jobs are created. Incomes grow. Innovations contribute to increased standards of living. The workplace is an important part of many people's lives and their community. While business can be exhilarating, creative, and challenging, it also is extremely competitive and time-consuming. The conflict with family life is a constant, and adding another dimension of considering religious values while making decisions may be too daunting. Somehow the value aspect must become second nature to the businessperson.

Business people do gather in groups where religion and spirituality are involved. However, I think that the predominant groups, prayer breakfasts and lectures, create only awareness, and that is not enough. Somehow, moral decision making must become routine in a person's business life. This process may be second nature for some people, but for most people the ability to make decisions by looking through a moral lens must be developed.

Although the obstacles are considerable—time, misunderstandings, attitudes, overriding pressures of business—what moves to the top of the priority list usually gets accomplished. The challenge is how to make the connection between religion and business a top priority.

ELEVEN

The Spirituality of Henri Nouwen

Some Case Studies

CLAUDIA MCGEARY

This chapter reports some conversations with several persons who have had significant corporate careers in the business community. The participants were familiar with the spirituality of Henri Nouwen. They also viewed two four-minute segments of Henri Nouwen's lectures at the University of Notre Dame that were recorded in the 1980s and were given selected readings from his book *Life Signs—Intimacy, Fecundity, and Ecstasy in Christian Perspective*.

The focus was on Henri Nouwen's spirituality as it relates to four central points:

1. Upward mobility versus downward mobility.
2. Productivity versus fruitfulness: How is success measured?
3. Recognizing the House of Fear and moving to the House of Love, thus leaving the static life and creating ecstasy.
4. What advice would you offer to the next generation of people entering business today in light of your experience and wisdom?

Nouwen Spirituality

Nouwen understood that spirituality is not something you do on the side. It is the heart of humanity. As members of local and global communities, we live and contribute to society in *chronos* time (our daily responsibilities), but we must find *kairos* (appreciation of the here and now) in

221

every moment. Our chronos calendars are linear indicators pressuring us to keep our time between the boundaries of the past and the future. Our kairos lives are dancing with angels, imagining what could be, creating poems, envisioning a new world order of justice and peace. By Jesus' example, we live in the point of the present moment, as a gift from God. We should forget our mistakes, reconcile with other people, other countries, and embrace healing and forgiveness. In Nouwen's words, "We would move from the House of Fear to the House of Love."

Celebrating Intimacy in Our Local and Global Environment

Nouwen was a boundary breaker. But how do we break out of our boundaries to avoid being trapped in the house of fear? Fear that pervades our family, career, community, national and global security? How do we become fear-less? How do we move to the house of love to become grounded and become the beloved?

How do we break out of these patterns and enter the ecstatic life? Nouwen said that ecstasy is the essential joy in a truly Christian spirituality. It is the constant moving away from the "static places of death toward the house of God," where an abundant spiritual life can be recognized and celebrated.

It is a struggle for a new freedom, a "new international order." We "claim the global as well as the personal dimension of the ecstatic life." We leave the static place behind and become new, resurrected in Christ.

Our challenge is how to gain the courage to take new directions, to enter the places we earlier did not dare to go, to places we couldn't have imagined or dared to dream were possible—to the house of love? How do we recognize our vocation, our calling? From where does it flow? How are we seen through the lenses of our public lives, professional lives, and private lives? How do we vote with our lives? Do we keep Christ in the closet for our private life only? Does he miss us during the busy week, like an unintentionally neglected child with working parents, wistful for more attention, but loving and forgiving nonetheless? Or do we take him to work and our daily mission or vocation as our intimate partner?

The challenge is to live a spiritual life of love, ministry, and witness to Christ in a competitive and increasingly secular and fearful world. We are soul mates in the Eucharistic life of thanksgiving and celebration, thus resurrecting ourselves to live in the moment with ecstasy and gratitude.

Upward Mobility versus Downward Mobility

In today's society we are challenged by the addictive drive for individual or group power, success, control, and compulsive competition. Jesus didn't have a job description. He preached downward mobility. We are one with each other in a community of love. He loved the poor. "Amen, I say to you, as long as you did not do it for one of these least ones, you did not do it for me" (Matthew 25:45).

The secular world preaches upward mobility. The relentless pursuit of "more" for the individual. Thus our local and global conscience is stretched taut; a bipolarization that contributes to individual and community stress and mental illness. Some say we are already at the breaking point.

From our childhood we learn that to make it in this world means competition and productivity, and these bring success, popularity, and social acceptance. Our self-image comes to depend on questions such as: Are we noticed? Are we appreciated? Are we rewarded? Are we smarter, stronger, faster, prettier, more popular, more successful, richer, and *sexier*?

Jesus' primary identity is the Son of God. We are the sons and daughters, disciples of Jesus Christ. What is the core of our identity, no matter what others may say? How can we practice downward mobility in spite of our upward movements? What "little steps" can we take in that direction "towards the places where God prefers to dwell"?

Productivity versus Fruitfulness. How is success measured?

Our chronos time, as lives measured by society, emphasizes the productive, not the fruitful. We pursue the material at the expense of the spiritual. Nouwen said, "Fruit is something you receive in gratitude." Young professionals spend eighty hours a week working, burning out, earning money their parents couldn't imagine, much less at that age. Older people are caught in the job squeeze and age bias, working longer hours for less without much negotiating ability, just to keep up. We are up against deadlines and the fear of not delivering on time. From working in a prestigious law firm in New York to producing designer sneakers in a sweatshop in Asia, we're up against the clock. All of this results in a fractured family and community life, pitting one group against the other, thus increasing fear and reducing love.

Productivity is repetition at least cost with consistent quality. What is my value? What is it to society, the community, the firm, the family, myself? Am I only measured in billable (productive) time? Am I measured in my ability to create (and consume) products and services? Do I measure other people in this way?

When did we cede our unique identities as human beings to being viewed as mere productive units? Have you ever heard the words, "I need a body by next Tuesday to handle the work flow"? And then you are dismissed as no longer needed. How do we reclaim our*selves* in an increasingly impersonal world?

Recognizing the House of Fear and Moving to the House of Love

Our intimate, communal, and global house of fear includes all that shapes us in inhumane ways. We are shaped, consciously or unconsciously, by the power of politics, ambition, economics, tyranny, physicality, influence, and knowledge. Vote for me! Do my work for me! Don't work for me! Help me! Listen to me! Buy me! Love me! Die for me! Sleep with me! (Paraphrased from Henri Nouwen, *From Fear to Love: Lenten Reflections on the Parable of the Prodigal Son*).

We are bombarded with impersonal electronic communications and phone solicitations. We are blocked by voice mails. Phone calls are not returned or are not returned promptly. Public cellular phone conversations pollute our peace and privacy. Impersonal rudeness seems to prevail as a daily frustration. We cannot personally communicate with our various communities. We have no time to nurture intimacy at all the levels of our relationships. We see love used as power, abuse of power and religion seemingly in the service of God. All of these, when used without balance, produce instability, dysfunctionality, fear, envy, helplessness, and communal and global mental illness, in a word—*brokenness*. How do we, Nouwen asks, *care* in kairos time, instead of seeking a chronos cure? Heal, as opposed to fix? Find God in the small places?

"On an international scale this means a foreign policy that goes far beyond the question, 'How can a nation survive?'" Nouwen says. "It would be a policy that seeks to liberate nations from their mutual fear and offers ways to celebrate our common humanity." We are engaging in a vicarious prosperity. There are people who are starving, in jail, living under tyranny, fear, and isolation. People are using power and influence abusively to keep us in place. Peace can't be fruitful if it happens out of fear. The question is how we can take personal and community responsibility to create a global spirituality, what Nouwen calls a "global ecstasy . . . people who belong to one human community."

Advice for the Next Generation
Each case study ends with the question: In light of your experience and wisdom, what advice would you offer to the next generation of people entering business today?

The Case of Loida Nicolas Lewis
(Chairman of TLC Beatrice International Holdings, Inc.)

Loida and I became friends through church. We are members of the Spiritual Life group at St. Vincent Ferrer Church in New York City. Loida exemplifies the joy of ecstatic living. If they had met, Loida and Henri Nouwen would have gone on for days discovering new ways to describe it. To know her is to understand that mountains are there simply to be moved by faith alone.

Loida Nicolas Lewis was born and educated in the Philippines. She grew up in the countryside, where her father built a successful furniture business. Her mother had a traditional upbringing. Both Loida and her sister, Imelda, who also works at TLC Holdings, were raised by the rule of "you can do anything." Instead of becoming a nun, Loida studied law to become a lawyer and planned to go into Philippine politics.

That all changed when she met Reginald Lewis during her "graduation gift" trip to New York. She soon became the devoted wife and partner of the late Reginald F. Lewis, founder of TLC Beatrice, a multibillion-dollar leveraged buyout food company with wide distribution in Europe and Asia. Reginald Lewis died of a brain tumor in January 1993, shortly after diagnosis. Loida Lewis's world and that of her two daughters, Christina and Leslie, changed almost overnight.

Loida grieved for a year and brought the extended Lewis family together through her love of the Lord. Then she saw that the company had been drifting without direction because its strong leader had died. He was the company. After prayer in December 1993, she decided to take over the company. In five years, she cut costs, reversed mounting losses into profits, sold TLC Beatrice at a profit in 1999, and paid off investors. Loida had no previous business experience, and she was not involved in TLC Beatrice prior to taking over. Loida Lewis is now moving on to a new life. She is fond of saying that she is "going where the spirit moves me."

The secret of her success in the TLC Beatrice turnaround was trusting in God completely. Loida started every board meeting with a prayer that included, "Lord, you are the true chairman and CEO of TLC Beatrice." She believes that the Lord was and is working with her in all facets of her life.

When her husband bought Beatrice Foods, the Lewis family lives changed markedly. When Loida was a wife and mother living in Paris, she found herself challenged by a world perfumed by fame, fortune, glamour, and all that comes with it. A group of women in the same precarious glamour boat formed a faith-sharing group that still communicates to this day. "We discovered the Lord," she said, "and you cannot help but be transformed."

The Paris life could have become a series of French doors opening on to twenty-four rooms filled with empty fancy chairs with signatures underneath. But Loida did not let that happen to her or her daughters. She said no, they would pray as a family and keep their faith communities.

Loida recalled St. Paul's letter to the Corinthians: "Love is patient, love is kind. It is not jealous, [love] is not pompous, it is not inflated, it is not rude, it does not seek its own interests, it is not quick-tempered, it does not brood over injury, it does not rejoice over wrongdoing but rejoices with the truth. It bears all things, believes all things, hopes all things, endures all things. Love never fails. If there are prophecies, they will be brought to nothing; if tongues, they will cease; if knowledge, it will be brought to nothing" (1 Cor. 13:4–8). As Loida says, "Love is a higher standard, God loves me in those terms. That's how I have to love, love unconditionally."

Loida Lewis began to read Henri Nouwen after her husband died, and he has become a new companion to her. She said, "Downward mobility is to remember who you are and to remember those who have less in life and in law, no matter who you are." We discussed the paradox of upward mobility versus downward mobility in the framework of power, drive, ego, control, and success. The role of chairman and leader brings many temptations. "If I did not root myself in the Lord, I would lose perspective. I might become someone else. Fame and power are seductive companions." Indeed, they are smooth dancing partners who lead you where *they* want to go, and before you know it, you're over the cliff.

Loida chose to become chairman and trusted in God completely to chart her course to avoid the entrapment of power addictions by those who were comfortable with such behavior. She made tough decisions in tough times and prayed her way through it, along with her own intuition, natural business acumen, and trusted counselors.

We discussed productivity and fruitfulness in her role as leader and provider for her employees, customers, and suppliers. "You have to bear the major responsibility for the company to be productive," Loida says. "You are running the business for your constituencies. But the employees also have to come to work with a sense of pride and satisfaction. If they are treated with respect, recognition, and remunerations, they will return it with their actions. That is fruitfulness.

"CEO is just a title. I have been given the chance to drive 'a rocketship to the stars' in a manner that reflects me. Who am I? A daughter of God, redeemed by Christ by his blood, because he loves me. What else do you need?" At various times in her life, Loida recognized the House of Fear and refused to let it be built on her land. She has created a House of Love for her various communities through "walking in the presence of the Lord in the land of the living" (Psalm 116).

Loida Lewis, paraphrasing St. Paul, has this advice for the next generation of people entering the business world: "May your roots go down deep into the soil of God's marvelous love. And may you know and understand how long, how wide, how deep and how high this love truly is and may you experience this love for yourselves."

The Case of Allerton "Jay" Cushman Jr.
(Morgan Stanley Dean Witter)

Jay Cushman's principal ministry in this fruitful and productive part of his life is St. James's Episcopal Church in New York City. Jay is a reader of Henri Nouwen and plays a major role in building servant leadership at St. James's. He is passionate about creating and nurturing a spiritual life of discipleship in Christ within the church community. For Jay, caring, compassion, and community are not buzzwords from spiritual books, nor catch phrases from Sunday sermons. They are visceral. They are gifts to share abundantly, particularly during the times when the House of Fear seems to be a city block long.

Jay remembers Henri Nouwen speaking at St. James's in the early '90s: Nouwen, with a small microphone, striding up and down the center aisle, personally addressing the people seated nearby, intent on emptying himself. "Henri was exhorting us to let God in, to create the building blocks of our relationship with God. His simplicity came from his struggle to squeeze out the heart of the truth."

When Jay retired in 1994, he became an advisory director at Morgan Stanley. With his wealth of experience, he was asked to speak one summer afternoon to the firm's new MBAs. His core message was, "If you care about being successful, you have to live a life outside the firm. This life has to be fruitful to develop your life inside the firm." Productivity is not the sole measurement of success and is certainly antithetical to spirituality. "You have to have a powerful understanding of human relationships and communicate within a larger framework to do well in your business life." As Jesus taught his twelve disciples by example to be servant leaders, a mentor-protégé relationship needs to be open to give and receive gifts from each other."

Asked what advice he would offer to the first generation of the twenty-first century's business schools graduates, he observed, "Technology reinforces our sense of power and omnipotence; it makes us think we are Godlike or close to it. That's a snare and a delusion. At best, technology is a means to an end; it doesn't put us on an equal footing with God. Concentrate on what's important. Accomplish the mission and take care of the troops. Do that and you can live in a virtuous circle, with Jesus and his disciples as your mentors."

The Case of William Saunders
(Attorney and Law Professor)

William Saunders, a former law professor at Catholic University, Washington, D.C., has served on the Family Research Council, Foreign Policy and Human Rights Counsel, and is now the executive director of Sudan Relief and Rescue, Inc., Washington, D.C.

I met Bill Saunders by inviting him to speak on Sudan at our Africa Action study group at St. James's church. I left the next day to participate in the Sudan Catholic Bishops' Conference in Nairobi, thus beginning the journey to Sudan. There is a genocide of holocaust proportions in southern Sudan. The radical Islamic-front government in Khartoum is annihilating Christians and animists for religious reasons as well as human displacement for development of oil and other natural resources. Bill Saunders dedicates more than half his time to work for religious freedom in Sudan, particularly for Bishop Macram Gassis of the El Obeid diocese in southern Sudan.

Bill has read and studied Henri Nouwen, participating in meetings with a group of people who met for a year, traveling deeper into "the return of the prodigal son." Nouwen's writings have opened spirituality for Bill as a "continuous encounter with God."

Bill's life blossomed from productivity into fruitfulness over the course of ten years as he embarked on a spiritual journey that took him deeper into Christianity through mystical experiences, retreats, and prayer. He prayed for one year to be directed by God and to reveal his will so that Bill could know what to do. He read a story written by a Protestant pastor in Sudan about the suffering and persecution of Sudanese Christians and animists. The pastor said, "We know there are Christians in the West, why won't they help us?" That was it for him. Bill spent Christmas 1998 participating in mass under a canopy of trees in the El Obeid diocese in Sudan with Bishop Gassis and over five hundred people, praying that the bombs from the Antonov planes sent by the radical Islamic front from Khartoum would miss them. They did. Everyone was full of joy to be there. The bishop, Bill, and everyone else were ready to accept death, but there was no house of fear because God was with them. Bill quoted from the Luke Beatitudes: "When men persecute you in my name . . . leap for joy."

After his Sudan experience, Bill spent two weeks in a monastery leading the contemplative life with the monks. Henri Nouwen taught him the deepness and richness of the resources we have and how we must be in constant spiritual renewal. Bill said, "Satan tries to snatch defeat from the jaws of our victory. He tries to get you so busy that you forget God. You do the right thing for the wrong reasons." Henri Nouwen teaches us to "put first things first." Bill Saunders's road that he prayed for so fervently is named "passionate action." He found his house of love in

Sudan, where others would rightfully call it a house of fear. Bill, Bishop Macram Gassis, and some of us are bringing light to one of the darkest places on earth, Sudan, by being a witness to Christ.

Conclusion

Henri Nouwen brings out the best in people, the spiritual dimension. He reflects light where some of us may have experienced darkness—in ourselves, in our jobs, and in our local and global communities. Some light is buried pretty deep, but it's there. He was a visionary who saw a broken world and said it didn't have to be broken. It's ours to heal; indeed, it's our responsibility to heal. He said it's not only OK to bring our light, our spirituality into the world, not to keep it for church and private times, but that as living, breathing disciples of Christ we must do this. Whether we live in a tribal village or a skyscraper, we are a part of God's plan in the world community.

In one of his tapes, Nouwen said, "We love one another because we love one another because we love one another." This is our spiritual survival strategy in living joyfully with our Christian, Jewish, Islamic, and Eastern religious communities as women and men of equal identity before God, honoring multicultural and racial diversities as gifts to be shared and respected.

That is Henri Nouwen's gift to us, a gift we *must* share with other people, with the confidence and grace of God that we are good.

TWELVE

Morals Adrift

Professional Ethics, Community, and Religion

BUZZ MCCOY

Modern society has tended to break areas of knowledge down into narrower and narrower specialties and to build walls around such areas of knowledge. This is certainly true in the area of professional ethics. Despite widespread efforts over recent years, business ethics remains a difficult subject to teach in most graduate schools. This is so in part because of the fragmentation of knowledge. Ethics is per se an integrative discipline. It crosses over many lines and loses the benefits of the focused attention of an established university department. This is also so because of the premium on "values-free" education. We find it difficult to criticize the actions of others. We also lack a common language in which to discuss proper or improper behavior in a nonemotional, disinterested manner.

Attempts to link business ethics with deeper philosophical or theological roots have most often failed. This is so, in part, because most business school professors are generally not familiar with philosophical and theological concepts and, in part, because business school administrators are careful not to impose values upon their students.

As a result, ethics taught in business schools tend to derive from everyday moral norms, that is, from whatever values society adopts at a particular period of time. In this perspective, there is no "right" answer. Ethics is viewed as value-free, and therefore deals only on a surface level of social relativism and utilitarianism, as against being grounded in the wisdom of the ages.

This article proposes the need for a return to the traditional grounding of ethics. It will attempt to do so without espousing a particular religious or political point of view. It will also make the suggestion that an underlying ethic is what differentiates a profession from a job.

A Brief Look at History

Only two hundred years ago, Western society was centered on God. Universities had been founded especially to teach theology. In our country, institutions such as Harvard, Yale, Princeton, Andover, and Columbia were founded with the primary purpose to train clergy. With the Enlightenment, theology was broken off from philosophy, psychology, sociology, economics, and politics. Religion became, for many, separated from inwardness and faith; thus religion became social ethics. Society became centered upon the individual human being. Reason replaced faith, and values became matters of changing tastes and preferences. The Enlightenment was supposed to "free" us from prior constraints. Human moral and religious autonomy became the foundation of our intellectual life. People forgot that "goodbye" is a contraction of "God be with you," and "adiós" a contraction of "to God." Language expresses cultural orientation. Those simple words relating to God lost their fundamental meaning as cultural orientation changed.

Freud, Tillich, and Sartre reminded us of our alienation and loneliness from self, community, and the divine presence—our lostness; but the universal search for origin and meaning, for orientation, continued.

In business education, we could say theology evolved into ethics, which itself evolved into political economy, then into economics, and finally into management "science." As we became more and more specialized, we were further removed from the source of faith and ethical action. It is interesting to note that both Adam Smith, at the beginning of the evolution of ethics, and Peter Drucker, at this point in the evolution of ethics, were both trained in theology and ethics. Now social norms have become the real religion of the times. We look to current values to integrate all the other aspects of existence, as religion once did.

The Sources of Social Norms

For purposes of this article I shall define *morals* as that behavior that society condones at a particular time (externally driven), and *ethics* as responsive behavior based upon faith (internally driven). We are each individual moral agents with great potential to do good as well as evil. The problem is that we rarely live up to our potential, and we too readily give up our moral authority to others, including the organizations where we make our living. Bad practices grow incrementally. Each small twist of the wheel goes unnoticed. People are often rewarded for behavior that reinforces bad practices instead of good practices. Entitlement replaces responsibility. We each have our own vision of organizations gone awry; and as we wonder how senior management could have condoned such bad practices, perhaps the answer is the incremental gradualism of evil where there is a lack of ethical awareness or imagination, which results in a lack of diligence.

Good organizations where bad practices are condoned, and even rewarded, develop a culture of bad morality and common ignorance. Individual ethics and good practices have been drowned out by the cultural norm of the group by being ignored. Sometimes a single individual can change the course of an organization, though he or she takes great risk in doing so. When the entire group is moving in the same direction, the one who stops can become a fixed point from which the others can regain their bearing. Vaclev Havel terms politics "the art of the impossible." I am reminded of Hannah Arendt's amazing tribute to William Shawn, the great editor of the *New Yorker*: "He had perfect moral pitch."

I have found it useful in discussing morality to attempt to frame a language by discussing types of moral systems. The following list is by no means inclusive. It is meant only to gain a primitive hold on a possible common language.

Contextual morality is that behavior which society condones as proper at a particular time. These norms may be codified as the law, but they embrace large areas of behavior not codified by the law. Cultural relativism is a current norm, as is situational ethics. There are those who would say that today's norm is that there are no rules, no easily identifiable, broad set of values to which we can all agree. It is easy to go along with the norm; but the norm can easily lead to the incremental gradualism of bad practice as well as pluralistic ignorance.

An important aspect of contextual morality is that it changes over time as people's attitudes change. Sociologists have even described long-wave rhythms of societal norms swinging back and forth between conservatism and liberalism. Thus, if we base our behavior purely on societal norms, we must be prepared to have the rug pulled out from beneath us. Somewhat arcane, but valid, illustrations of the social "morality" would include price fixing, trusts, insider trading, or nonpayment of social security taxes for part-time domestic employees. If we base our behavior on current norms, we might find ourselves behind bars twenty years into the future.

Kantian ethics, named after the famous eighteenth-century moral philosopher, has come to mean rigid universal rules or duties. Philosophers term such an ethic deontological, or duty-bound. Attributed to Kant is the categorical imperative, which says there are certain things we simply must do in order to maintain our basic humanity. As much as certain elements of our normative society are crying out for at least some rules to live by, others would say that Kant's approach is too rigid and legalistic for contemporary society.

All of us, to a certain extent, are Kantians. The trouble is, we are each Kantian about different things. For each of us there are certain things we could never allow ourselves to do. In doing them, we would lose our humanity. Yet for each of us the limits are somewhat different. This is what makes governance so difficult for any type of social structure and why, in an age of cultural relativism, we often come together at the lowest common denominator or at the worst practice.

Utilitarian morality is a branch of teleological ethics in which the "rightness" of an act is linked with the "goodness" it brings about. It stems from Jeremy Bentham and John Stuart Mill. The utilitarian norm, the greatest good for the greatest number, is a powerful shaper of our current morality. Utilitarianism drives much government policy making and economic input-output modeling. Cost-benefit analysis basically determines how our world works. We can calculate the value of a human life and enter the sum into our input-output models to determine how many kidney dialysis machines we can afford economically.

Utilitarian morals are pervasive in our society. The majority vote wins. The only real losers are the minority. The powerful issue for the majority is, Where do I stop trading off in order to win? Where do I set the limits?

Social justice morality is an antidote to the excesses of majority-rule utilitarianism. It takes care of those who lose out to the mainstream of society. The social safety net is a good example of social justice. Critics of social-justice politics brand it as single-issue politics, or the tyranny of the minority. More and more often we find ourselves in the minority on a specific issue that matters to us, and we attempt to use pressure to overthrow the majority. As we see in our daily newspapers, process overwhelms purpose. There results a loss in civility.

A recent book by David Harris, *The Last Stand*, tells the story of the conflict between Pacific Lumber and Earth First. Both groups want to save some of the redwoods in California and the Northwest. There is obviously a trade-off between preservation and economic vitality in the Pacific states. Both sides used power and tried to hurt the other side. Some people got blown up by a car bomb, and many workers lost their jobs. Few redwoods were actually saved. The process became the overriding issue. There appeared to be no underlying ethic on either side.

Communitarian ethics: More recently, the respected economist Amatai Etzioni has given a name to another moral system. In *The Moral Dimension* he describes communitarianism as relying on the individual, society, and transcendent values. For Etzioni, transcendent values can be any of the world's religions, or even a deeply rooted humanism.

To those coming from a Christian background, communitarianism resonates with the one great commandment of the New Testament: We must love our neighbors as we love ourselves (which means, implicitly, that we must first love ourselves), and we must love the Lord our God with all our heart and all our mind and all our strength and all of our soul. This commandment may be found in the Jewish and Islamic religions as well. The universality of this idea cannot be completely accidental.

The great theologian Paul Tillich discussed evil in terms of isolation, loneliness, and alienation. We must be in community with ourselves, our society, and our God. Such a theology is validated by the great psychologists.

In a recent article Peter Drucker stated that the three qualities for the leader of the future are: (1) belief in oneself (self), (2) love of people (community), and (3) passion for the job (transcendent value). Thus, once again, we encounter the three self-orienting principles of the Bible. In addition, Drucker mentions the need for emotional strength to manage anxiety and change, which is another way of saying that one must be at peace with oneself and in a trust relationship with some form of God.

The Sources of Ethics

Many of the commentators on Dante's *Divine Comedy* or T. S. Eliot's *Four Quartets* state that these great poems can be read on four different levels. The first is the literal level: What is actually going on, on the surface of things. The second is the allegorical level: How does this great poem mimic other great heroes of literature? In a business sense, this might be thought of as how the present situation resonates with the informal cultural myths and heroes. The third is the moral level, which in a business sense would include the determinants of moral behavior cited above. The last, and most profound, is the theological level, or what I have here termed "ethics" based on transcendent faith, as differentiated from cultural, contextual norms.

On this fourth level, ethics becomes a by product of religion. Religion becomes a means by which we decide what we shall value and how we shall live out our lives at the deepest and most personal level. It is a means by which we determine what is right and what is wrong and so create morality. Our understanding of who we are in relation to ourselves, our communities, and our God allows us to reconstruct models of proper conduct and principles on which to build our relationships. When such understanding begins to inform us, we might cease making moral trade-offs in a utilitarian society.

Such a point of view is not popular in our highly secular society, yet we remain informed by the Western Judeo-Christian tradition, which is deeply built into our morality. So much of our art, literature, and even normative behavior is derived from this cultural heritage. We implicitly inform and are informed by the religious culture of Western pre-Enlightenment. As it is stated in Deuteronomy: "The word is very near you, in your mouth and in your heart, that you may observe it." And Pascal wrote: "If I had not known you, I would not have found you." Indeed, as the English language and Western business practice dominate global trade and business, so do the normative Judeo-Christian beliefs that underlie that culture. The great critic George Steiner has written that every true work of art has moral, spiritual, and psychological meaning, which is to say, transcendent value.

This is by no means meant to be evangelistic. In the plurality of the modern world, one need not be a Christian to be successful or even ethical or moral. It is important, however, that those Westerners doing business (which is just about everyone, at a certain level) as well as those doing business with Westerners, become informed of the implicit ethics imbedded in Western culture. Christianity has shaped our secularism, even our atheism. To separate cultural morals from the ethics of faith, whether articulated or implied, is to leave cultural morality rootless and without foundation or constancy.

I am reminded of the German woman who joined the resisting church in the 1930s, saying: "In my father's house, we were taught morality, to respect the law, but not religion. Morality without religion does not stand up."

What Is a Christian Ethic?

If one is to take this argument seriously and admit that normative behavior must be connected somehow to the Judeo-Christian ethical mainstream, what does this mean? What is a Christian ethic?

In a profoundly simple sense, it is the communitarian ethic cited above with the replacement of the word "transcendent" with the word "God," meaning God as believed in by the Judeo-Christian faith. If one can live in harmony with oneself, all of one's various communities, and with one's God, one is in harmony ethically, spiritually, and psychologically. Of course, such consistent behavior is impossible, but it can be a goal.

In the Christian tradition, theologians have long stated that the greatest sin against God is to be ruled by one's personal ego, to make of oneself a God. We all know that the more we can relate to others and to values beyond ourselves, the greater chance there is that we will do the right thing (for example, bring out a product that people may eventually wish to purchase because it is good for them).

A sense of discipleship or stewardship, a sense of overall purpose and mission, once again, beyond the self, reaching out to the other, can point people toward success in business and draw others to them.

A decision is most likely to be ethical if it encompasses the broadest possible group of stakeholders, considers imaginative options (rather than the binary Are you for me, or are you against me?), and merges individual ego and emotion into the larger community.

We tend to diminish one another (and ourselves) by stereotyping people and reducing them to labels. The more obvious labels are "liberal" and "conservative." What we call today "conservatism" started out two hundred years ago as "liberalism" attempting to free up power from kings, bishops, popes, and despots and give it to the common man. We are each a bundle of liberalism and conservatism. As Larry Pickering points out so well in his book *Beyond Left and Right*, these labels become a convenient way of keeping us from seriously considering the issues.

Paul Tillich, in his book *The Courage to Be*, writes of the creative excitement of moral life: "Moral decisions involve moral risk. Even though a decision may be wrong and bring suffering, the creative element in every serious choice can give the courage to decide. . . . The mixture of the absolute (Kantian) and the relative (social norms) in moral decisions is what constitutes their danger and their greatness. It gives dignity and tragedy to man, creative joy and pain of failure. Therefore one should not try to escape into a willfulness without norms (anarchy) or into a security without freedom (legalism)." Thus we require both virtues and sanctions in order to operate in communities.

In our secularized world, we have trivialized sin. We confuse pride with self-esteem. Sin becomes converted to crime, then sickness, and finally to low self-esteem. Everyone's OK, everything's OK, we just have to do a little work on our self-esteem once in awhile.

Carl Jung, in his autobiography, *Memories, Dreams, Reflections*, writes that good and evil are no longer so self-evident: "One must have the freedom in some circumstance to avoid the known moral good and do what is considered to be evil, if an ethical decision so requires. As a rule, however, the individual is so unconscious that he altogether fails to see his own potential for decision. . . . Instead he is constantly looking around for external rules and regulations which can guide him in his perplexity."

Admiral James Stockdale, confined for seven years in prison in Hanoi, with three years in solitary confinement, writes in *The Principles of Leadership*:

> To handle tragedy may, indeed, be the mark of an educated man or woman, for one of the principal goals of education must be to prepare people for failure. . . . To say, "I spilled my guts because I was being tortured" is never an adequate explanation. To what degree were you incapacitated? How much information did you give? Whom else did you endanger by providing information? A disciplined life will encourage a commitment to a personal code of conduct, and from good

habits a strength of character and resolve will grow. This is the solid foundation by which good is made clear, by action and by example. A moralist can make conscious what lies unconscious among his followers. Another duty of a leader is to be a steward. This requires tending the flock—"washing their feet," as well as cracking the whip. . . . The test of our future leaders' merit may well not lie in hanging in there when the light at the end of the tunnel is expected but rather in their persistence and continued performance of duty when there is no possibility that the light will ever show up.

Stockdale goes on to suggest that ethics is living free of stated rules and having the courage and conviction that allows one to improvise.

Thus a Christian ethic embodies a sense of worldliness. A faith without community, without issues, without reality is worthless. As Dietrich Bonhoeffer, the Word War II German theologian-martyr, once said, "It is only by living completely in the world that one learns to have faith."

Application of Christian Ethics to Business

It is possible to interpret great leadership textbooks such as Drucker's *On Management* or Peters and Waterman's *In Search of Excellence* from a Christian, or a religious, point of view. There is much in these books that resonates with the Western Judeo-Christian tradition. "Management by walking around" can be interpreted as sublimation of the personal ego, attentiveness, openness, and living in community. It is not by accident that the first word of the rule of the Order of St. Benedict is: "Listen!"

Discipleship, or the notion of the servant leader, as demonstrated by Robert Greenleaf, formerly of A.T.&T. and Lilly Endowment, in his writings, can be thought of as illustrating the Christian belief in unconditional love.

Obedience and submersion of the ego to a higher cause, an all-motivating set of transcendent values, is a characteristic of the "good" enterprise. This concept is validated by *Fortune Magazine's* annual poll of the most admired companies, which invariably have superordinate goals, which are included in the vision of most of the employees.

Christian ethics has to do with having the confidence to know what to do even when the situation seems to have no allegorical meaning or

fixed reference points. One never acts out of uncertainty (lack of harmony with the self), nor does one act alone (lack of harmony with the
group), and one allows God to open up that which is otherwise locked
up inside us (the vision which is beyond that transmitted by cultural
norms).

Obviously the current trend toward empowerment of workers and
semiautonomous teams can be tied to the caring and compassionate
model of religious life. Trust-based organizations tend to work better than
command- and control-based organizations. They are much cheaper to
administer, they attract the best employees, and turnover and dissatisfaction tend to be lower. The irony is that, as human beings, we need both
virtue and sanctions to operate at our highest level. This paradox is also
contained within the Judeo-Christian tradition.

We speak of covenantal leadership, which obviously has Old Testament origins and permeates the federal, covenantal societies of today. A
good manager realizes that many of the covenants are implied and not
spelled out; but if they are broken, there is hell to pay. Such a manager
has the imagination to understand the implicit and explicit covenants of
an organization and to adopt a style that resonates with the covenants,
rather than attempting to manipulate them.

The best leaders are tolerant of ambiguity and paradox, just as the
mature person of religious conviction learns that one cannot know everything in a post-Enlightenment sense. There remains some aura of mystery, luck, chance, or fate to the enterprise.

Suggestions for Teaching Ethics

In terms of getting across the literal story line, examples of the best practices can form the bedrock of class discussion. Abundant material is
available on the Johnson & Johnson Tylenol series of decisions and the
background of discussions that provided support for them. The Business
Roundtable has published a report on the ethics programs of several
major corporations in *Corporate Ethics: A Prime Business Asset. Business
Week* has termed this report "a landmark study."

On the allegorical level, stories of individual corporate heroes are not
only a very traditional, but also an effective, method of transmitting interpretations of ethical (or moral) behavior.

Students often feel that if they conform to cultural norms, they act ethically. Useful learning can be accomplished by showing them where culturally based morals are often not enough, especially where they have been developed by unanchored, self-validating individuals. There is more than ample material depicting situations gone awry where players have pushed currently accepted practices of insider trading, price fixing, trusts, and the like to the limits and suddenly discovered that the culturally based rules have been changed, so they are now protesting their fate from inside a prison.

The conclusion of this article is that in order to truly probe ethical issues, the wisdom of the ages must be affirmed as input. Students need to be free to discuss their religious values and those matters that are of the deepest concern to them. Such discussions are not easily engendered. The instructor needs a high level of self-confidence, a sense of personal values, an open disposition, as well as tolerance for a wide variety of religious beliefs and a keen ability to listen. They can take place only where there is a high degree of trust and a sense of integrity in the classroom. Although the Judeo-Christian tradition is still a precondition of the Western cultural belief system, such discussions must include a broad range of input from atheists, agnostics, Muslims, Buddhists, Hindus, Confucians, spiritualists, and undoubtedly several others as well. To be effective, discussions should be neither pious nor didactic. Theological concepts can be discussed in the vernacular. Perhaps Dietrich Bonhoeffer's concept of "religionless religion" may serve as a model for these discussions.

Bonhoeffer felt that the organized church had abandoned him in his struggle against the Nazi regime. In a concrete sense, the post-Enlightenment church had become trapped in its own processes and culture and no longer expressed the voice of Jesus in the secular world. To find the voice of Jesus, Bonhoeffer suggested one must immerse oneself in the suffering of the secular world. One must listen to the voices of the secular world and be prepared to take daily, disciplined, right action. Thus, religionless religion for Bonhoeffer was a deeply worldly faith, come of age, in the center of life, beyond the man-made constraints of organized religion.

One method of teaching ethics is the use of literature, as Robert Coles has done so well at Harvard Business School. Religion-based, albeit secular, writings abound, ranging from Tolstoy and Dostoyevsky to Flannery O'Conner and Walker Percy. Such writings can be read on a literal, allegorical, or even a secular moral level, but to fully comprehend them, one must place oneself in the situation of the writer. Flannery O'Conner wrote that she interpreted herself as a "Christian-southern" writer, but that she felt few of her readers interpreted her that way. Once again, one needs to probe beneath the surface in order to truly confront oneself and become engaged in discovering one's value system.

Stories, assuming they are relevant and well told, can be effective means of transmitting the ethical foundations of organizational culture. When A.T.&T. attempted to incorporate the former National Cash organization into its global culture, they went to considerable effort and spent a year facilitating small discussion groups among some fifty thousand new employees scattered throughout the world. As the focus of the discussion, they utilized "The Parable of the Sadhu," a Harvard Business School ethics case, which presents a life or death situation suddenly imposed upon a group that has no basis for a common culture or an agreed-upon process for dealing with a crisis.

Another method of getting deeper into ethics is to study case situations that are truly ambiguous and that present a truly ethical conflict. So often what we deem to be ethical issues are merely those situations where we find ourselves losers in a society that has agreed-upon processes for allocating scarce resources or services. It is rare that one is confronted with a true ethical dilemma, where each of two choices is compelling at the deepest level. One example that comes to mind is the decision of the German theologian Dietrich Bonhoeffer to assist in the plot to assassinate Adolf Hitler. If we can push students to the point that Admiral Stockdale identifies as being beyond the limits of culturally accepted alternatives, where one must choose freely and without constraint, we can begin to approach a discussion of true ethical responsibility.

Ethics is taught most often as consideration of individual, isolated, ethical issues; yet social scientists and businessmen have come to realize the importance of organizational ethics as well. Organizations do have value systems that transcend the personal values of the individual actors. Such values may exist only by default, or they may have been effectively and sensitively developed and managed. A corporate value system invariably reveals itself when the organization is under stress. The stories people tell, rather than the printed materials, transmit their conception of what is proper behavior. A leader understands, develops, and responds to these organizational values.

The Practice of Christian Ethics in a Secular World

The purpose of teaching professional ethics is not to teach rules of behavior, but to attempt to increase one's level of ethical awareness and imagination. Though rules and laws are helpful, Christian ethics takes us deeper than the rules and the laws to discern what Jesus Christ would call us in love to do in the concreteness of the situation. In order to be truly ethical, we must take the risk of making the wrong decision. We must not allow the rules to become so important that we never pierce the surface of the concreteness of the situation. If we are in harmony with Jesus Christ in our daily lives and spiritual practice, perhaps we can become agents of his love in interpreting and applying the rule and the law to the specific situation.

In *My Search for Absolutes,* Paul Tillich states:

> Listening love takes the place of mechanical obedience to moral commandments. . . . No moral code can spare us from a decision and thus save us from moral risk. It can advise, but it can do no more. . . . Moral commandments are the wisdom of the past as it has been embodied in laws and traditions, and anyone who does not follow them risks tragedy. . . . Laws are not absolutes, but they are consequences derived from the absolute principle of agape-love united with justice and experience in innumerable encounters with concrete situations in human history. . . . Those who make genuine moral decisions courageously, guided by agape, looking with listening love into the concrete situation, helped by the wisdom of the ages, do something not only for themselves. They actualize possibilities of spiritual life.

As Christians, we should always broaden the list of stakeholders as imaginatively as possible before reaching a decision. This is another facet of living in community and relating our ethical acts to as broad a community as possible. If we must do layoffs, can we keep health benefits in place for a year afterward? What about the families of the affected parties? What about our own families? The more broadly one considers the affected parties in a decision, the more likely the decision will be ethically valid. What does this particular decision I am making do to enhance community rather than take away from community?

Have a peer group with whom you can be in community and discuss ethical issues. Do not share every concern with your superior. Share it with a peer or a friend or a fellow church member. The broader the community of discussion, especially within a Christian setting, the better chance that the love of God will prevail. Test out your creative ethical judgments in community. Also, do not think that every time you lose a utilitarian argument, you have been treated unethically. Become an active participant in developing the ethical quality of the culture of the organizations and groups of which you are a part.

Another valuable book is Sissella Bok's book *On Lying*. She says we lie so much to one another in our daily currency that the word "truth" is totally debased. She recommends instead the word "trust." Trust is candor, total honesty. Bok further points out that trust is so precious and all-encompassing that we can only be in a trust relationship with a handful of people. Otherwise we begin trading off once again. Confucius stated that trust is of greater importance to a nation state than food. If there is underlying trust, almost anything can become accomplished. Without it, little can be accomplished, no matter how weighty the law code books. As I have said before, social enterprises ruled by trust, rather than by rules, are cheaper and easier to manage and much more fun to work in. Trust derives from a common pur pose, a common set of values, a common ethic, or perhaps even a common faith or a covenant.

What are you willing to lose? To be in Christ, we must first lose ourselves. We must replace our egos with the love of Christ. Are we really willing to lose the goods and chattels of the secular world to live in Christ? Christian ethics is not about always winning, but about losing in the short term for longer-term values and commitments.

When Warren Buffet was named the richest man in America, he said something deceptively simple. He said one only makes about twenty major decisions in a full-term career. In a fifty-year career, that is one every two and one-half years. If I may paraphrase Buffet for my own purpose, we cannot wear our ethics on our sleeve. If everything that is going on appears unethical to us, we are in the wrong job. Not everyone is suited to be an investment banker or a litigator. We must know who we are. We must know where we stand. We must not let the really big issues drift by while we are in an unconscious state. If we are going to operate in the secular world, we must *be* in the secular world. We must also know when and where we are going to make our stand as Christians. Our faith is not transparent unless it is real to us in the secular world.

When a Profession Lacks an Ethical Base

Let us briefly examine the profession of economics, as a basis for evaluating the importance of an ethical underpinning in order for a line of work to become entitled to term itself a profession. Classical economics, from Adam Smith and David Ricardo through Alfred Marshall to John Maynard Keynes, was rooted in the social-political needs of their respective times and cultures. Economics through the time of Marshall was basically microeconomics, based upon individuals and their choices as unique moral agents. With Keynes, economics became macroeconomics. The individual lost relative importance to powerful institutional forces. Keynes's theories themselves became discredited by his lack of attention to inflation, stagflation, the role of money, and a failure to reconcile the collective forces back to the individual. Deficiencies in Keynes's systematic economics were explained away as uncertainties, propensities, risks, animal spirits, and chaos.

A number of theories have come forth to replace Keynes's, but none has prevailed. The monetarists floundered in the Volcker crisis of 1982. Rational expectations have been deemed overly cynical and uprooted from social, political, and historic forces because rationality alone has no binding ethic. The efficient market theory treats each individual as a perfectly substitutable factor or actor. Systemic market clearing is all-important. There is no moral basis. There are those who believe that economics is professionally in a state of confusion and failure of vision. There is no conceptual center. Econometrics can prove almost any hypothesis. There is no more solid theory. Economics is performed at the margin. We are now focused on the calculus of change. These theoretical exercises teach us nothing about the world in which we live. Economics has become mostly marginalized. A recent study indicates that 68 percent of economics graduates view it as unimportant to know how the economy itself works in order to be successful economists. There is no compelling center of vision. We are enthralled with the lure of technique.

Markets are not resource allocation machines; they serve a social function. In order to become valid, economics must be connected with the underlying social order. There must be an underlying faith-based ethic—a theology, if you will, providing commitments that guide the science of economics, or any profession. It is interesting to me that in the writings of Nobel laureates in economics there are almost always essays on the ethics of economic systems. Thus the recognized great minds are still orienting their economic theory to basic societal values.

Conclusion

We have compartmentalized our lives and separated out our interior life from our exterior life, our faith from our work. Academic theology, with the Enlightenment, has been broken up into philosophy, psychology, sociology, economics, and politics. Religion has often become separated from morality. Business people find it difficult to talk about ethics or about God with their game face on. We want to be reintegrated into community—with ourselves, with others, and with our God.

With Bonhoeffer, we need to live in the polyphony of life, where everything that informs us, including our faith, is relevant at all times. We must reject the either-or dualism of God or life, of God or work. We do not always know what is the correct thing to do. An isolated, alienated, personal orientation to life without God and community is disaster. We need others and the divine Other.

We must respect the orientation and values of others. We must respect Jews and Muslims and Hindus and all the rest. We must respect the rights of individuals and communities in their discernment about issues such as abortion or assisted death. We need also to have our own systems of values to add to the mix—values that we are prepared to live with and to defend. Only then can we hope for a true sense of *civitas*—of community. Only then can we be prepared for that critical moment of ethical decision when we stop trading off our value system for gain, ignoring the call to serve others.

PART V

The Development of Spirituality in Managers and Organizations

THIRTEEN

Spirituality and Business

The Latest Management Fad
or the Next Breakthrough?

STEPHEN J. PORTH, DAVID STEINGARD, & JOHN McCALL

"Spirituality in the workplace is exploding," as Laura Nash has rightly observed. Signs of it are everywhere (Cavanagh 1999; Mitroff and Denton 1999a; Porth 1997). But is spirituality in the workplace just another whim in a long line of business fads, or is this the next breakthrough in management thinking and practice? The purpose of this paper is to analyze the spirituality and business phenomenon, to identify both the risks and the promise of spirituality in business. Three types of risk—management, market, and employee—are described. These risks are juxtaposed against the breakthrough potential of a spirituality movement in business, a potential for transforming the ways that organizations are managed. Catholic Social Teaching (CST) is used as a foundation to illuminate the distinctions between an authentic spirituality of business and a trendy, superficial new management approach.

Risks of Spirituality in Business

In this section, we propose three specific risks that potentially threaten the authenticity and viability of a genuine spiritual transformation of business theory and practice.

Management Risk: Spirituality as an Exclusively Instrumental Tool to Enhance Employee Productivity, Creativity, Morale, and the Bottom-Line

> But perhaps the largest driver of this [spirituality and business] trend is the mounting evidence that spiritually minded programs in the workplace not only soothe workers' psyches but also deliver improved productivity. (Conlin 1999, 153)

If spirituality in business is considered to be nothing more than a tool to enhance employee productivity, it will soon find its rightful place in the management fad hall of fame. Instrumental spirituality renders employees and managers valuable only insofar as they are efficient and effective tools or agents of corporate financial performance. When human beings are reduced to instruments made more productive by applying scientific management (Taylor 1911) and management techniques (Ellul 1964), the risks of management abuse and employee manipulation are high. Mitroff's pioneering research into spiritual values in corporate America amplifies this point: "Spirituality could be the ultimate competitive advantage" (Conlin 1999, 154). Similarly, McKinsey and Co. Australia has determined that spiritually oriented management techniques and systems lead to improved productivity and decreased turnover (Conlin 1999, 153). But as soon as spirituality fails to produce the expected benefits of increased productivity, better morale, enhanced creativity, and decreased turnover, it will be abandoned as a management tool. A tool is only as good as the results it produces.

Despite this risk, it is becoming increasingly clear that attending to the spiritual and emotional well-being of employees and management is of paramount concern in today's economy. Bartlett and Ghoshal (1995) claim that the role of top management has changed due in large part to the new information economy: "The most basic task of corporate leaders is to unleash the human spirit, which makes initiative, creativity, and entrepreneurship possible" (132–33). Conlin echoes a similar point:

> Unlike the marketplace of 20 years ago, today's information and services-dominated economy is all about instantaneous decision-making and building relationships with partners and employees. Often, spiritual approaches can be used to help staffers get better at the long-neglected people side of the equation. (1999, 156)

If spirituality in business is to be a positive breakthrough for the evolution of management and not another tired fad, it must speak to "the long-neglected people side of the equation" (Conlin 1999, 158) and avoid the very real management risk of employee manipulation.

Market Risk: Spirituality as a Commodity—The Selling of "Total Spiritual Management" (TSM)

> For success in the $20 billion-a-year management consultancy business, find a fad. In recent years total quality, culture change, core competencies, organizational flattening, benchmarking, outsourcing, and downsizing have all been touted as the sole path to corporate salvation. . . . Is management really so easy? (*Economist*, 25 January 1997, 57)

Spirituality cannot be bought and sold. In the worst-case scenario, spirituality in management gets reduced to a dehumanizing (Alvesson and Willmott 1996) and desacrilized (Fox 1994) management fad—Total Spiritual Management (TSM). Like the passing specter of Total Quality Management (TQM), when spirituality becomes a commodity, it is destined to crash and burn [See Steingard and Fitzgibbons (1993) for similar arguments deconstructing TQM].

The unraveling of TSM is an all too familiar story. Management ideas and techniques are regularly launched with great fanfare. They are touted as the next business breakthrough and sold by consultants to corporate clients searching for a quick fix. Quick-fix solutions help drive the growth of the consulting industry and line the pockets of happy consultants, but they tend to be superficial and rarely work in the long term. Managing people and organizations is a complex proposition. Fad-based management simplifies and even trivializes the complexity of the management process.

Endemic to the risk of spirituality as commodity is a ubiquitous, wholesale application of spiritual approaches regardless of context. Years of research in management have yielded a few truths, one of which is the contingency approach (Lawrence and Lorsch 1967). The contingency approach recognizes that context matters—what works for one organization may be a complete failure for another because of situational differences. Similarly, the systems approach to management (Senge 1990) recognizes that new management approaches, such as spirituality, must be supported and aligned with other components of the organization.

If spirituality in management is to transcend the proclivity of becoming a useless, generic commodity, then it will have to both fit and transform the organization as a system. While this is a lofty ambition for any approach to management, there is some evidence that spiritually imbued approaches to management can provoke radical changes in organizational functioning. [For examples, see research on the Transcendental Meditation technique in business (Schmidt-Wilk et al., 1996; Schmidt-Wilk et al. forthcoming; Harung 1999; and King and Herriott 1997)]. To avoid the market risk of spirituality, the spiritual imprint must be evident throughout the organization (e.g., job design, culture, management style, reward system, vision, and mission), and the organization must avoid the temptation to revert to its old ways once the spiritual impulse is out of favor.

Employee Risk: Spirituality as Euphemism for Individualism

To the average person, "religion" is churches and hierarchy and people telling you what to do, and "spirituality" is "I do what I want to do." It's [baby] boomer narcissism. (Grossman 1999a, quoting Ken Wilber 1999)

Perhaps the most insidious and pervasive challenge to a non-faddish approach to spirituality is the risk of spirituality turning inward to the self-glorification and narcissistic narrowness of individualism (Lasch 1979). Similarly, America's predominantly materialistic culture threatens to embrace spirituality in a materialistic fashion, another product to be purchased and flaunted in an unfulfilling game of conspicuous consumption (Veblen 1924) and civilly destructive behavior (Bellah et al. 1985).

Once the dominant intermediary for spirituality, organized religion may be ceding its stronghold to individual appropriation and expression. There is a growing trend to describe oneself as "spiritual" but not "religious" [30 percent of respondents according to a recent *USA Today*/CNN Gallup Poll survey (see Grossman 1999a)]. Mitroff and Denton (1999a) found that about 60 percent of their sample had positive views of spirituality and negative views of religion. Grass-roots movements of individualized spirituality abound (Creedon 1998, 44). Without the built-in social connection and mission inherent in socially oriented religious institutions, however, spirituality on its own may render individual practitioners disconnected from and uninterested in social change. As Joan Brown Campbell, general secretary of the National Council of Churches, admonishes: "The cost of being spiritual is rather low. It means to many people being happier, being more content, more related to other persons. . . . Real faith is not about 'me and mine,' but about community" (Grossman 1999a, 2A).

If employees embrace a genuinely nonegocentric, contributive spirituality (with or without the structure of organized religion), narcissistic spirituality masquerading as stewardship and service (Block 1993) can be subverted. Distinguishing between authentic and self-serving forms of spirituality, however, is not a simple task (as discussed later in this paper). Nevertheless, making this distinction is necessary to prevent spirituality in management from becoming a potentially dangerous fad that separates employees and managers from their larger responsibilities and accountability to society.

In summary, spirituality in the workplace is vulnerable to several risks. Table 1 outlines three of these risks as a precursor to discussing our thoughts on how spirituality can eschew its fad possibility and catalyze an authentic spiritual breakthrough in management thinking and practice.

Table 1. Risks of Spirituality in Business

	Management Risk	Market Risk	Employee Risk
Uses of Spirituality	Instrumental tool	Commodity	Euphemism for individualism
Risks	Dehumanization of the employee; subtle manipulation	TSM: Total Spiritual Management	Narcissism; lack of social stewardship and responsibility

The Promise of Spirituality in the Workplace

If there is something authentic to spirituality in business, spirituality must be more clearly defined if we are to avoid the risks described above. What are the hallmark attributes of an authentic spirituality of business?

How does it differ from the merely trendy, and what meaningful contributions might it make for the theory and practice of management?

Mitroff and Denton (1999a) defined spirituality in terms of two fundamental components: the existence of a supreme guiding force and a sense of the interconnectedness of things. Our working understanding of spirituality avoids defining the concept in terms of a metaphysics of the supernatural. In fact, such a metaphysical starting point seems doomed if we admit, as we must, that there are authentic exemplars of spirituality in traditions with incompatible metaphysical assumptions. Rather, our understanding is based on an attribute common to paradigmatic instances of spiritual persons from Ghandi to Christ to the Buddha. Our working understanding of spirituality identifies it with a deep commitment to the equal humanity of others. Spirituality in this sense forces people fundamentally to be concerned not just about themselves but about others; it causes them to respect and promote the full flourishing of other humans. We take this commitment to the dignity and flourishing of the whole person, of both oneself and others, to be emblematic of authentic spirituality.

The promise of such spirituality in business is not as a benign management tool for increasing employee productivity; it is to promote management of a different sort where spirituality transforms the very nature of the management game itself. That is, if spirituality is to touch management in some authentic way, the basic agenda of management must radically change. Management must be transformed from a purely instrumental attitude toward "human resources"; it must instead exhibit a fundamental and abiding concern for the humanity of those whom its actions affect. Table 2 shows the differences between a faddish TSM and an authentic spirituality in management.

Table 2.   Total Spiritual Management versus Authentic Spirituality

	Total Spiritual Management (TSM)	Authentic Spirituality (AS)
View of employee	Instrumental value	Intrinsic value
View of Spiritual Practices	Good insofar as they improve organizational performance	Good insofar as they promote thedevelopment of the whole person

| Purpose | Maximize shareholder value | Create sustainable value for people, including shareholders |
| Ethics | Doing good in order to do well | Doing good with or without doing (maximally) well |

In the following section, we attempt to amplify this working understanding of spirituality and to give it clearer implications for management practice by considering principles of Catholic Social Thought (CST). We appeal to the prescriptions of CST as one possible tradition capable of infusing management practice with an authentic spiritual foundation. We recognize and appreciate the important contributions that other spiritual and religious traditions can make to this discussion and do not intend to privilege Catholicism as the sole authority. Rather, we use it to illustrate how a traditional religion's spiritual concerns can have implications for business practice (Porth et al 1999).

Catholic Social Teaching (CST) as a Foundation for Authentic Spirituality

In the following paragraphs, key principles of CST are introduced and briefly described. A set of corresponding diagnostic questions derived from each of the principles is identified. These questions may be useful in assessing the authenticity of spiritual practices for managing.

The Principle of Human Dignity

The first principle of CST, the principle of human dignity, is the core, foundation, and pinnacle of the Catholic understanding of social issues, including the practice of managing people. All other principles are anchored in and flow from the fundamental primacy of the individual person.

This principle holds that every human being is created in the image and likeness of God and is therefore a sacred being. The individual is worthy of respect and dignity as a member of the human family. "It is not what you do or what you have that gives you a claim on respect; it is simply *being* human that establishes your dignity" (Byron 1998, 10).

Because of this dignity, the human being is never a means, always an end. TSM relies on spiritual practices not primarily out of respect for the employee, but as a tool to increase employee productivity. Spiritual practices, just like employees themselves, are viewed as an instrumental good to be used so long as they produce the desired outcomes. Authentic spirituality, however, treats the employee as intrinsically good. Spiritual approaches are used out of respect for the inherent goodness of the employee, even if they do not always produce the expected gains for the organization. This deep respect for the human being would manifest itself in a concern for employee growth and development.

Diagnostic questions for Authentic Spirituality in business:

- What are the management systems, practices, and requirements for the flourishing of employees in organizations? Do our employees develop and grow on the job?
- What are the life-giving qualities of work? Are our employees energized or drained by their participation in the organization?

The Principle of Association

Human beings are not only sacred; they are social. Human flourishing in life occurs at both the personal and communal levels (Barrera 1997, 4), and employee development is necessarily social as well as personal.
This principle emphasizes the sense of community, the "spirit," of the organization. People need to work in community with others to achieve shared goals. An authentic spirituality of business nurtures the esprit de corps.

Diagnostic questions for Authentic Spirituality in business:

- How is the business structured and how are jobs defined to either promote or hinder community building?
- Do working conditions promote healthy and productive relationships in the organization?

The Principle of Human Equality

"Equality of all persons comes from their essential dignity. . . . While differences in talents are part of God's plan, social and cultural discrimination in fundamental rights . . . are not compatible with God's design" (Byron, 1998, 11). The implications of this principle for organizations are quite clear—racism, sexism, and all forms of bias violate the dignity of the individual and undermine the social fabric of the organizational community.

Diagnostic questions for Authentic Spirituality in business:

- Does participation in the organization ennoble each employee, or are some ennobled while others are demeaned?
- Are subtle or not so subtle forms of discrimination tolerated in the organization?
- How is diversity embraced?

The Principle of Participation

Human flourishing requires meaningful participation in the life of the organization, including an equitable distribution of both the responsibilities and benefits of organizational affiliation. "Work is more than a way to make a living; it is a form of continuing participation in God's creation. If the dignity of work is to be protected, then the basic rights [of employees] must be respected," including the right to productive work, fair compensation, and economic initiative (*Sharing Catholic Social Teaching*, 5, quoted in Byron, 1998, 10).

Diagnostic questions for Authentic Spirituality in business:

- What is the earnings gap between senior executives and operating employees?
- Are employees given appropriate opportunities to participate in the organizational decision-making process?
- Do employees receive a commensurate share of the value created by the organization?

The Principle of Solidarity

The welfare of the individual and the good of the broader community in which the organization exists are inextricably intertwined. This principle concentrates on those aspects of organizational life that may advance or hinder the welfare of the global community (Barrera, 1997, 11). Solidarity calls for organizations to consider the implications of their decisions and practices for society. Corporate citizenship and socially responsible behavior are necessary to preserve and respect solidarity.

Diagnostic questions for Authentic Spirituality in business:

- What practices of the organization emphasize the interdependence of stakeholder interests?
- How are members of the organization encouraged to relate to the broader community? For example, are there expectations or incentives for community service and acts of corporate citizenship?

The Principle of Stewardship

The natural environment and our personal talents are gifts bestowed on us by a loving God. We do not own these gifts. They are to be used in wise and prudent ways to build the common good. "The steward is a manager, not an owner. In an era of rising consciousness about our physical environment, our tradition is calling us to a sense of moral responsibility for the protection of our environment. . . . Stewardship responsibilities also look toward our use of our personal talents" (Byron, 1998, 11).

Diagnostic questions for Authentic Spirituality in Business:

- Are the organization's business practices consistent with a sustainable economy and ecology?
- Do the organization's products and services promote the well-being of humanity?

Indicators of an Authentic Spirituality in the Workplace

While Catholic Social Teaching and other spiritual and religious traditions may help to distinguish between Authentic Spirituality in business and Total Spiritual Management, the task remains a difficult challenge. The differences between AS and TSM are generally not observable since they tend to exist at the level of motives and core values. They may look alike on the surface and even produce very similar measurable outcomes, at least in the short run. To qualify as truly authentic, however, they must be undertaken for the right reasons, including a deep, abiding commitment to respect the individual person, as described above.

No empirical test exists to determine conclusively whether a company is practicing Authentic Spirituality. Certainly, the test is not whether a given organization is using spiritual practices such as transcendental meditation. However, knowing the scope of the practices and the core values and motives that underlie them would help. Therefore, the following indicators are proposed to help distinguish between Authentic Spirituality and Total Spiritual Management.

1. *Longevity.* Authentic Spirituality passes the test of time in varying organizational contexts, including varying financial conditions. TSM is dropped when it fails to produce expected results or when the organization is experiencing financial concerns.
2. *Systematic Approach.* Authentic Spirituality is not programmatic, it is systematic. It is not introduced piecemeal but infused throughout the organization's culture, core values, reward system, and management style.
3. *Cura Personalis* (care for the person). If there is a litmus test for Authentic Spirituality, it is how the organization treats the people with whom it interacts—employees, customers, suppliers, owners, and so forth. Authentic Spirituality respects the whole person and the profound dignity of each person. The test is not whether customers complain or not, but how the organization responds to customer complaints. What is the organization's position on employee layoffs? The test is not whether employee layoffs have ever been made, but how and why? This includes whether employees are given a reasonable severance package and support system to find new work. But it goes beyond the question of *how* employees are laid off to *why* they were laid off. Authentic Spirituality is undermined when layoffs, even if done humanely, are done for the sole purpose of increasing shareholder value.

Conclusion

Spirituality in management is fraught with risks, including the management, market, and employee risks described in this paper. In addition, the very concept of spirituality in business is understood differently by different people, and Authentic Spirituality is difficult to identify without knowledge of the organization's values and motives. Notwithstanding these challenges and risks, spirituality in business has the potential to transform our understanding of the purpose and practice of management. Furthermore, the human spirit seems to have an unquenchable desire for personal integration and meaning in life (Frankl 1963). These needs are so deep and fundamental to human nature that they will not fade. Any sane approach to management will have to recognize and address these human needs one way or another.

Is the spirituality phenomenon a potentially dangerous fad or an enlightened breakthrough? We argue here that it is both. On balance, then, do the risks of the fad outweigh the promise of a breakthrough? We believe this may be the wrong question. Perhaps the question should be reframed to avoid the pitfalls of the spirituality movement while trying to capture its promise. We suggest that, instead of cloaking the issue in the language of spirituality, we focus on a concept of management based on a deep, abiding commitment to respect the intrinsic value of the human individual. This shift might divert the focus away from the question whether an organization's approach is "spiritual" to the more practical and discernable diagnostic questions identified above. The essence of these questions may be summarized as follows:

- What are the life-giving qualities of work?
- What management systems, values, beliefs, and practices foster these life-giving qualities so the human being can develop and flourish in organizations?

Answers to these questions might shift the focus of investigation away from potentially instrumental and superficial uses of spirituality in organizations to more observable management systems and practices that respect the inherent dignity of every employee. In addition, these systems and practices would resonate with the spiritual dimension of the human individual but avoid the potentially ambiguous and divisive language of spirituality.

REFERENCES

Alvesson, M., and H. Willmott. 1996. *Making Sense of Management: A Critical Introduction*. Thousand Oaks, Calif.: Sage Publications.

Barrera, A. 1997. "Analytical Framework for Business Ethics: Catholic Social Principles." Paper presented at the Second International Symposium on Management Education and Catholic Social Teaching, Antwerp, Belgium.

Bartlett, C. A., and S. Ghoshal. 1995. "Changing the Role of Top Management: Beyond Systems to People." *Harvard Business Review* (May–June 1995): 133–42.

Bellah, R. N., R. Madsen, et al. 1985. *Habits of the Heart*. Berkeley and Los Angeles: University of California Press.

Block, P. 1993. *Stewardship: Choosing Service over Self-Interest*. San Francisco: Berrett-Koehler.

Byron, W. J. 1998. "Ten Building Blocks of Catholic Social Teaching." *America* 179 (13): 9–12.

Cavanagh, G. F. 1999. "Spirituality for Managers: Context and Critique." Special Issue, Work and Spirituality. *Journal of Organizational Change Management* 12 (3): 186–99.

Conlin, M. 1999. "Religion in the Workplace: The Growing Presence of Spirituality in Corporate America." *Business Week*, 1 November, 150–58.

Creedon, J. 1998. "God with a Million Faces." *Utne Reader* 88 (July–August): 42–48.

Ellul, J. 1964. *The Technological Society*. New York: Knopf.

Fox, M. 1994. *The Reinvention of Work: A Vision of Livelihood for Our Time*. San Francisco: HarperSanFrancisco.

Frankl, V. E. 1963. *Man's Search for Meaning: An Introductionn to Logotherapy*. New York: Simon and Schuster.

Grossman, C. L. 1999a. "In Search of Faith: For Many, Self-Defined 'Spirituality' Is Replacing a Church-Based Faith." *USA Today*, 23–26 December, 1A–2A.

Grossman, C. L. 1999b. "An Unbounded Spirit: Religious Leaders Seek a Place for God." *USA Today*, 23–26 December, 1A–2A.

Harung, H. 1999. *Invincible Leadership: Building Peak Performance Organizations by Harnessing the Unlimited Power of Consciousness*. Fairfield, Iowa: Maharishi University of Management Press.

Hilmer, F. G., and Donaldson, L. 1997. "Instant Coffee as Management Theory." *Economist* (London), 25 January, 57

King, K., and S. Herriot. 1997. "Beyond the Current Paradigm in Management Thought: Alignment with Natural Law through Maharishi Vedic Management." *Modern Science and Vedic Science* 7 (1): 224–37.

Lasch, C. 1979. *The Culture of Narcissism: American Life in an Age of Diminishing Returns*. New York: Warner Books/Norton.

Lawrence, P. F., and J. W. Lorsch. 1967. *Organization and Environment: Managing Differentiation and Integration*. Boston: Harvard University.

Mitroff, I. I., and E. A. Denton. 1999a. *A Spiritual Audit of Corporate America*. San Francisco: Jossey-Bass Publishers.

Mitroff, I. I., and E. A. Denton. 1999b. "A Study of Spirituality in the Workplace." *Sloan Management Review* (Summer): 83–92.

Porth, S. J. 1997. "Spirit, Religion, and Business Ethics: A Crossroads?" *Journal of Human Values* 3 (1): 33–44.

Porth, S. J., J. McCale, and T. A. Bausch. 1999. "Spiritual Themes of the Learning Organization." Special Issue, Work and Spirituality. *Journal of Organizational Change Management* 12 (3), 211–20.

Schmidt-Wilk, J., C. Alexander, et al. 1996. "Developing Consciousness in Organizations: The Transcendental Meditation Program in Business." *Journal of Business and Psychology* 10 (4): 429–44.

Schmidt-Wilk, J., D. Heaton, et al. "Higher Education for Higher Consciousness: Maharishi University of Management as a Model for Spirituality in Management Education." *Journal of Management Education*. Special Issue, *Spirituality in Management* Education. Forthcoming.

Senge, P. 1990. *The Fifth Discipline: The Art and Practice of the Learning Organization*. New York: Doubleday/Currency.

Sharing Catholic Social Teaching: Challenges and Directions. Reflections of the U.S. Catholic Bishops, June 1998. Washington, D.C.: United States Catholic Conference.

Steingard, D., and D. Fitzgibbons. 1993. "A Postmodern Deconstruction of Total Quality Management (TQM)." *Journal of Organizational Change Management* 6 (5): 27–42.

Taylor, F. 1911. *Principles of Scientific Management*. New York: Harper and Row.

Veblen, T. 1924. *The Theory of the Leisure Class: An Economic Study of Institutions*. New York: B. W. Huebsch.

Wilber, K. 1999. *One Taste: The Journals of Ken Wilber*. Boston: Shambhala Publications.

FOURTEEN

Religion and Spirituality in Business

Obstacles and Opportunities

GERALD F. CAVANAGH, S.J.

The current interest in spirituality among managers is manifested in the multitude of prayer groups, conferences, books, and articles in both popular and academic journals. The interest spans the globe, from Europe to India and the United States. Well over a dozen organizations with Protestant, Jewish, or Catholic roots seek to integrate faith, spirituality, and work for business people.[1] *Forbes* shows that this new interest is a large and growing market niche for firms with annual sales of more than $1 billion in Christian publishing and $200 million in religious radio stations, along with religious music, toys, videos, and CDs for kids.[2]

On the other hand, some two hundred years ago, at the time of the Enlightenment, the Western world separated religion and spirituality from public life. This was done officially in the United States Constitution. Hence, to many this new interest in spirituality in business is surprising and even dangerous. To them it seems like a step backward into the Dark Ages.

To help us understand better and appreciate this phenomenon, I would like to address several questions:

- Is this current interest appropriate, rooted, and growing or is it merely a superficial fad?
- What are the obstacles to the development of spirituality among managers?
- What role might religion play in the development of spiritualities for managers?
- Among the many Christian spiritualities, how might Ignatian spirituality be of help to managers?

263

Definitions

The terms spirit and spirituality are widely and loosely used. It is therefore important to clarify the meaning of the term. There are many definitions, but I find Andre Delbecq's definition of spirituality to be clear,
complete, and contemporary:

> The unique and personal inner experience of and search for the
> fullest personal development through participation into the tran-
> scendent mystery. It always involves a sense of belonging to a greater
> whole and a sense of longing for a more complete fulfillment through
> touching the greater mystery (which in tradition I call God). My test
> of authenticity is the extent to which progress in the spiritual journey
> manifests itself in loving and compassionate service.[3]

Let us now proceed to the questions listed above.

Is Manager Spirituality a Fad?

Interest in spirituality has been present as long as people have existed.
Spirituality meets a deeply rooted and genuine need in people and thus
goes beyond being a fad. The need for spirituality can be stated as simply
the need that all human beings have to recognize that they are dependent
on someone or some force greater than they and are connected to every
other person in the world:

> The needs that businesspeople often feel are a separation from other
> people, alienation from their work, and a lack of meaning in their
> lives. They often experience their work, family life and their faith to
> be in separate compartments—50 to 70 hours per week at work, an
> hour on weekends for worship, and the time left over for family. This
> separation leaves one feeling dry, unfulfilled and unhappy, and is
> often experienced as a profound absence or vacuum in one's life.[4]

The above is a statement of the need for connectedness. It is deeply
rooted in human nature. Mature people feel this need and respond to it
in some fashion—many today with some type of spirituality. Moreover,

spirituality provides benefits to the firm. Managers in organizations that they regard as open to spirituality feel that their firm is more profitable. These managers say that they can bring more of their "complete selves" to work. They can use "more of their creativity, emotions, and intelligence; in short, organizations viewed as more spiritual get more from their participants and vice versa."[5]

Nevertheless, the fact that spirituality satisfies a deep human need and enables an organization better to tap participants' creativity and intelligence does not guarantee that the current interest in spirituality will not fade. The movement could evaporate because of a number of obstacles that are in its path, some new and others quite old.

Obstacles to Developing Spirituality among Managers

These are the obstacles to developing spirituality among managers: (1) historical attitudes in Western nations that spirituality has no place in work or in any public life; (2) much of the attention to spirituality for managers is from New Age advocates, and it tends to be amorphous, shallow, undeveloped, and thus open to criticism; (3) if managers have a spirituality, currently it is most likely not connected to religion; in fact, some managers who favor spirituality are antagonistic to religion.

The most obvious obstacle is the commonly held conviction that spirituality has no place in business and public life. This attitude is prevalent not just in the United States, but in much of the Western world. Spirituality is considered to be a private affair, perhaps to be discussed with like-minded friends, but not to be brought into the workplace. It is a personal matter, to be spoken about on one's own time, at church or at home. In this view, spirituality has nothing to do with designing, making, financing, and marketing goods and services.

A second obstacle is that New Age enthusiasts often give spirituality a bad name. For many of them, spirituality is any feeling, sentiment, or emotional experience. An early critique of New Age managers in the *Harvard Business Review* says that "if everyone follows their own path to bliss then anything goes—from a hermetic mountaintop existence to Ivan Boesky's 'greed is good.'"[6] New Age proponents often report uncritically without any attempt to separate the valid from the spurious "past-life experiences and out-of-body experiences, speaking in foreign languages and reincarnation."[7] Although personal experience and emotions are components, they are by no means the substance of spirituality.

Third, proposing or advocating a specific religion in the workplace can be divisive. Most countries today are pluralistic, that is, made up of people of many religions, so it is important to maintain respect for all legitimate religions. Mitroff and Denton's recent study of several hundred managers found that 30 percent of the managers had positive views of both religion and spirituality. However, and to our point here, more than a majority, that is, 60 percent, had a positive view of spirituality but had a *negative* view of religion. These managers see religion as "organized, close-minded and intolerant. Spirituality, on the other hand, is extremely individualized."[8] One of the managers in this study spelled out his notion of religion:

> Organized religion . . . is more concerned with maintaining itself. It cares more about the organizational aspects of religion and with ritual and dogma than with serving people irrespective of their beliefs. Not only do you *not* have to be religious in order to be spiritual, but it probably helps if you are not religious, especially if you want your spirituality to grow and be a basic part of your life.[9]

Given the above difficulties, much of the interest in spirituality today among managers and others is separated from religion. But it is important to note that most spiritualities that have lasted more than a generation or so are rooted in one of the great religions of the world. Is it possible to tap these rich resources without also activating the divisive elements of religion?

Religion and Spirituality: The Severed Root

Severing the link between religion and spirituality means that contemporary managers must discover anew and alone the insights, techniques, and riches that have been discovered countless times in a variety of styles in many cultures. The religious heritages, of Judaism, Christianity, Buddhism, Taoism, Hinduism, and the other great religions of the world provide a rich variety of spiritualities that some contemporary managers find very beneficial. Not building on these riches of the past may make a contemporary spirituality temporarily attractive, but it will also result in that spirituality most likely being superficial and shallow.

Historically, spirituality has been rooted in religion. However, much of the current use of spirituality in business does not stem from a particular religious tradition. There are several reasons for this:

- Most Western societies are pluralistic; there is no one dominant religious tradition that can be cited as common to all.

- A specific religious tradition most often cannot be used as the foundation for a firm's mission or vision statements; all people in a particular firm do not share the same religious tradition, so citing one tradition would be divisive.

- Citing one religious tradition can encourage distrust and dislike of "outsiders," that is, those not sharing the same religious convictions. In civil society, this can undermine democracy and even lead to civil war.

- Finally, as indicated earlier, the nineteenth-century European Enlightenment has led many to distrust religious values. Religion is thought to be opposed to rationality and science and the source of superstition and the irrational.

Some have challenged this relegating of religion to private corners of one's life and thus separating it from public life. Yale law scholar Stephen Carter calls it "trivializing" of religion.[10] Nevertheless, it is difficult or impossible to gain a consensus in any large, random group of U.S. citizens on common religious beliefs.

Thus it is a challenge to utilize a particular religious tradition and its spirituality without seeming to imply that it is the only valid tradition. To do so would be divisive in the firm. Let us now examine some of the elements that will contribute to the spirituality of managers.

Elements Common to Spiritualities for Business People

There are common features that we find in most religions. They are especially obvious in the religions that share common roots, "the religions of

Abraham," that is, Judaism, Christianity, and Islam. The following elements are also found in most of the spirituality of business movements that we are experiencing:

- Belief in God or a "supreme force" on whom all of us are dependent.
- Recognition of the importance of quiet time, contemplation, and prayer in one's life.
- Emphasis on the centrality of persons and being sensitive to the needs of others.
- A commitment to better relations among all peoples and trying to bring justice to all, regardless of status, nationality, sex, or race.
- A commitment to a sustainable environment, thus to pass on a better world to our grandchildren. This is called ecospirituality, and it has its own literature.[11]

Thus it is appropriate to briefly probe some of the major religious spiritualities. The Jewish tradition that contributes to a spirituality for business people is gaining wider recognition in recent years.[12] Epstein points out that "all wealth originates in God alone." Since the earth is the Lord's, all human ownership is temporary; we are but custodians or stewards. Judaism is a communal, rather than an individualistic, religion, and society is thus a partner in this wealth. Therefore all wealth is subject to the needs of the community.[13]

The Christian tradition stems from the same experience and prophets. So it is not surprising that the Christian tradition supports this same vision. The Protestant ethic is a much later development, and it has been cited as the foundation for the market system. The Protestant ethic encourages hard work, self-discipline, saving, and planning ahead. This was the predominant vision or spirituality for business people for several centuries.[14] This spirituality is based upon the theology of the sixteenth-century Reformer John Calvin and is predominantly individualistic. Benjamin Franklin later secularized the Protestant ethic. One commentator contrasts what he calls the Catholic ethic with the Protestant ethic:

> The Catholic ethic views the world through the lenses of family and forgiveness. The Protestant ethic views it through lenses of individualism and immutability. In the Catholic ethic, life in this world is a process, a journey, in which forgiveness is always possible. In the

Protestant ethic, one's efforts to "succeed" may help in this world but have less influence on the next. . . .

The merciful culture of the Catholic ethic has many elements that make the sharing of resources natural and ordinary and that temper hostility toward the needy, and these elements guide the daily decisions of those who are influenced by this ethic.[15]

There is a multitude of Catholic spiritualities that have developed over the last two thousand years. These spiritualities are rooted in saints and scholars like Augustine, Francis of Assisi, Benedict, and many others. Each of these spiritualities has unique elements, some of which are potentially beneficial for the contemporary manager. For example, a spirituality for managers has been elaborated over the last century by the popes in their many encyclicals, from *On the Condition of Work* (1891) to *The One-Hundredth Year* (1991). This tradition presents a spirituality that places emphasis on the person as a cocreator with God and the dignity of working persons and the respect due to them. However, before embracing a spirituality, it is first important to know where one is led by one's own personal goals and values.

Probing One's Roots

Many of people's personal goals and values develop from the actions and attitudes of their parents, family, and friends, along with the culture and the people in their workplace. Schools, including most U.S. universities, do not often encourage students to articulate their own personal goals. This allows many people to be victims of the pervasive, value-forming elements of our popular culture, such as advertising, TV, film, and popular magazines. These values support a consumer culture and are generally self-centered and shallow.

A simple exercise can enable individuals to articulate their own goals and values and thus clarify personal priorities.[16] This, in turn, empowers people to choose a preferred lifestyle and to specify what time and effort they want to spend in various life activities.

I have used this exercise with university students, both undergraduate and MBA. It asks each person to list three major goals in each of five categories: (1) career, (2) personal relationships, (3) leisure satisfactions,

(4) learning and education, and (5) religion and spirituality. A second part of the exercise asks each person to rank-order sixteen personal values. Individuals then identify their own value-forming, life-changing experiences, reflecting on how these experiences have shaped their goals and values. They then compare their current goals and values to see if there is support or conflict among them. Finally they write a brief paper on the results of their inquiry, specifying their current personal goals.

Surprisingly, up to one-half of even the graduate students had never reflected in any systematic way on their personal goals, in spite of the fact that they had spent four years in an undergraduate college or university. For many, the results of this personal reflection open doors to a new freedom. Each term several students, generally male, who are well into their career will realize that "family is very important to me, but up to this point in my life, I have spent most of my time pursuing my career. I am going to change that and spend more time with my spouse and children." Many have parallel realizations with regard to their own spiritual life and their religious observances.

We have examined the need for personal spirituality, along with mechanisms that enable us to reflect on our own lives. It is useful now to examine a specific, tested spirituality that may be of some use to business people: the spirituality of St. Ignatius Loyola.

Ignatian Spirituality for Business People

Ignatian spirituality and the Society of Jesus (Jesuits) have had a widespread and deep impact on the far corners of the world since the Society began spanning the globe more than 450 years ago. St. Ignatius Loyola developed Ignatian spirituality; he communicated it to his first companions and they to others to this day. The Society of Jesus has been banished, sometimes repeatedly, from many countries, and its members have been imprisoned and murdered for their work even in recent years. Yet it continues to flourish, largely because of its mission and spirituality. The success of Ignatian spirituality prompts us to inquire what lessons it might have today for business people. But first, some background on the Society of Jesus itself.

Ignatius Loyola (1491–1556) gathered a group of ten men at the University of Paris to form the Society of Jesus in 1540. The Society was founded to be of service to people and the Catholic Church. Loyola and these first Jesuits had a global vision, which was demonstrated by St. Francis Xavier's being sent to India in 1542 and to Japan in 1549.[17] By the time of Loyola's death in 1556 there were 1,000 members, scattered across Europe, North and South America, and Asia. On 1 January 2000 there were 21,354 Jesuits working in 115 countries.

Integration into the Catholic Church

The superior general of the Society of Jesus reports directly to the head of the Catholic Church, currently Pope John Paul II. A regional superior, a "provincial," leads each Jesuit region (there are ninety "provinces" in the world; ten in the United States). Each Jesuit is a member of a local community, which has a local superior. Thus there are only three levels of "management" between the individual Jesuit and the head of the Catholic Church, the pope.

Jesuits[18] were trained to be flexible and to bring the "good news" of the gospel of Jesus to people wherever they were. Ignatius Loyola insisted that each Jesuit make a special vow to do whatever work in whatever place the pope requests. Over the centuries, popes have given Jesuits various special missions. After World War II, when Japan was devastated, Pope Pius XII asked Jesuits to begin a university in Tokyo. Staffed by men from dozens of countries, Sophia University is now among the finest universities in Japan. Over the last two decades the Jesuit superior general has asked Jesuits to help refugees in Rwanda, Burundi, Bosnia, Kosovo, Sudan, Ethiopia, and other places. Jesuits have been aid workers, medical doctors, and other specialized personnel in these efforts. More recently, Pope John Paul II has asked Jesuits to begin an ecumenical university in Jerusalem, Palestine, as a model of interfaith cooperation.

Some Distinguishing Characteristics of Jesuits

Jesuits are distinguished from other religious communities in the Catholic Church by their flexibility. They are ready to go anywhere and do any work as long as it contributes to the "greater glory of God" (in Latin, Ad Majoram Dei Gloriam, or AMDG). Jesuits have no specified house as a permanent home base as do Catholic religious orders founded earlier, such as those of the Benedictines, Franciscans, or Dominicans. For Jesuits, apostolic work takes precedence over living together in community. The individual Jesuit will go where the needs are the greatest and his talents can be used best.

Another distinguishing element of Jesuit spirituality is that they see themselves as "contemplatives in action." This contrasts with the rule and lifestyle of other Catholic religious orders. Benedictines, Franciscans, and others have a regular daily order that they observe, which includes work, prayer, and meals together. On the other hand, Jesuits were the first to emphasize that each person must pray even while in the midst of activity, thus being a "contemplative in action." Daily quiet is sought, but not for long periods. Jesuits have no set prayers, except that Ignatius Loyola urged each Jesuit to do some daily prayer, "find God in all things," and do a brief daily examination of conscience.

In the *Spiritual Exercises*[19] of Ignatius Loyola, Jesuits are urged to "discern" (prayerfully determine) God's will for them in a particular situation. The *Spiritual Exercises* are designed to equip the one undertaking the exercises to be able to better understand himself and his strengths and weaknesses and to determine what God is asking of him. Discernment is often done with the help of another, a spiritual director or a friend. Prayerful discernment in groups is also done, when a group is about to make a difficult major policy decision.

Each Jesuit is expected to be open and honest with his major superior. This enables the superior to suggest work and a life that is most compatible with each person's strengths and weaknesses. This demands much trust between these two people. Perhaps surprisingly for most Americans, this trust is generally present between the individual Jesuit and his superior.

A final element of Jesuit spirituality is "finding God in all things," that is, affirming the goodness of the world. This view leads Jesuits to bridge the sacred and the secular; to interpret each to the other, and to work against an artificial separation of the two, such as we have experienced in the post-Enlightenment West. Thus Jesuits as early as the sixteenth and seventeenth centuries were accomplished in the sciences and the humanities, with unique expertise in architecture, astronomy, drama, music, and seismology.

Education was seen as a vehicle to find God in all things and to communicate the "good news." Schools were begun by 1547. The establishment of a worldwide system of schools demonstrates Ignatius Loyola's vision:

> By the time the Society was suppressed by papal edict in 1773, it was operating more than 800 universities, seminaries and especially secondary schools almost around the globe. The World had never seen before nor has it seen since such an immense network of educational institutions operating on an international basis. The schools were often at the center of the culture of the towns and cities where they were located. They might produce several plays or ballets per year, and some maintained important astronomical observatories.[20]

Let us now turn to the lessons this Ignatian spirituality might have for contemporary business people.

Lessons for Business People

The Society of Jesus, in preparing and socializing its members, offers numerous lessons for the business manager. Among these lessons are (1) extensive training and trust of members, (2) working cooperatively, (3) full communication with superiors, and (4) heroes as models. Let us examine each.

Extensive Training and Trust for Subordinates
The flat organizational structure of the Society of Jesus requires that individual Jesuits be trusted in their lives and their work. There are only three levels of "management" between the individual Jesuit and the pope: local, provincial, and general superiors. The local superior has a full-time job, in addition to being local superior. Hence, the individual must have initiative, competence, and good judgment to carry on his work largely without direction. The work is thus entrusted to the individual Jesuit, in some cases working alone. The individual Jesuit has a regular conference with his local and provincial superior only once a year. Moreover, the education and training Jesuits receive empowers them to be competent self-starters.

Jesuits receive extensive education and training for their work. Most men who enter the Society of Jesus already possess an undergraduate degree and often a graduate or professional degree. These men initially learn Jesuit spirituality and personal development in the "novitiate" for two years. The young Jesuit then studies philosophy and liberal arts at a university for two to three years, after which he does an internship ("regency"), often teaching at a Jesuit high school or university for two to three years. Theology studies come next (four years). Many Jesuits will then do specialized studies, generally toward a doctorate, in order to better equip them to do their lifework. A Jesuit then begins his major work, and, after a half dozen years or so, it will take him one additional year to work on Jesuit spirituality ("tertianship"). The total education and training requires eleven to fifteen years after the bachelor's degree. The Jesuit is then entrusted with a major work, sometimes in another region a long distance from any Jesuit superior. The long education in both spirituality and secular subjects is designed to equip a Jesuit to deal sensitively and competently with people and affairs of many cultures.

The lengthy investment in spirituality, training, and education provides lessons for the businessperson. If executives really believe that people are vital to the success of their firm, they will fund resources to provide those people with education and competencies. Unfortunately, in recent years, with an eye on the bottom line, many firms have retreated from their earlier commitment to support graduate business education for their employees. Nevertheless, Ford, Motorola, and many other firms continue to be models in business for their willingness to invest time and resources in their people.

Working Cooperatively

With Jesuits widely separated, communication among them in the early days was difficult and limited. Messages sent via sailing ships could take up to a year to reach them. Hence, once a man began a work in a distant land, there was little direct oversight. Thus it is essential that each person have a common sense of mission and goals.

Today we find that Jesuits working in an American university constitute only 5–10 percent of the teaching faculty. Jesuits know that it is vital to work cooperatively among themselves and with others; this is somewhat easier among them because there is little motivation to gain more money or power. Since Jesuits have a vow of poverty, they do not get individual paychecks. Their pay goes to the Jesuit community in a lump sum. The community uses what is needed to support the men and contributes the rest to support the school.

Jesuits also cooperate with the entire faculty and staff in pursuing the mission of the institution. This has become a major effort in Jesuit high schools and universities, especially in the last twenty years, and is called "collaboration." A journal that is dedicated to collaboration, *Conversations,*[21] is sponsored by the twenty-eight U.S. Jesuit colleges and universities.

Firms have developed clearer missions and goals in recent years. Jesuit efforts to communicate the mission, goals, and values of their work provide models and techniques for business people.

Communication with Superiors

Each Jesuit annually meets with his superior to report on and discuss the important elements in his life. Jesuits call this "the account of conscience." This is another element that enables the Jesuit superior to know his man and to trust that he is making balanced decisions on many questions, even when far away from "headquarters." This trust is reinforced by the knowledge that each Jesuit is pledged to seek solitude and to pray in some fashion daily. Moreover, each Jesuit knows that the success of his work is ultimately in the hands of God, and this lessens stress and can give him balance.

This sort of communication and trust is possible because the individual Jesuit knows that his superior's primary goal is the welfare of the individual Jesuit and the good of the work. There is no fear that his revelations will be used in a shortsighted way against him.

Such openness in communication with one's superior is a model for any organization. In business, this is more difficult if members perceive it as a competitive, win-lose environment, as opposed to a win-win one.

Heroes as Models

Jesuits have many models, beginning with Ignatius Loyola himself.[22] Another is the brilliant and talented Francis Xavier, who received his degree from the University of Paris and sailed for India. Xavier is still revered by all, including Hindus, in Goa, India, which was his home base. The Jesuit church there, which contains his remains, is a world historical site and is maintained by the government of India. Matteo Ricci brought astronomy and mathematics to China a generation later, and there is a monument to his life and work in Beijing even to this day.

Saints John De Brebuf and Isaac Jogues sailed to what is now Upper New York State and Ontario, Canada, to work with the American Huron Indians in the 1630s. They, like other Jesuits of their time, were the first to record the language and customs of the native tribes.

In recent years, Ignatio Ellacuria was president of the University of Central America in El Salvador. He and the other Jesuits at the university had protested the government's brutal treatment of 80 percent of their people, the local peasants and farmers, by the military dictatorship of that country, which was supported by the United States. In 1989 he, along with seven companions, was awakened in the middle of the night, dragged outside their house, and murdered by soldiers trained by the United States at the School of the Americas.

An organization needs heroes to communicate values and to encourage members. Bill Hewlett and David Packard are legendary heroes of Silicon Valley; they received hero status because of their openness, wisdom, vision, and generosity. It is difficult to respect a hero who does not have those qualities.

Conclusion

Spirituality can expand a businessperson's horizons, stimulate creativity, and relieve stress. People throughout all ages and cultures have treasured their spiritualities. Religion generally contributes to one's spirituality, but in a pluralistic society religion's use in the public workplace is limited. A person's explicit awareness of personal life experiences, goals, and values enables him or her to build a firmer foundation for a spirituality.

Ignatian spirituality is a well-known and proven spirituality that can be easily adapted to the contemporary businessperson's needs. Its emphasis on training and trust, cooperation, open communication, and heroes as models is especially helpful to the businessperson.

NOTES

1. Stephen J. Porth, "Spirit, Religion, and Business Ethics: A Crossroads?" *Journal of Human Values* 3, no. 1 (1997): 34.

2. Tim W. Ferguson and Josephine Lee, "Spiritual Reality," *Forbes*, 27 January 1997.

3. Andre L. Delbecq, "Christian Spirituality and Contemporary Business Leadership," *Journal of Organizational Change Management* 12, no. 4 (1999): 345.

4. Gerald F. Cavanagh, "Spirituality for Managers," *Journal of Organizational Change Management* 12, no. 3 (Summer 1999): 186.

5. Ian I. Mitroff and Elizabeth A. Denton, "A Spirituality in the Workplace," *Sloan Management Review* 40, no. 4 (Summer 1999): 83.

6. Martha Nichols, "Does New Age Business Have a Message for Managers?" *Harvard Business Review* 72, no. 2 (March–April 1994): 56.

7. Ian I. Mitroff and Elizabeth A. Denton, "Spirituality in the Workplace," 84.

8. Ibid., 90.

9. Ibid., 87.

10. Stephen Carter, *The Culture of Disbelief* (New York: Basic Books, 1993).

11. See, for example, two classic and perhaps best-known books on eco-spirituality, both by Catholic priests: Pierre Teilhard de Chardin, S.J., *The Divine Milieu* (New York: Harper and Collins, 1957) and Thomas Berry, *The Dream of the Earth* (San Francisco: Sierra Club Books, 1988).

12. See Edwin M. Epstein, "Contemporary Jewish Thought on Business Ethics: Some Perspectives and Reflections" (paper presented at the Society for Business Ethics Meetings, Boston, 1997); Meir Tamari, *The Challenge of Wealth: A Jewish Perspective on Earning and Spending Money* (Northall, N.J.: Jason Aronson, 1995); and Moses L. Pava, *Business Ethics: A Jewish Perspective* (Hoboken, N.J.: KTAV Publishing, 1997).

13. Epstein, "Contemporary Jewish Thought," 5, quoting Tamari, *The Challenge of Wealth*.

14. For more on the influence and decline of the Protestant ethic, see Gerald F. Cavanagh, *American Business Values: With International Perspectives*, 4th ed. (Upper Saddle River, N.J.: Prentice Hall, 1998), 114–38, 228–29.

15. John E. Tropman, *The Catholic Ethic in American Society* (San Francisco: Jossey-Bass, 1995), 99.

16. See the exercise "Personal Values and Life Goals Inventory" in Cavanagh, *American Business Values*, 33–36. This exercise is adapted from David Kolb et al., *Organizational Behavior: An Experiential Approach*, 6th ed. (Upper Saddle River, N.J.: Prentice Hall, 1995), 128–36; and Milton Rokeach, *The Nature of Human Values* (New York: Free Press, 1973).

17. *Constitutions of the Society of Jesus and Their Complementary Norms* (St. Louis, Mo.: Institute of Jesuit Sources, 1996) and James Broderick, S.J., *The Progress of the Jesuits (1556–1579)* (Chicago: Loyola University Press, 1986).

18. The term "Jesuit" was first intended as a term of opprobrium at the time when Queen Elizabeth was persecuting Catholics and executing Jesuits in sixteenth-century England. The term has stuck.

19. Ignatius Loyola, *The Spiritual Exercises of Saint Ignatius*, trans. and with a commentary by George E. Ganss, S.J. (St. Louis, Mo.: Institute of Jesuit Sources, 1992).

20. John W. O'Malley, *The First Jesuits* (Cambridge: Harvard University Press, 1993), 15–16; see also Wilfred L. LaCroix, *The Jesuit Spirit of Education* (Kansas City: Rockhurst College, 1989).

21. For additional information, contact Brennan O'Donnell, ed., Department of English, Loyola College in Maryland, 4501 N. Charles St., Baltimore, Md. 21210–2699; e-mail: bodonnell@loyola.edu.

22. Joseph N. Tylenda, *Jesuit Saints and Martyrs* (Chicago: Loyola University Press, 1984).

FIFTEEN

Business, Religion, and Spirituality

Reflections of a Catholic Health System CEO

PATRICIA VANDENBERG, C.S.C.

The beginning of a new millennium provides a critical moment to pause and reflect together on a topic with tremendous implications in our world—business, religion, and spirituality. My reflections come from spending the past twenty years in health services administration.

It is fascinating to me to note that during my graduate studies at Duke University virtually no consideration was given to this critical topic. The closest we came to this domain was in Human Resource Administration courses where we briefly touched on the meaning of work to the individual and then quickly moved on to issues of managing the workforce to achieve the objectives of the firm. As CEO of a national Catholic health system, I've been concerned to create a culture and develop and implement a framework within the corporation that focuses decision making and engages the workforce in mission fulfillment. Our corporation has been a laboratory for a pragmatic effort at linking business, religion, and spirituality.

And so I applaud Notre Dame for bringing together a collection of articles from business leaders and scholars to discuss a theme that is too frequently shunted aside in the world of American commerce. Religion in American life, as Robert Bellah and his coauthors so clearly demonstrated in *Habits of the Heart*,[1] is assigned to the realm of privacy, of the personal. Religion, for the governor of Minnesota, is a crutch for the weak, a mechanism that enables some individuals to cope with the stresses of life, the fear of an empty existence. Such views relegate religion to the personal and private; they deprive religion of any public meaning or significance. The world of business and commerce, on the other hand, is an inherently public world constituted by exchanges and relationships between corporations. The world of business relies on shared meanings and expectations, a world governed by law and economics. If religion indeed pertains to the world of privacy, what role might it play in the public world of commerce?

I would like to suggest to you an alternative view of religion, spirituality, and business. I will then attempt to relate this understanding of religion and spirituality to the contemporary American workplace, to the current environment of American health care, and, finally, to a series of programs initiated within the Holy Cross Health System which have created a corporate architecture that supports a platform for a corporate spirituality.

Religion, Spirituality, and Work

Chapter 3 of the Book of Genesis provides one view of the relationship between religion and work. As a result of his sin, Adam was cursed by God. "Accursed be the soil because of you. With suffering shall you get your food from it every day of your life. It shall yield you brambles and thistles, and you shall eat wild plants. With sweat on your brow shall you eat your bread until you return to the soil as you were taken from it."[2] According to this view work is a punishment, it is incapable of producing the lushness and copious bounty of the Garden of Eden. Work as toil is imposed on humankind as a consequence of sin. This is the view of work Studs Terkel mirrors in the opening paragraph of his book *Working*:

> This book, being about work, is by its very nature, about violence—to the spirit as well as to the body. It is about ulcers as well as accidents, about shouting matches as well as fistfights, about nervous breakdowns as well as kicking the dog around. It is above all (or perhaps beneath all), about daily humiliations. To survive the day is triumph enough for the walking wounded among the great many of us.[3]

This negative and pessimistic interpretation of work, however, must be taken in its theological context. The Garden and its richness is a symbol of humankind's pristine relationship with God, a relationship lost through original sin. The theological meaning of this text suggests that the endeavors of men and women, their striving for a life of meaning and significance, cannot be accomplished through their own efforts, but rather requires the work of redemption.

A second interpretation of the relationship between religion and work has been suggested by Max Weber[4] and R. H. Tawney.[5] These early-twentieth-century authors portray the powerful influence of Calvinism on the development of capitalism. Calvinism, they suggest, encouraged its adherents to live a life of hard work and frugality. Such a lifestyle, coupled with the accumulated wealth that resulted from it, was deemed a sign of salvation, a sign of God's blessing upon an individual. This same view of the relationship between work and salvation was a key element in the New England theology of the Puritans. This theology played an important role in the lives of many nineteenth- and early-twentieth-century American entrepreneurs, men such as Andrew Carnegie, John D. Rockefeller, and Henry Ford.

Such a view of the relationship between religion and business is no longer adequate to the needs of American commerce. Although the American economy remains fertile soil for the entrepreneur, as Silicon Valley clearly demonstrates, the bulk of American business is conducted through large, complex organizations. Indeed, perhaps the highest hurdle for the successful entrepreneur is the transition from a sole-proprietor organization to a successful corporation. What is the model of religion and spirituality that might be consistent with and beneficial to large American corporations?

When I speak of religion, I take a cue from William James's *Varieties of Religious Experience.*[6] Like James, I propose to set aside the various denominations and ecclesiastical organizations and to say as little as possible about systematic theology. Although as a Catholic woman and a Sister of the Holy Cross, these themes are profoundly important to me. Rather, when I speak of religion I am referring to the common core latent or patent in human experience that seeks meaning and purpose in life. The Protestant theologian Paul Tillich referred to this as one's "ultimate concern."[7] What is it that provides focus, direction, and purpose to the multiple activities of life? Bernard Lonergan, a Catholic theologian, points to a similar dynamic in human transcendence.[8] Within human life there is a longing for the intelligible, the true, and value that impels human beings to issues of ultimacy. The works of Jewish scholars such as Martin Buber's *I-Thou*[9] and Victor Frankel's *Man's Search for Meaning*[10] are also attuned to this fundamental dynamic of human existence. The dynamic to which these authors call our attention is not experienced exclusively in churches and synagogues, but rather its exigency is discovered in the day-to-day activities of life—in our families, in our clubs and associations, in our work and business activities and then perhaps celebrated and named in denominational settings. From this perspective, to return to Studs Terkel once again, work "is about a search too, for daily meaning as well as daily bread, for recognition as well as cash, for astonishment rather than torpor, in short, for a sort of life rather than a Monday through Friday sort of dying. Perhaps immortality, too, is part of the quest."[11] The same theme is also reiterated in the writings of contemporary psychologists such as Karl Jung[12] and Abraham Maslow.[13]

Thus, by "religion" I mean this fundamental dynamic of human beings for meaning, purpose, value, and ultimacy in their lives. But there is one further characteristic of religion that I wish to articulate. There is a common, shared, indeed public dimension to the meaning, purpose, value, and ultimacy toward which religion draws us. This is certainly a touchy subject in American society. American political philosophy and our own Constitution prohibit the government from fostering such shared concepts. Nor is it the role of corporations to impose religious beliefs upon its employees. Nevertheless, if we are to live together as a people, part of the glue that holds us together is some basic, shared meaning, purpose, and value. A primary duty of every corporation is the development of processes that enable employees to become acculturated to its meaning, purpose, and values and to contribute to value creation. Civic and corporate meaning, purpose, and value cannot claim for themselves the ultimacy associated with the tenets of organized religion. But they certainly are mediating institutions that need to mirror and give expression to these fundamental dynamics of human well-being. The religious exigency for meaning, purpose, value, and ultimacy are intertwined with the civic and corporate lives of citizens and employees. Such is the theme of Robert Bellah and his colleagues in *The Good Society*.[14] Perhaps latent within the reflective, value-orientated citizen or employee is, as Turkel suggests, the quest for immortality.

Finally, "spirituality," as I understand the term, pertains to two related notions. First, spirituality is the practices persons engage in to foster and enhance the religious dimensions of their experience. In organized religions such practices include liturgies, preaching, and a variety of rituals. In civic religion spirituality is associated with special holidays, the secular translation of holy days, patriotic events, and recollections of our national history. In the corporation, spiritual practices include events to heighten employees' awareness of the meaning, purpose, and values at the heart of the corporate enterprise. Second, spirituality refers to the sentiments, not sentimentality, occasioned by spiritual practices. Feelings as intentional responses to the value of other persons and to the significance that life is lived in a realm of meaning and purpose provide human life with its dynamism and drive.

Contemporary American Business

It is not my purpose to delineate an overall vision of the present trends and currents in the contemporary American business environment. In fact, many of you are more familiar with these issues than I am. However I do think it is important to identify at least some elements in the current business world that affect American corporations generally as well as the health-care segment of the economy. I will focus on three issues: the consolidation of corporations, the tension between cost and quality, and the evolving nature of the corporation and corporate leadership.

For the past thirty years or so corporations have grown through mergers and acquisitions. The reasons for the acceleration of mergers and acquisitions are multiple and complex. At least two of these reasons are intriguing to me. The first is that there are efficiencies to be achieved through the creation of larger organizations. The cost associated with redundant corporate leadership and overhead can be eliminated. The cost of materials can be reduced through large-scale purchasing. Large corporations can provide a range of goods or services that smaller organizations cannot. Second, the size and pooled resources, including intellectual capital, of large national or multinational corporations make them better equipped to enter new markets and to develop new products.

However, alongside these important benefits there are side effects that pose new challenges to the social structure. Several familiar examples come to mind. Banks and grocery stores were once the economic centerpieces of the communities they served. Both were owned and operated by residents of the community. In many ways they were the economic bulwarks of a locality. Today these enterprises are owned by distant investors and operated by persons who may well have no roots in or loyalty to the community. An organization such as the South Shore Bank in Chicago or the mom and pop grocery store remain as mere reminders of an earlier era of American economic life. My point here is neither to praise nor blame, but simply to indicate the social and economic change that has occurred. In the language of sociologists such as Zygmunt Bauman such change results in the fragmentation of the institutions of a community. Residents become alienated from, distrustful of, indeed even fearful of the very institutions essential to the well-being of individuals and communities. Yet, if they wish to eat or secure a loan they must do business with these organizations. And when they do business with these organizations, the decision maker is usually not the person with whom they meet.

The "coin of the realm" in American business is quality. But the "coin of the marketplace" is cost. In the past thirty years American business has learned from Demming, Drucker, and others the importance of quality and the steps essential to producing quality. The promise of every consultant throughout the land is that, if you retain my services or buy my program, your enterprise will experience quality enhancement. Quality is demanded, but quality is questioned when it entails an increase in costs. My suspicion is that every corporation in America is affected by this tension between cost and quality.

Collins and Porras's *Built to Last*[15] provides one insightful manner in which a group of companies have addressed this tension. They depict visionary companies as adhering to a core ideology, to a vision or mission statement in good times and in hard times. Notions such as "contribution," "service to the customer," "being on the creative or cutting edge," and "responsibility to the community" are frequently found in the core ideologies of visionary companies. The core ideology of a corporation identifies the explicit purpose of an organization, the reason for its existence, what it intends to accomplish. Peter Senge appears to have a similar concept in mind when he writes, "One is hard pressed to think of any organization that has sustained some measure of greatness in the absence of goals, values, and mission that become deeply shared in the organization."[16] The tension between quality and cost cannot be resolved by eliminating one horn of the dilemma. Rather, the tension must be managed through adherence to the core ideology, the mission, of the corporation.

My third observation on the current business environment is that the nature of the corporation, and thus the nature of corporate leadership as well, is in a period of rapid evolution. Many Americans still view the corporation as the rationalized bureaucracy portrayed by Max Weber. According to this view the apex of the corporation, the CEO, is the sole decision maker. Managers simply implement the plan dictated by the corporate leader. The flow of the organization is exclusively from the top down. Many corporations, however, have migrated to new models of how the work of the company can best be accomplished. In *Competing by Design*, Nadler and Tushman[17] provide an array of organizational architectures through which corporations can accomplish their specific goals. If there is one theme to their work, it is that one organizational structure cannot meet the diverse goals of different types of corporations. The structure of the corporation must be tailored to meet its specific objectives. In many of these new corporate structures managers are not viewed as executors of a CEO's directives, but rather as decision makers with responsibilities and accountabilities.

If the CEO is not the sole decision maker in the organization, what is his or her role? The CEO, I believe, has two principal roles. The first is to be herald of the core ideology and mission of the organization. The CEO is responsible for the effective communication to the entire staff that the core ideology or mission defines the business of the corporation. Managers need to know that as long as they are operating within that core ideology they will fulfill their accountabilities. No incentive should be offered, no rewards accorded to individuals who compromise the core ideology of the corporation.

The second task of the corporate leader is to be the sponsor of change in the organization. Market dynamics change, new opportunities as well as new threats present themselves in a competitive environment. The one constant in American corporate life is that change will continue. The leader, in conjunction with senior staff and the endorsement of the board, must identify the changes that the company must introduce in order to continue to be successful. Change is not a modification of the core ideology, but rather a modification of the means through which the ideology is brought to life in the activities of the organization. In addition, the corporate leader must communicate to the staff that change is both permissible and required. Everyone is resistant to new ways of doing things. The CEO is the sponsor of change. As Daryl Connor has pointed out, only the CEO has "the power to sanction and legitimize change."[18]

Contemporary American Health Care

If change has become endemic to American business, it continues to be pandemic in American health care. Only at the beginning of the previous century did the formal organization of the American hospital begin to occur. Prior to this, hospitals were, for the most part, community institutions for the indigent dying or mentally ill. Following the lead of Florence Nightingale and drawing upon the experience of creating field hospitals during World War I, American hospitals gradually assumed the bureaucratic, hierarchical models associated with American business. The acceptance of the importance of a sterile environment for surgical patients greatly improved survival rates. In the late 1930s and early 1940s penicillin and its derivatives made possible the successful treatment of infections. Hospitals increasingly became institutions in which persons got well, not died. In the late 1940s and early 1950s new surgical procedures were performed. The '60s and '70s introduced new radiology processes—ultrasound, CAT scans, and an array of technologies that make it possible to view and diagnose human organ systems without the risks of exploratory surgery. The scope of new drugs, most recently, genetically produced drugs, that physicians are requesting for hospital and managed care formularies is staggering. All of which merely sets the stage if one is to comprehend the current environment of American health care.

In the 1970s the for-profit hospital companies emerged, followed in the '80s by the gradual consolidation of the hospital sector. The industry leader among hospital companies has been the Hospital Corporation of America. During the decade of the 1990s the Catholic health systems formed in the '70s began to consolidate, forming large multistate corporations. Twenty years ago each of these hospitals was locally operated. Local boards have been either replaced by corporate boards or their powers curtailed and conditioned by corporate approval. Just as banks and grocery stores were once the focal institutions of local communities, so too were hospitals. Alienation from the local hospital is perhaps even more threatening than alienation from the local bank and grocery store.

The vertical integration of American health care is a key aspect of the economic and social status of hospitals. Simultaneously, at the market level, horizontal integration is also occurring. Until the late 1980s American health care could be characterized as fragmented, as a system of independent competing entities where divergent and redundant forms of health services were available to the public. Sanford Grey has described the situation thus:

Until recent years the U.S. health care system could be fairly described in terms of independent nonprofit and small proprietary institutions and independent physicians practicing alone or in very small groups.[19]

Under pressure from managed-care companies and other payers of health benefits these multiple independent entities are being brought together into organized or integrated delivery systems. Steven Shortell and his coauthors define an organized delivery system as "a network of organizations that provides or arranges to provide a coordinated continuum of services to a defined population and is willing to be held clinically and financially accountable for the outcomes and health status of the population served."[20] Thus an array of local health services is moved from a fragmented to a coordinated system. Physicians, hospitals, outpatient services, long-term care, rehabilitation facilities, and home health and hospice care are brought under one corporate umbrella. There are several implications associated with organized delivery systems that I would like to discuss.

The traditional goals of medicine have generally been recognized as illness treatment, rehabilitation, chronic-disease management, and palliative care. While retaining each of these traditional responsibilities of heath-care providers, organized delivery systems also assume responsibility for "improving community health and well-being through disease prevention and health promotion."[21] The older standards of care presumed that health-care providers did not intervene until someone was sick. Further, traditional standards focused the attention of health-care providers exclusively on the needs of individuals. Contemporary standards require that organized delivery systems, and thus each of the practitioners within them, extend their attention to the healthy as well as the sick, that they extend their attention to communities and not just individuals. I would suggest to you that these are not small, incidental changes but in fact go to the core of what the health-care delivery system is about.

In the fragmented delivery system, the provision of health services was financed on a fee-for-service basis. As long as hospital and physician bills stayed within the "reasonable and customary" range, they could expect reimbursement for whatever services were rendered. Organized delivery systems, however, assume clinical and fiscal accountability. On the basis of a managed-care contract or a negotiated contract an organized delivery system agrees to provide a range of services for a stipulated fee. This entails two new features for organized delivery systems. One, they are now expected to manage risk. A new set of skills must be developed in the corporate leadership. Second, the management of such contracts requires new levels of financial and clinical management. Again, sets of new skills, policies, and procedures need to be developed if these organizations are to succeed. These policies and procedures cannot be promulgated by a traditional CEO directing a rationalized bureaucracy. Rather, they can only be created, implemented, and managed by drawing upon the pooled financial and clinical expertise within the organization. The pressures to find the match, the level of market responsiveness to the tension between cost and quality, needs to be identified and resolved.

In the former system of care, individual physicians, in conjunction with their patients, were the decision makers concerning modalities of treatment. They determined the length of a patient's hospital stay, recommended surgery or pharmaceutical interventions, and ordered radiological studies and laboratory tests. In an organized delivery system, physician treatment plans are tracked by risk managers and precertification programs. As Ezekiel Emanuel, a physician, comments:

> Physician-patient interaction no longer occurs in a practitioner's office in which the practitioner, alone or a small group of colleagues, has control over the structures that influence the interaction. Instead these interactions occur within large organizatzions in which the practitioner or a small group of colleagues does not control the rules of the engagement. The context of medical ethics can no longer be cases, but institutional structures.[22]

Thus, just as the organized delivery system assumes financial accountability for the health services it provides to a population, it also incurs, along with its physicians, clinical accountability. This requires physicians and other leaders within the organized delivery system to create care plans, clinical outcome studies, and clinical pathways which are financially responsible and at the same time meet the health needs of the population. Corporate entities rather than individuals have accepted clinical responsibility and accountability for patient care.

Finally, Shortell challenges organized delivery systems to become holographic institutions. A holographic organization is one in which the whole is present in each of its parts. The vision, culture, leadership, and strategy of the integrated delivery system must be present in each of its parts; it must be equally operative in its physician practices, its acute-care services, rehabilitation, and long-term care partners, and its outpatient services, home health care and hospice care.[23] The vision and culture of the integrated delivery system is the heart of the mission of the organization, including the redefined goals of medicine. The strategy of the organization is constituted by the plans, policies, and procedures it adopts in order to incorporate the mission into the day-to-day activities of the organization. The challenge of leadership is to introduce these enormous changes effectively and uniformly into each point of service. Given the demands of an organized delivery system, the management of change is the first and primary responsibility of its chief executive officer. The same vision, culture, leadership, and vision must be operative at each point of service.

Corporate Spirituality

In the beginning of this chapter I shared with you some ideas about religion and spirituality. Then I attempted to identify several business issues that I believe are common to the current American marketplace. In this final section, I will link together these two themes, which at first blush may appear to be unrelated.

As the changes in health care evolved over the past several decades, it became clear that a new approach would be needed to fostering the culture and managing decision-making processes in health systems if one held out any hope of avoiding having a business model completely overrule the historic service culture of health care.

My first systematic reflection in this area was stimulated in 1984 by reading Peters and Waterman's *In Search of Excellence*.[24] The framework they offered for achieving excellence spoke to me of the need to engage the workforce individually and collectively to achieve the corporation's mission.

Over the past ten years the Holy Cross Health System has introduced a series of procedures or practices that provide the basis of a corporate spirituality. Earlier I defined spirituality as "the practices persons engage in to foster and enhance the religious dimensions of their experience." I proposed that we think of religion in terms of humankind's longing for meaning, purpose, and value in everyday life. The procedures or practices I wish to share with you have as their common goal the objective of instilling in the workforce and among physicians, patients, and communities served an awareness of a shared corporate meaning, purpose, and values.

The foundation of these activities is the mission statement of the Holy Cross Health System, which declares:

Faithful to the spirit of the Congregation of the Sisters of the Holy Cross, the Holy Cross Health System exists to witness to Christ's love through excellence in the delivery of health services motivated by respect for those we serve. We foster a climate that empowers those who serve with us while stewarding our human and financial resources.

I believe that my principal task as CEO is to ensure that the mission not be seen as a static statement, but rather be integrated into the complex strategic decisions as well as day-to-day operations of the corporation. As acquisitions were assessed, as the plans for the development of new delivery systems were being developed, as the pressures to maintain effective operations while achieving profitability were being addressed, it was my principal responsibility to guarantee, to the extent possible, that all these decisions would be consistent with the mission of the organization. In focusing on the mission of the Holy Cross Health System, I do not want you to think that my concerns were focused on denominational issues. Rather, I would have you think about Collins and Porras's emphasis on the business significance of the core ideology of the corporation for its long-term success. The practices and procedures I wish to share with you are good business practices, not vehicles for the promotion of denominational beliefs.

The Mission Assessment and Development Process, the Leadership Formation and Development Program, the Mission Discernment Process, and the Organizational Integrity Program are the four initiatives I sponsored to assist me in managing the mission of the corporation. I would like to discuss each of them briefly.

The Mission Assessment and Development Process is a systematic assessment throughout the corporation culminating in a report submitted to the board of directors every five years that details the organization's successes and failures in living out its mission. Boards are accustomed to receiving financial reports, approving mergers and acquisitions, and reviewing operating performance reports and strategic plans. Of course, the board fulfills these traditional tasks on a regular basis. The Mission Assessment Process enables the board to step back from its focus on these important pieces of the puzzle and to get a view of the whole.

The Mission Assessment Process begins with the corporate mission statement. Then, in a collaborative effort on the part of corporate office staff and mission executives in member organizations, specific mission standards, each with a subset of criteria, are identified. The standards along with their criteria become benchmarks against which the performance of a member organization can be assessed. At each member organization an internal team is assembled that conducts a self-assessment including interviews with a sampling of the leadership and staff of the organization. The on-site teams submit a report to an outside review team composed of a staff member from the corporate office and a mission executive from another organization. There is a meeting between the two teams that reviews the report from the member organization. The result is a report on the mission effectiveness of each organization. The report contains commendations for the successes and innovations individual member organizations might have achieved as well as recommendations for areas that require additional attention. At each organization there are rituals to both kick off and conclude the process.

Besides the obvious value of informing the board of which member organizations are doing well and which require further attention, the Mission Assessment and Development Process has an additional benefit. Across the Health System, the process entails the work of several hundred staff members and collaborators in conscious reflection upon the mission of the organization. They are charged to evaluate the mission integration and effectiveness of their place of work. A by-product of their involvement is an enhanced awareness of the meaning, purpose, and values of the organization in which they work. They are brought into contact not only with the words of the mission statement but also the activities of the organization through which the mission statement is mediated. These same themes are reiterated at the opening and closing of the process, which large numbers of employees attend.

In his book on not-for-profit organizations, Peter Drucker points out that the success of such organizations cannot be assessed on the basis of their bottom line alone at the end of a fiscal year. His point was that their success can only be measured in relation to the reasons for their existence.[25] Collins and Porras's *Built to Last* suggests that the same reasoning applies to for-profits. Companies that focus exclusively on the bottom line fail; companies that attend to their core ideology succeed and endure over time.

The second process is associated with Leadership Formation and Development. The Holy Cross Health System recruits women and men with highly developed professional skills. When the women and men join the Health System, they are frequently unfamiliar with the underlying values of the organization. If they are to function successfully in the organization, they must not only acquire the skills and knowledge to perform their responsibilities well but also develop the capacity for leadership consistent with the mission of the corporation. Leadership Formation and Development is a core process that provides for the identification of the core competencies that are critical for the successful performance of a leadership role. Specific competencies are associated with particular positions in the organization. Gap analysis is performed in order to develop a personal/professional development plan appropriate to the person's role in the organization. Mission education, ethics, and values are an integral component of such developmental plans. The organization then deploys internal and external resources to assist the leader to fulfill his or her development plan. In this way the organization attempts to develop competencies within its leadership that result in well-honed professional skills nuanced by an awareness of the mission, ethics, and values of the Health System. The Leadership Formation and Development Process is an exercise in corporate spirituality, inculcating within the leadership an awareness that the business of the corporation and the work of its leadership must serve as mediations of the mission, the core ideology of the organization. Leaders with such refined competencies are essential to the success of the Mission Discernment Process and the Organizational Integrity Program.

The third practice of corporate spirituality at Holy Cross is the Mission Discernment Process. This process is used whenever the corporation or its member organizations have to make strategic decisions or a decision of some substance that lies outside the scope of routine operational decisions. Such issues would include mergers and acquisitions, adding or deleting service lines, staffing redesign projects, or major capital requests. The process requires the assembling of an appropriate team, persons with the skills and knowledge to review the multiple technical, financial, and human resources, and the strategic and mission issues a particular proposal might entail. The team engages in a collaborative reflective process until each aspect of the decision has been appropriately investigated and resolved. The mission dimension of the process requires participants to evaluate the manner in which the proposal is consistent with or is an enhancement of the mission of the organization. Further, the impact of the decision upon the workforce, the community, patients, physicians, and other relevant stakeholders is evaluated. At times, representatives of these various constituencies are invited to participate in the process. The process is similar to what Patricia Werhane has recently referred to as moral imagination: the ability to understand "a set of activities from a number of different perspectives, the actualizing of new possibilities that are not context-dependent, and the instigation of the process of evaluating those possibilities from a moral point of view."[26] The results of the process are integrated with the business plan and submitted to the board for its approval.

The Mission Discernment Process is intended to ensure that corporate decisions are embodiments of the mission of the organization. The board values the process because it provides evidence to them that corporate decisions are not simply market driven, but are consistent with the corporation's mission. A by-product of the process is that senior and mid-level managers are required to bring mission, ethics, and values explicitly to bear upon their work and the business of the company. The Mission Discernment Process is an exercise in corporate spirituality.

The fourth initiative in corporate spirituality is the Organizational Integrity Program. The program not only fulfills the government's requirements for a corporate compliance program but also goes much further. Its focus is on the integrity of day-to-day operations of the organization. The Organizational Integrity Program goes further than standard compliance programs. The program is a public announcement to government agencies, local communities, patients, accrediting organizations, physicians, and other relevant stakeholders that "the Holy Cross Health System is committed to complying with all ethical professional and legal obligations, and to fostering a climate that enables all those associated with Holy Cross to fulfill these obligations."[27] I mentioned earlier that the formation of organized delivery systems requires a corporation to assume fiscal and clinical responsibility. The Organizational Integrity Program is our public statement that we will fulfill these duties in a manner consistent with our mission.

It is also a statement to our employees that we expect them to fulfill their duties in a manner consistent with the core ideology of the organization and that we will provide a culture to support them in this regard.

The Organizational Integrity Program contains the federally mandated requirements for a compliance program. I am sure that many of you are familiar with these, and I will not review them again here. Rather, I would like to highlight how the program deepens the commitment to compliance and goes beyond mere legal compliance. One of the requirements of a compliance program is the publication of a code of business practices. The code of the Organizational Integrity Program addresses questions of ethics. For instance, the code stipulates that "[m]anaged care contracts must clearly identify a Holy Cross member organization's professional obligations toward enrollees. Contracts that fail to provide reasonable health benefits to enrollees, plans that are effectively open only to the healthy or which in some demonstrable way fail to respect the human dignity of enrollees shall not be entered into."[28] This provides a clear directive to staff in the evaluation of pending managed-care contracts that such contracts need to be evaluated from the perspective of the mission, the core ideology of the organization.

An objective of the program not yet fully realized is that the job description of every employee will contain all relevant compliance issues that he or she might confront. In addition, the clinical, professional, and ethical obligations of their role in the organization will also be specified. At the time of the annual performance evaluation all these factors will be taken into consideration.

Conclusion

Corporate spirituality can be a critical success factor in American business. Spirituality is not something abstract or something relegated to times of private worship. Corporate spirituality is the creation of exercises and practices that draw upon a people's need for meaning, purpose, and value in their professional lives. Corporate spirituality mediates the mission or core ideology of the organization throughout the staff in a manner that ensures that the goals of the company will be achieved. These are not incompatible goals, but rather ones that are mutually reenforcing.

Mission Assessment and Development, Leadership Formation and Development, Mission Discernment, and the Organizational Integrity Program are aspects of corporate spirituality that have evolved and been effective in my organization. They are corporate infrastructure initiatives that attempt to create linkages and foster integration of spirituality and business practice.

NOTES

1. Robert N. Bellah, Richard Madsen, William M. Sullivan, Ann Swidler, and Steven Tipton, *Habits of the Heart* (Berkeley: University of California Press, 1985).

2. Genesis 3:14–15.

3. Studs Terkel, *Working* (New York: Pantheon Books, 1972), xi.

4. Max Weber, *The Protestant Ethic and the Spirit of Capitalism*, trans. Talcott Parsons (New York: Charles Scribner's Sons, 1958).

5. R. H. Tawney, *Religion and the Rise of Capitalism* (West Drayton, U.K.: Pelican Books, 1922).

6. William James, *The Varieties of Religious Experience* (New York: Collier Books, 1961).

7. Paul Tillich, *Systematic Theology*, vol. 1, *Reason and Revelation* (Chicago: University of Chicago Press, 1951), 12.

8. Bernard Lonergan, S.J., *Method in Theology* (New York: Herder and Herder, 1972), 101–24.

9. Martin Buber, *I-Thou*, trans. Ronald Gregor Smith (New York: Scribners, 1958).

10. Victor Frankel, *Man's Search for Meaning* (Boston: Beacon Press, 1962).

11. Studs Terkel, *Working*, xi.

12. Karl Jung, *Psychology and Religion* (New Haven, Conn.: Yale University Press, 1938).

13. Abraham Maslow, *Toward a Psychology of Being* (Princeton: Van Norstrand, 1968).

14. Robert N. Bellah, Richard Madsen, William H. Sullivan, Ann Swidler, and Steven Tipton, *The Good Society* (New York: Vantage Books, 1991).

15. James Collins and Jerry I. Porras, *Built to Last* (New York: Harper Business, 1997).

16. Peter Senge, *The Fifth Discipline* (New York: Currency Doubleday, 1990), 9.

17. David A. Nadler and Michael L. Tushman, *Competing by Design* (New York: Oxford University Press, 1997).

18. Daryl R. Connor, *Managing at the Speed of Change* (New York: Villard Books, 1992).

19. Bradford H. Gray, *The Profit Motive and Patient Care* (Cambridge: Harvard University Press, 1991), 3.

20. Stephen M. Shortell, Robin R. Gillies, David Anderson, Karen Morgan Erickson, and John B. Mitchell, *Remaking Health Care in America* (San Francisco: Jossey-Bass Publishers, 1996), 7.

21. Ibid., 8.

22. Ezekiel Emanuel, M.D., "Medical Ethics in the Era of Managed Care: The Need for Institutional Structures Instead of Principles for Individual Cases," *Journal of Clinical Ethics* 6, no. 4 (1995): 335.

23. Shortell et al., *Remaking Health Care in America*, 7.

24. Thomas J. Peters and Robert H. Waterman Jr., *In Search of Excellence: Lessons from America's Best-Run Companies* (New York: Harper and Row, 1982).

25. Peter Drucker, *Managing the Nonprofit Organization* (New York: Harper Collins Publishers, 1990).

26. Patricia H. Werhane, *Moral Imagination and Management Decision Making* (New York: Oxford University Press, 1999), 5.

27. "Standards of Conduct," *Organizational Integrity Program* (privately published by the Holy Cross Health System), 6.

28. Ibid., 23.

Three Responses to
Patricia Vandenberg

Response by Mary Kathryn Grant

Health care, like other arenas of the service sector of the United States economy, has generally attracted people looking for workplaces where they can exercise their faith, live their values, and serve others. Consequently, their expectations of the workplace are shaped accordingly: they seek meaningful ways to contribute to the life of the organization and to the betterment of the lives of others, of both those they serve as well as those with whom they work. This is true whether they be trustees, physicians, housekeepers, health-care providers, or administrators.

When one thinks of spirituality and the freedom to exercise one's spirituality at work in health care there are two distinct areas: the delivery of health services and the arena of management and operations. The following remarks will deal with the reality of management and operations, leaving comments on health-care delivery to other respondents.

For more than a decade, the Holy Cross Health System has systematically endeavored to nurture workplace spirituality. When we first embarked on this path, we recognized the need to lay building blocks very carefully. From the outset, we recognized that such an initiative would require a careful articulation of what precisely we meant by spirituality, an articulation not in words only but in actions as well.

To set the context for this challenging first step, it may be helpful to give a snapshot of the pluralism of the more than twenty thousand employees of the health system. One of our hospitals was actually founded by Jewish physicians at the height of anti-Semiticism following World War II. Today its medical staff is made up of the sons and daughters, granddaughters, and grandsons of these physicians. Its patient and workforce

297

populations contain at least twenty-seven language groups—and there is no way of knowing how many religions.

I cite this example only to stress that it was imperative for us to assure our colleagues that we were not trying to convert them. We had to state very clearly in words and in actions that, while we were first and foremost a Catholic health-care system, we respected the diversity of faiths and religious practices among these more than twenty thousand colleagues.

A basic premise of our effort was that spirituality and religious faith were different realities. This was a critical first step in our effort to create and nurture a spirituality in the workplace. Nor did we want in any way to diminish the strong Catholic identity of our enterprise. We not only promote but also require adherence to the social and biomedical moral teachings of the church. We have Catholic chapels, most of which have been designed for flexible ecumenical liturgical usage; we have Catholic chaplains serving along with rabbis, Mormon bishops, Baptist ministers, and a variety of trained chaplains in the various faith traditions of each location.

So how then do we promote spirituality? First, through building on the notion that we are an ecclesial community, a "community of persons committed to a common mission." We endeavored to downplay the notion of family—with its attendant notions of paternalism and maternalism that often lead to codependency and unreal expectations of the workplace. In place of the image of family, we advanced the notion of a community of persons freely choosing to serve in an organization, striving to live its mission and values, and holding themselves and one another accountable for personal commitment to mission and values and collective organizational fidelity.

Replacing the notion of family with community has had its own challenges: these include defining a core set of beliefs to serve as the basic building blocks for a workplace spirituality. This was a relatively easy task. We used our mission statement, two simple, easy-to-remember sentences:

Faithful to the spirit of the congregation
of the Sisters of the Holy Cross,
the Holy Cross Health System exists
to witness Christ's love
through excellence in the delivery of health services
motivated by respect for those we serve.

> We foster a climate that empowers those who serve with us
> while stewarding our human and financial resources.

In order to make this statement accessible to and capable of being put into operation by employees at all levels of the organization, we further identified four components: *fidelity* to the spirit of the congregation; *excellence* in health services; *empowerment* of those with whom we serve as well as those we serve; and *stewardship* of the scarce and valued resources entrusted to us. Fidelity, excellence, empowerment, and stewardship became the four foundations of our workplace spirituality.

Fidelity gives us an avenue into the meaning of our work: faithful to the gospel and to the spirit of the founders. We stress the words and spirit invoking identification with the selflessness, courage, dedication, and commitment of the founders and sponsors, the Sisters of the Holy Cross. This notion of fidelity appealed greatly to our employees and associates because it touched their own motivation for choosing health care as a profession and easily related behaviors flowing from faithfulness to the spirit and tradition of the congregation.

Excellence speaks to the compelling need to strive for the best possible outcomes—be they clinical results, operational performance, financial results, or decision making. There is essentially no aspect of work life unaffected by the concept of excellence. This notion, too, was accessible to the rank-and-file health-care worker. No one comes to work—especially in a field such as health care—to do a mediocre job. This aspect of excellence as a component of our corporate spirituality also ties into the respect for coworkers and patients and self-respect for a job well done.

Empowerment addresses the notion of how we work together— respecting both the individual dignity and differences between us, shaping goals together, sharing accountabilities, nurturing the spirit as well as the bodies and minds of those with whom we come in contact and with whom we connect. In this regard, we invite others to share their faith traditions through prayer, mission retreats, and other events structured to enable each individual to be comfortable within an overall Catholic tradition.

Stewardship concerns all the resources entrusted to us—financial, environmental, and human, as well as the intangible resources of time and the stewardship of the very health-care ministry itself. This latter dimension of stewardship has been tested in the crucible of our current merger and raises the fundamental question of ownership of assets and resources. A discussion of this particular application of stewardship would take us afield; suffice it to say that coming to terms with the belief that the assets of the health system are held in trust within the greater healing ministry of and for the church takes its share of prayerful discernment.

Five initiatives within the corporation support the goal of mission integration and accountability: the Mission Assessment and Development Process; the Mission Discernment Process; Mission-based Performance Management; the Organizational Integrity Program; and Workplace Spirituality. Each of these is built around the mission and articulates interdependently with one another, much like a hologram wherein each part contains in some measure the whole. The Mission Assessment Process illustrates how this may be achieved.

It should be clear how inspiring and inspiriting these four fundamental concepts are: how they might inform workplace spirituality and touch the deepest values of those serving in this work. To take this to a practical level, we translated these four elements into a set of Mission standards and, in turn, into criteria for periodic assessment. The standards are concrete, tangible, measurable applications of each element of the mission to action in the work setting. The standards themselves serve as a teaching aid, as it were, describing the culture, the spirit, and hence the spirituality of the workplace culture.

The standards were created by our local-facility mission vice-presidents and reflect their vision and struggle to create authentic, mission-based work sites. They are instructional insofar as they detail how the mission informs and shapes the culture, defines both individual and institutional accountability, and assists in decision making grounded in the organization's mission. For example, the concrete expressions of fidelity may be measured in symbols and rituals, stories exemplifying mission effectiveness, as well as education in and adherence to the Ethical and Religious Directives for Catholic Health Care Services; excellence in continual attention to process improvement, monitoring improvement of clinical outcomes, and strategic planning; empowerment in personnel policies, grievance procedures, diversity initiatives, and the like; stewardship in fiscal accountability; and commitment to levels of charity care and community benefit.

As we continually seek to read and reflect on the signs of the times, the standards are regularly revised to meet the changing demands of health care. How does all this relate to workplace spirituality? First, by continually struggling to live the mission in everyday practice, actions, attitudes, and decisions, we hold before ourselves an ideal. And we hold ourselves individually and collectively accountable for "walking the talk." We also invite deeper reflection of the meaning of a healing mission in today's world. This self-reflective process calls for individual and organizational assessment of the integrity with which the mission is imbued, implemented, and then assessed and deepened.

The ultimate value of this process, however, is not found in the accountability report nor even in the resultant action plans. It is in the process itself. Conducted periodically and involving literally thousands of persons within the system, this Mission Assessment Process derives its principal value from providing the opportunity for individuals and groups to reflect on the meaning of the mission and to identify better ways to live it out in meeting the pressing demands of health-care delivery.

Our goal has been to create workplaces animated by our mission in which persons form a community and in turn nurture and renew one another in the demanding ministry of health care in order to better serve the needs of those who come to us for care. We believe that processes such as our Mission Assessment Process work to inspire and animate the workplace. They serve to ground our workplace spirituality in four values—fidelity, excellence, empowerment, and stewardship.

The rewards of this effort are manifold: employees are able to express their personal values and faith traditions in concrete ways at work; the work environment is animated by the organization's mission and values; and a commitment to continually seek ways to deepen and extend the mission permeates all decision making. In the end, patients, clients, employees, and families experience the tangible effects of spirituality at work.

Response by Peter J. Giammalvo

There are two crises in American health care: a crisis of strategy and a crisis of spirit. The crisis of spirit is evidenced in a number of sectors: public ratings of hospitals are at an all-time low (close to the ratings of the IRS and airlines); doctors and nurses are dispirited as shown by the increase in union activities throughout the country; boards and consequently executives are too focused on financial performance and not sufficiently focused on the quality of care and service to patients; and there is a growing distrust between doctors and hospitals.

Success at the beginning of the new century and beyond will be accorded to those leaders who focus their energy on a mission that is deeply held, establish and communicate a vision, embrace innovation, focus on patients through excellence in both service and outcomes, and nurture the spirit of their organizations and their people.

Successful leadership is a combination of experience, intelligence, and reflection. Therefore, leadership development must primarily focus its attention on leadership and not on management. The manager relies on control, the leader inspires. The manager maintains, while the leader develops. The manager asks how and when, the leader asks why and why not. The manager administers and the leader innovates.*

The goal of Leadership Formation and Development at the Holy Cross Health System is to integrate fully the lessons cited above and, in doing so, ask the leader to probe his or her own values and goals. Ultimately the process will evolve to a point where transactional leaders become transformational leaders.

The leadership program incorporates mission, vision, and values. The mission states why an organization exists and what it is about, the values articulate how the organization goes about fulfilling its mission, and the vision specifies the direction. The leader is the steward of these three realities. To help leaders achieve these goals, the requisite competencies need to be identified.

As part of the Leadership Formation initiative at Holy Cross, specific components address each of the areas. These include, but are not limited to:

- Articulation of competencies
- Competency assessment and development planning
- Programs, retreats, and seminars to reinforce lessons
- Systemic integration of mission in all aspects of organizational life
- Research and development
- Internships and residencies

In health care, leadership is presented with a unique set of challenges. Even when the United States was experiencing a booming econ-

---

*From Warren Bennis, *Managing People Is Like Herding Cats* (Provo, Utah: Executive Excellence Publishing, 1997), chap. 13.

omy, health care itself did not participate in this boom. And, at the same time, the numbers of the uninsured and underinsured are growing exponentially.

The marketplace is not an adequate platform for strategic planning and decision making while the system itself is artificially controlled by constraints such as revenue flow from federal programs like the Balanced Budget Act and other governmental regulations that limit resources. Providers are squeezed between drug companies, equipment manufacturers, insurers, and government payers. Often the largest line item in a hospital's budget is its information technology.

What is needed to address these challenges and form leaders for today and tomorrow are opportunities to probe, examine, and evaluate one's personal values and to integrate these values into the workplace and one's own work life. A similar process of reflection, probing, and integration must take place within the organization itself.

A Response by John A. Gallagher

I would like to comment on three issues and draw out their implications for this topic. First, I want to focus my comments on the similarity of the Holy Cross Health System and other corporate enterprises; second, I would like to explore briefly the relationship between corporate spirituality and holistic approaches to health, and last I will touch on the accountability to the corporate board.

As one ponders the processes mentioned earlier, the Mission Assessment Process, Leadership Formation and Development, and the Organizational Integrity Program, it is easy to fall into the misconception that such programs can only be implemented in faith-based organizations. While it is certainly true that the Holy Cross Health System, inherited from the Congregation of the Sisters of the Holy Cross, is a culture amenable to such practices and activities, it is equally true that the health system exists in the same environment of accreditation, fiscal responsibility, professional accountability, and community expectations faced by any other provider of health services. The Holy Cross Health System goes to the same bond market and is under the same stringent review as any other not-for-profit organization. The Joint Commission on the Accreditation of Healthcare Organizations regularly reviews the operations of its members with the same scrutiny it uses throughout the industry. My point, in other words, is that the system is in many ways the same as that of other providers of health services across the nation. Indeed, in general, it is more *like* any large American corporation than it is different. Thus, it is my conviction that activities and programs similar to those discussed here should be possible in any corporation—for-profit, not-for-profit, faith-based, or secular.

There is, however, a special reason why attention to corporate spirituality is particularly important in the health-care industry. There is a small, but growing, trend in American medicine that deems the mind-body relationship to be essential to health and well-being. I am thinking in particular of Harvard University's Mind-Body Health Institute. The premise of this approach to medicine is that there is an essential relationship between physical health and mental or spiritual health. If American health-care organizations are to mediate such an approach to health and well-being, they must be able to mirror that understanding in their approach to corporate life and their attention to the holistic needs of their staff and stakeholders. The mind-body approach to health care is not just a new fad among practitioners; it is not a new drug *de jour* or a surgical technique that a physician must learn. It is a fundamentally different way of viewing health and healing. It can be mediated by organizations imbued with such a philosophy. If the mind-body philosophy is only practiced in the offices of primary-care physicians but not in the offices of the specialists or the management offices, it is on a terminal course. Corporate spirituality across the health-care setting can provide a firm foundation for such programs.

Finally, I would like to develop briefly a point alluded to earlier. An element common to the Mission Assessment Process, Mission Discernment Program, and Organizational Integrity Program is that of accountability to the corporate board. Corporate boards, particularly in the not-for-profit sector, should require evidence that management is achieving the mission of the organization. Profit-and-loss statements, analyses of market share, and reports of staff-to-patient ratios are important, but not sufficient, manifestations of mission for a board to effectively discharge its fiduciary responsibility.

The Mission Assessment Process provides reliable information concerning the extent to which each member organization is effective in the fulfillment of its mission and where it is challenged. Mission Discernment develops information that assures the board that in approving a new undertaking it can be confident that the initiative will be consistent with or even enhance the mission of the organization. The Organizational Integrity Program informs the board on a regular basis that the operations of the company are being performed in a manner consistent with its mission, values, and code of conduct. The financial soundness of a corporation is obviously important to its board of trustees, and equally important to the board should be the soundness of its mission.

Contributors

JAMAL A. BADAWI teaches courses in the areas of management and religious studies at Saint Mary's University in Halifax, Canada. He holds MBA and Ph.D. degrees from Indiana University at Bloomington and has written numerous works on Islam, including "The Application of Tawheed in the Natural and Social Order," *Humanomics*, vol. 1, and *Gender Equity in Islam*. He is a member of the Islamic Juristic Council of North America, the founder of the Islamic Information Foundation, and a frequent speaker on Islam in North America and abroad.

JOHN CARON is the retired president of Caron International, a textile manufacturing firm. He is a life trustee of the University of Notre Dame and past chairman of its Academic and Faculty Affairs Committee, as well as a founding member of the Notre Dame Program on Multinational Managers and Developing Country Concerns. He is a former chairman (now vice-chairman) of Technoserve, whose aim is to improve the economic and social well-being of low-income people in developing countries, and a former chairman and current board member of the National Catholic Reporter Publishing Company.

GERALD F. CAVANAGH, S.J., holds the Charles T. Fisher Chair of Business Ethics and is professor of management at the University of Detroit Mercy. He is the author of numerous articles and five books, among them, *American Business Values: With Global Perspectives; Ethical Dilemmas in the Modern Corporation; Blacks in the Industrial World*, and *The Businessperson in Search of Values*. Cavanagh has lectured and given workshops on business ethics throughout the United States, Mexico, Indonesia, Australia, and India. He received the Most Outstanding Faculty Award in 1998 from his colleagues at the University of Detroit Mercy. Cavanagh holds a B.S. degree in engineering, graduate degrees in philosophy, theology, and education,

306

and received his doctorate in management from Michigan State University. He is an ordained Catholic priest in the Society of Jesus. Cavanagh received the highest award in his field, the Sumner Marcus Award, from the Academy of Management for his writings, teaching, and other contributions to business ethics. He has served on the boards of trustees of Fordham, Santa Clara, Xavier, and as a board chairman of the University of Detroit.

LAWRENCE S. CUNNINGHAM is professor of theology and former chairman of the Department of Theology at the University of Notre Dame. He is the author or editor of eighteen books, including *Thomas Merton and the Monastic Vision*. A lecturer both in the United States and abroad, he writes the "Religion Book Notes" for the *Commonweal* magazine and has written more than three hundred articles and reviews. He currently serves as a consultant for matters Catholic for the new edition of the Encyclopedia Britannica. Cunningham has won two teaching awards at the University of Notre Dame for excellence in undergraduate instruction.

ANDRÉ L. DELBECQ is the director of the Institute for Spirituality and Organizational Leadership and the J. Thomas and Kathleen McCarthy University Professor at Santa Clara University, where he served as dean of the Leavey School of Business from 1979 to 1989. His research and scholarship have focused on executive decision-making processes, organization design, and managing innovation in rapid-change environments. Recently he has conducted research on the role of CEOs in technology firms, the business culture of Silicon Valley, and innovation in both high technology and health care. He is the eighth dean of Fellows of the Academy of Management. Delbecq is recognized nationally for executive programs delivered to high-technology industries, as well as health, human services, and government organizations. He has served as member of three corporate boards of directors and twice as board chair. During 1997–1998 the American Council of Learned Societies awarded him a Contemplative Practice Fellowship. In addition, he studied at the Graduate Theological Union at Berkeley in preparation for teaching spirituality for business leadership. For more than twenty years Delbecq was a member of the Estes Park Institute faculty for medical staff and trustee education. He was named an Honorary Fellow by the American College of Physician Executives in recognition of service in the education of physician managers. He is currently a faculty member of the college.

KRISHNA S. DHIR is the dean of the Campbell School of Business at Berry College in Mount Berry, Georgia. He has been on the faculty of Pennsylvania State University at Harrisburg, the Citadel, Medical University of South Carolina, University of Denver, and University of Colorado. Dhir has been a senior executive with CIBA-GEIGY AG in Basle, Switzerland; a pilot plant manager with Borg-Warner Chemicals' International Division in Parkersburg, West Virginia; and has been associated with BioStar Medical Products in Boulder, Colorado. He has published widely and received a Ph.D. in management science and administrative policy from the University of Colorado, an M.B.A. from the University of Hawaii, an M.S. in chemical engineering and physiology from Michigan State University, and a B.Tech. in chemical engineering from the Indian Institute of Technology.

EDWIN M. EPSTEIN was appointed dean of the School of Economics and Business Administration and Earl W. Smith Professor at Saint Mary's College of California in 1994. He is responsible for both undergraduate and graduate programs at the college. Epstein is noted internationally for his efforts to infuse ethical inquiry and socio/political analysis into management education. From 1964 until 1991 he was professor of business administration at the Walter A. Haas School of Business at the University of California at Berkeley and is currently professor emeritus. At Berkeley he served as the chair of the Academic Senate, associate dean of the Haas School, and chair of the Political Economy of Industrial Societies major. A member of the California, Pennsylvania, and Supreme Court of the United States bars, he serves as a consultant to business firms and non-profit organizations. His teaching and scholarship over thirty-five years have earned him a number of significant awards. His book *The Corporation in American Politics* won the Howard Chase Book Award from the Social Issues in Management Division of the Academy of Management for making "a significant and lasting contribution to the study of business and society." He is a former chair of the academy's Social Issues in Management Division, a recipient of the division's Sumner Marcus Distinguished Service Award, and a past Fellow of the Woodrow Wilson International Center for Scholars in Washington, D.C.

JOHN A. GALLAGHER founded the Institute for Health Care and Organizational Ethics in 1999. The mission of the institute is to collaborate with health-care and business organizations in the creation and development of organizational ethics programs. The institute works with clients in the development and refinement of mission/vision statements and the creation of programs, procedures, and policies that ensure that the ethical aspects of the organization's business are realized in its day-to-day activities. Prior to founding the institute, Gallagher served as vice-president, in the field of system organizational integrity and system ethics for the Holy Cross Health System. In that role, he provided overall direction and coordination to the Organizational Integrity Program, Holy Cross's corporate compliance program.

PETER J. GIAMMALVO was vice-president of leadership formation and development of the Holy Cross Health System Corporation from 1991 to 2000. In that role he was responsible for the development and implementation of mission-based education programs and consulting for executives, trustees, and physician leaders. He later assumed responsibility for organizational development, focusing his efforts on the area of change management. Previously, Giammalvo was visiting associate professor of the Health Services Administration, Department of Public Administration, at West Virginia University, teaching advanced-study courses in health administration. He also served for thirteen years in various capacities, including vice-president of operations, at Saint Thomas Hospital, Nashville, Tennessee. He is a member of the American Academy of Medical Administrators and a diplomat in the American College of Healthcare Executives. He currently serves as a member of the board of trustees at Mount Carmel College of Nursing, Columbus, Ohio. Giammalvo holds a doctorate in education and a master's degree in theology from Vanderbilt University, Nashville. He completed a certification program in health services administration at the University of Alabama at Birmingham. His bachelor's degree in philosophy is from the College of the Holy Cross, Worcester, Massachusetts.

MARY KATHRYN GRANT was executive vice-president of Sponsorship and Mission Services for the Holy Cross Health System Corporation in South Bend, Indiana. Prior to joining the Health System in 1990, Grant was a principal with Consolidated Catholic Health Care, Westchester, Illinois; director of sponsorship for the Catholic Health Association, St. Louis, Missouri; and executive director of Mercy Health Conference,

Farmington Hills, Michigan. Prior to a career change in health care, Grant was involved in Catholic higher education. She is a prolific author and conference and seminar speaker on a wide range of topics, particularly in the areas of mission and sponsorship and health-care planning and development. Grant is a member of the American Hospital Association, the Forum for Healthcare Planning, the American Public Health Association, and the Canon Law Society of America. Grant holds a doctorate degree in English and American Studies from Indiana University, Bloomington.

ROBERT G. KENNEDY is an associate professor in the Department of Management at the University of St. Thomas, St. Paul, Minnesota. He received his Ph.D. degree in medieval studies (with a concentration in philosophy and theology) from the University of Notre Dame and holds master's degrees in both biblical criticism and business administration. At St. Thomas, Kennedy was the founding director of the Institute for Christian Social Thought and Management, which aims to bring the principles and insights of Christian social thought to bear in constructive ways on business and professional issues. He teaches courses in general management and business ethics, as well as philosophy, and has coordinated the university's required undergraduate course in business ethics. He has been a visiting professor in theology at the University of Dallas, and in business ethics at the Instituto Panamericana in Mexico City. Kennedy is the co-author of a book on ethics and management, as well as the author of a number of case studies and journal articles on professional ethics and other various topics, such as "Executive Compensation," "Virtue and Corporate Culture," and "The Virtue of Solidarity and the Theory of the Firm."

MARTIN E. MARTY was ordained into the ministry in 1952 and served for a decade as a Lutheran parish pastor before joining the University of Chicago faculty in 1963. He has published numerous books and articles. His awards include the National Humanities Medal, the National Book Award, the Medal of the American Academy of Arts and Sciences, the University of Chicago Alumni Medal, and the Distinguished Service Medal of the Association of Theological Schools. He is an elected member of the American Antiquarian Society and of the Society of American Historians. He is also an elected Fellow of the American Philosophical Society and the American Academy of Political and Social Sciences, and he is an admiral in the Nebraska Navy. Marty has received sixty-four honorary doctorates.

JOHN McCALL is professor of philosophy and management at Saint Joseph's University in Philadelphia, Pennsylvania. His scholarly work is primarily in business ethics, with a special focus on issues of employee rights. He is coauthor/coeditor with Joseph DesJardins of *Contemporary Issues in Business Ethics*, now in its fourth edition. His articles have appeared in, among other venues, *Business Ethics Quarterly*, *Journal of Business Ethics*, *Social Justice Research*, *Journal of Change Management*, and *The Blackwell Encyclopedic Dictionary of Business Ethics*. He has taught at the McDonough School of Business of Georgetown University, the Wharton School of the University of Pennsylvania, and Iowa State University. He holds a Ph.D. in philosophy from the University of Notre Dame.

BOWEN H. "BUZZ" McCOY was employed by Morgan Stanley for twenty-seven years. He was an owner of the firm for twenty years and directed Morgan Stanley's real estate finance activities. In 1990 he retired and presently spends his time as a real estate and business counselor, an educator, and a philanthropist. McCoy graduated from Stanford University in economics and received his M.B.A. degree from Harvard Business School. He serves as a trustee for the Urban Land Institute and is president of the Urban Land Foundation. He is a member and past president of the Counselors of Real Estate. He has served on advisory committees for the Harvard University Graduate School of Design and as chairman for the Stanford University Center for Economic Policy Research. McCoy has published more than twenty magazine articles and has received writing awards from the *Harvard Business Review* and the *Real Estate Counselor*. He also has received professional awards in real estate from the University of Southern California and in business ethics from Arizona State University.

CLAUDIA McGEARY is vice-president, executive director, and trustee of the New Foundation for Global Management Studies. The New Foundation for Global Management Studies creates programs for global businesses based on multicultural communications—people in different countries engaging in business together. McGeary is a board member of the Henri Nouwen Society and is actively involved in the Sudan cause, working with several churches and constituencies in New York City and beyond. She also develops church programs in New York City, focusing on contemporary issues of interest to the Christian community.

JAMES J. McGEE is the associate director of the Institute for Spirituality and Organizational Leadership at the Leavey School of Business, Santa Clara University, California. His current research is in the emerging interdisciplinary field of spirituality and business with particular focus on issues of spirituality in management leadership and organizational culture. He has been assistant dean and director of continuing education at St. Mary's Seminary and St. Mary's University, Maryland, where he served as professor of Christian spirituality. He has extensive experience in ecumenical affairs, including appointments as research and program staff member at the Washington Theological Consortium and the Washington Ecumenical Institute. He has also been part of the teaching faculty of the National Conference of Christians and Jews Seminarian Interchange Program. He is a founding member of the executive committee for the Management Spirituality and Religion Interest Group of the Academy of Management. In his present capacity on that committee he has served as chair of the Professional Development Workshop and as program chair. He continues to serve as an organizational consultant, a retreat director, and a spiritual director.

IAN I. MITROFF holds the Harold Quinton Distinguished Professorship of Business Policy at the Marshall School of Business at the University of Southern California in Los Angeles. He is also the president of Comprehensive Crisis Management, a private consulting firm, and the author of twenty books, including *Smart Thinking for Crazy Times* and *A Spiritual Audit of Corporate America* (with Elizabeth A. Denton).

LAURA L. NASH is director of the Institute for Values-Centered Leadership at Harvard University. On the faculty at Harvard Business School, Nash has been teaching and acting as a consultant in the area of business ethics for twenty years with corporations and not-for-profit organizations. She is a past president of the Society for Business Ethics. Her views on ethics, religion, corporate culture, and business leadership have been featured on ABC News, NBC News, CNBC News, the Wall Street Journal Radio Report, Marketwatch, National Public Radio, the *New York Times*, the *Wall Street Journal*, the *Washington Post*, and the *Economist*, to name a few. Her views on spirituality in business have been quoted in *Business Week*. Her articles have appeared in a number of journals, including "Believes in Business" and "Good Intentions Aside." Nash received her doctorate in philosophy from Harvard University.

STEPHEN J. PORTH is a professor of management at St. Joseph's University in Philadelphia, Pennsylvania. His research and teaching interests are in the areas of strategic management, management consulting, and spirituality in business. He recently completed a book, *Management Consulting: Theory and Tools for Small Business Interventions*, and has published extensively in management journals, including *International Journal of Operations and Quantitative Management*. He has provided consulting services and leadership development programs for thousands of managers in the food, insurance, and pharmaceuticals industries. Some of his recent clients include Merck, Roche Laboratories, McCormick, and the Specialty Coffee Association of America.

JOHN T. RYAN III is chairman and chief executive officer of Mine Safety Appliances Company. MSA is the world's leading manufacturer of equipment and systems for worker and plant protection and has sales and manufacturing operations throughout the world in twenty-eight countries, with about half of its business coming from customers located outside the United States. Ryan graduated magna cum laude from the University of Notre Dame, where he received a B.A. degree in 1965. He served as an officer in the U.S. army in military intelligence and graduated from Harvard University with an M.B.A. degree in 1969. He is a member of the Council on Foreign Relations and of the Advisory Council of the College of Business Administration at the University of Notre Dame; director of the World Affairs Council of Pittsburgh; a member of the executive committee of the Allegheny Conference on Community Development; a trustee of the Penn's Southwest Association; director of the Regional Industrial Development Corporation of Southwestern Pennsylvania; chairman of the board of directors of the Industrial Safety Equipment Association; and chairman of the Pittsburgh branch of the Federal Reserve Bank of Cleveland.

DAVID S. STEINGARD is an assistant professor of management at Saint Joseph's University in Philadelphia, Pennsylvania. His current research and teaching interests include corporate spirituality and transformation, new paradigm and stakeholder management, consciousness-based organizations, the social and environmental responsibilities of business, alternative research methodologies, and the integration of science and spirituality in business and academe. His publication and conference presentations focus on the fields of organizational studies and management education.

PATRICIA VANDENBERG, C.S.C., is a sister in the Congregation of the Holy Cross and has been a leader in Catholic health care for more than twenty-five years, most recently serving as president and CEO of the Holy Cross Health System (HCHS) in South Bend, Indiana, one of the largest national Catholic health-care systems, with twenty thousand employees and more than $2.3 billion in assets. (HCHS recently merged with Mercy Health Services and became Trinity Health.) Under her leadership, HCHS was recognized for its efforts in mission integration, workplace spirituality, organizational integrity, as well as superior financial performance. She has published widely and acted as a consultant internationally on these topics as well as on sponsorship and the future of sponsored ministries. She sits on the boards of several health systems and the Catholic Health Association of the United States and holds an M.H.A. degree from Duke University.

OLIVER F. WILLIAMS, C.S.C., served as the Donald Gordon Fellow and visiting professor in a joint appointment from Stellenbosch University and the University of Cape Town from January 2003 to 2004. He is an associate professor of management and academic director of the Notre Dame Center for Ethics and Religious Values in Business. He was an associate provost of the university from 1987 to 1994. He was a visiting professor at the University of Cape Town, Graduate School of Business, during the 1995–1996 academic year and returns there every year for two months. He has published and lectured extensively in the field of business ethics and is the author of *The Apartheid Crisis* and coeditor or author of twelve books, including *A Virtuous Life in Business* and *The Moral Imagination: How Literature and Films Can Stimulate Ethical Reflection in the Business World*. His most recent works are *Global Codes of Conduct: An Idea Whose Time Has Come* and *Economic Imperatives and Ethical Values in Global Business* (with S. Prakash Sethi). He received his B.A. degree in chemical engineering and M.A. degree in theology from the University of Notre Dame and his Ph.D. from Vanderbilt University. He was ordained a Catholic priest in 1970.

Index

315